"If ever a story needs retelling, it is that of _____ n (John 4). Reeder sets the record straight—_____ al sinner alleged by previous commentators. Reeder brings to life the woman's historical circumstances and expertly locates this story within the overarching narrative and theology of John's Gospel. Reeder reclaims the Samaritan woman's voice for the church today. Beautifully written, pastors and lay leaders alike will be inspired and encouraged to raise up women theologians, teachers, and evangelists."

Lynn H. Cohick, provost and dean of academic affairs, professor of New Testament, Northern Seminary

"I've watched with shame and horror at the many stories of abuse exposed by the #MeToo and #ChurchToo movements. I was even more shocked when I saw the Samaritan woman among the abused and heard the church's Bible reading indicted. What happens when a careful New Testament scholar offers her prophetic voice at a critical, cultural moment? You get this amazing, convicting book and a better church."

Jon Lemmond, lead pastor of Trinity Covenant Church, Salem, Oregon

"In a world that is quick to dismiss the lived experience of women, Caryn Reeder's timely exploration of the woman at the well brings new insights to a familiar but often misunderstood story. She dives deep into the interaction between Jesus and a woman who is often sullied without cause. Applications to today's #MeToo world spring from each page."

Ruth Everhart, pastor and author of *The #MeToo Reckoning: Facing the Church's Complicity in Sexual Abuse and Misconduct*

"Prostitute and sinner or missionary and evangelist? It turns out that our categorization of the Samaritan woman reveals much more about our own view of women than it does about John's Gospel. In this book, Reeder has expertly traced the reception of John 4 and, more importantly, has used the Samaritan woman's story to raise hard and necessary questions about the ongoing objectification, sexualization, and abuse of women—abuse that has too often been perpetrated and enabled by the church and its leaders. Reeder's is a sobering and challenging account that demands to be taken seriously in the age of #ChurchToo."

Erin Heim, tutor in biblical studies at Wycliffe Hall, Oxford

"Exposing the sexualization of biblical women that stigmatizes them as immoral, *The Samaritan Woman's Story* liberates women as agents of justice, liberation, and redemption. Chapter by glorious chapter, Reeder upends their historic demeaning to recover women's calling as moral and spiritual leaders. An essential tool in overcoming prejudice, dominance, and abuse, this book is needed more than ever!"

Mimi Haddad, president of Christians for Biblical Equality International

"The Samaritan woman who speaks with Jesus at a well may be the most misinterpreted and mistreated individual character in the history of New Testament study. She has suffered continued abuse (the word is not too strong) at the hands of Christian preachers, teachers, and scholars who (mis)label her an egregious sexual sinner and social deviant. Aiming to right this wrong, Caryn Reeder boldly and brilliantly advocates for the Samaritan woman by exposing the long run of interpretive malpractice from early church fathers to present-day pulpiteers and by expounding the rich text of John 4 in its primary narrative and cultural contexts. Yet as she deftly deploys her impressive knowledge of the ancient world, Reeder is no antiquarian. She proves to be an adept prophet as much as an expert historian, proclaiming that the intertwined lives of the Samaritan woman and Jesus *matter* for the church today, not least concerning critical matters of sex and gender."

F. Scott Spencer, professor and author of *Dancing Girls, Loose Ladies, and Women of the Cloth: The Women in Jesus's Life*

THE

Caryn A. Reeder

SAMARITAN

WOMAN'S

Reconsidering John 4 After #ChurchToo

STORY

ivp
Academic
An imprint of InterVarsity Press
Downers Grove, Illinois

InterVarsity Press
P.O. Box 1400, Downers Grove, IL 60515-1426
ivpress.com
email@ivpress.com

InterVarsity Press® is the book-publishing division of InterVarsity Christian Fellowship/USA®,
a movement of students and faculty active on campus at hundreds of universities, colleges, and schools
of nursing in the United States of America, and a member movement of the International Fellowship
of Evangelical Students. For information about local and regional activities, visit intervarsity.org.

Scripture quotations, unless otherwise noted, are the author's own translation.

The publisher cannot verify the accuracy or functionality of website URLs used in this book
beyond the date of publication.

Cover design and image composite: Cindy Kiple
Interior design: Jeanna Wiggins
Image: illustration of a woman © lupashchenkoiryna / Digital Vision Vectors / Getty Images

ISBN 978-1-5140-0060-1 (print)
ISBN 978-1-5140-0061-8 (digital)

Printed in the United States of America ♾

InterVarsity Press is committed to ecological stewardship and to the conservation of natural resources
in all our operations. This book was printed using sustainably sourced paper.

Library of Congress Cataloging-in-Publication Data

Names: Reeder, Caryn A., author.
Title: The Samaritan woman's story : reconsidering John 4 after #churchtoo
   / Caryn A. Reeder.
Description: Downers Grove, IL : InterVarsity Press, [2021] | Includes
   bibliographical references and indexes.
Identifiers: LCCN 2021047376 (print) | LCCN 2021047377 (ebook) | ISBN
   9781514000601 (print) | ISBN 9781514000618 (digital)
Subjects: LCSH: Samaritan woman (Biblical figure) | Bible. John, IV,
   4-42—Feminist criticism.
Classification: LCC BS2520.S9 R44 2021 (print) | LCC BS2520.S9 (ebook) |
   DDC 248.8/43—dc23
LC record available at https://lccn.loc.gov/2021047376
LC ebook record available at https://lccn.loc.gov/2021047377

| P | 25 | 24 | 23 | 22 | 21 | 20 | 19 | 18 | 17 | 16 | 15 | 14 | 13 | 12 | 11 | 10 | 9 | 8 | 7 | 6 | 5 | 4 | 3 | 2 |
| Y | 37 | | 36 | | 35 | | 34 | | 33 | | 32 | | 31 | | 30 | | 29 | | 28 | | 27 | | 26 | | 25 | | 24 | | 23 | | 22 |

CONTENTS

PREFACE

Why John 4, Yet Again? Why Now?

THE LEAD PASTOR OF A MEGACHURCH. A youth conference chaperone. A Sunday school teacher, the president of an evangelical Christian university, a Catholic priest, a youth pastor. Beginning in the fall of 2017, the #MeToo movement and its offshoot, #ChurchToo, have given women and men who have been abused by sexual predators and opportunists in Christian communities a platform to share their stories. The crisis is not new. But the tidal wave of revelations and accusations has made the crisis impossible to ignore as easily as in the past.

"As easily": pastors, governing boards, and ordinary Christians have not always (perhaps even rarely) responded well to accusations, choosing to prioritize and protect the reputation of the abusers and the church. Christian communities have silenced victims and survivors by redefining abuse and assault as mutual sin or inappropriate relationships, a move that makes the person who was abused responsible for their own abuse—and then shames them for it. Sexual crimes have therefore gone unreported to law enforcement, and sexual criminals have been free to abuse others.

This situation is changing as a tidal wave of credible allegations has swept away willful ignorance. Key church leaders and even entire denominations have publicly recognized their errors. Christian churches and parachurch organizations are developing stronger policies and procedures for protecting vulnerable people from abuse.

But I confess that, as I have listened to survivors tell their stories of abuse and of mismanaged responses that have only added to the trauma, I have been deeply angry. How has the church created a space in which abusers are enabled and the people they abuse are silenced and shamed? Why has the church been so slow to acknowledge the evil we have done, repent, and change? I have wondered where my place is in this crisis. What can a biblical scholar contribute to the church's response to the crisis of sexual abuse?

There are two obvious possibilities. First, the Bible bears witness to people victimized by the powerful who ignore God's demand for justice: Hagar; Dinah; Tamar in 2 Samuel 13; women harassed at wells and assaulted in fields; slandered brides; women like Sarah, Rebekah, and Bathsheba, endangered because they were seen by men. Biblical narratives of sexual assault are written from and reflect the perspectives of men in patriarchal societies. But their presence in the church's Scriptures nonetheless demands that we hear and learn.

Second, a call for justice and the protection of the vulnerable runs straight through the Bible, from beginning to end. The commands of the Torah, the laments of the Psalms, prophetic indictments, Jesus' words and actions, the exhortations of Paul and James, and more challenge the powerful to give up their power for the sake of the powerless. Both of these are important elements of a Christian response to the crisis of sexual abuse, and many survivors, counselors, pastors, and theologians have taken up the task of reminding the church of these biblical messages.

This book addresses a third concern. The Bible itself is implicated in the problem. The Bible gives limited attention to women or women's perspectives in stories and laws, which all reflect patriarchal cultural norms. Biblical stories and laws also disrupt a male-centric world with strong women who speak, lead, seek God, and are valued for their words. But through the history of the church, readers with their own patriarchal assumptions have often missed these disruptions.

The Bible challenges us with a vision for God's love for the world, a love centered in justice and equity, in the thriving of those who have been oppressed. Its stories, commands, and prayers also show us the reality of life in a world ruled by sin and death. Unfortunately, tragically, the church throughout history has too often used the Bible to perpetuate abuse rather than protect the vulnerable. This book explores this space through one specific story: the woman at the well in John 4:4-42.

I have two purposes in this book. First, I survey the traditional Christian interpretation of the Samaritan woman as sexual sinner. This analysis particularly focuses on the intersection of women, sex, and sin in Christian understanding and the consequences of this intersection for women in the church. Second, I explore an alternate interpretation that centers the Samaritan woman's words, influence, and leadership in the story. This interpretation challenges the objectification of women with women's agency in and contribution to the church.

The structure of the book echoes these two purposes, with the first part (chapters two, three, and four) centering on historical interpretations of the Samaritan woman's story, and part two (chapters five, six, and seven) offering a reinterpretation of John 4:4-42. Chapter one explores the purposes of the book more fully, and brief introductions at the beginning of part one and part two explain what to expect in each section. Sidebars throughout the book provide supplemental information or draw attention to important questions and concerns. I also quote extensively from interpretations of John 4:4-42, and from sources that represent women's lives in the first century world. Many of these sources are accessible online, so you can explore for yourselves (links are provided in the bibliography).

Finally, in this book I will sometimes address historical and contemporary stories of assault. These stories may be difficult for readers who have experienced abuse, so please read with care. These stories may also be difficult for readers who have not experienced abuse. They should be. Listening to victims and survivors is not comfortable. But it is a necessary part of lamenting, repenting, healing, and changing our communal practices to prevent abuse and to support victims and survivors.

> *Victim* and *survivor* refer to the same person. As Anne Marie Miller explains, the language of *victim* emphasizes the traumatic experience of assault, while the term *survivor* offers a way to reframe the experience of assault.[1] Both terms are needed to express the complex realities of living with abuse, even after it has ended.

There are many good, useful resources available for understanding sexual assault and its effects on individuals and communities, the crisis of abuse in

---

[1] Anne Marie Miller, *Healing Together: A Guide to Supporting Sexual Abuse Survivors* (Grand Rapids, MI: Zondervan Reflective, 2019), 77-78.

the church, and how to develop safe communities in which vulnerable people are protected against abuse. Here are a few:

- Rape, Abuse, and Incest National Network (RAINN): www.rainn.org/
- Mary DeMuth, *We Too: How the Church Can Respond Redemptively to the Sexual Abuse Crisis* (Eugene, OR: Harvest House, 2019).
- Rachael Denhollander, *What Is a Girl Worth?* (Carol Stream, IL: Tyndale Momentum, 2019).
- Ruth Everhart, *The #MeToo Reckoning: Facing the Church's Complicity in Sexual Abuse and Misconduct* (Downers Grove, IL: InterVarsity Press, 2020).
- FaithTrust Institute: www.faithtrustinstitute.org/
- Marie Fortune, *Sexual Violence: The Sin Revisited* (Cleveland: Pilgrim Press, 2005).
- Godly Response to Abuse in the Christian Environment (GRACE): www.netgrace.org/
- Anne Marie Miller, *Healing Together: A Guide to Supporting Sexual Abuse Survivors* (Grand Rapids, MI: Zondervan Reflective, 2019).

ACKNOWLEDGMENTS

I BEGAN THINKING ABOUT THIS PROJECT as a way to channel my grief and rage in response to the #MeToo and #ChurchToo movements. I thank the many friends, colleagues, and students who have listened, debated, questioned, and contributed to the development of my ideas and arguments over the past few years, especially Deborah Dunn, Patti Hunter, and Helen Rhee. Anna Moseley Gissing encouraged the project from its beginning and expertly guided the editing process, and Aniel Morey assisted with research of contemporary interpretations.

Special thanks are due to the librarians at Westmont College. In the midst of the coronavirus pandemic, Richard Burnweit and Jana Mullen made my work possible through their exceptional efforts to collect books and find options for interlibrary loans. I am so appreciative of their dedication to the service of the library.

Finally, I wrote part of the book on my parents' farm during the long pandemic summer of 2020. My nieces contributed to the balance of research, writing, and life with dinosaur hunts, cookie baking, and bike rides. I offer this book in the hope that they will grow up in a church that recognizes and celebrates the women of the Bible as models for all people to follow.

1

WOMEN, SEX, AND SIN
IN THE CHURCH

IN MATTHEW, MARK, AND LUKE, Jesus talks about the kingdom of God. In John, Jesus talks about himself, often in lengthy sermons. Other people—John the Baptist, Martha, a man who was born blind—also talk about Jesus. The Gospel of John further explores Jesus' identity through the narrative structure of sacred times and spaces: Passover, Sabbath, the temple, the wilderness. This Gospel recenters the significance of Israel's sacred times and spaces on Jesus. He is the manna that feeds God's people (Jn 6:35). He works on the Sabbath because God is still at work (Jn 5:17). He is the living temple, the presence of God once again camping out among the people (Jn 1:14, 2:19).

This pattern is established in the narrative by John 4, when Jesus passes through Samaria on his way home from the Passover celebrations in Jerusalem. He sits down by a well to rest, and, as readers might expect, the location has theological significance. Jacob and his sons dug the well on the land they purchased from the people of Shechem (Gen 33:19). This place is one of the first pieces of the Promised Land that the people of God possessed, a sort of down payment on Abraham's covenant.

In this space, Jesus meets a woman. A single man meeting a woman at a well—in the Bible, stories that begin this way end with marriage (Gen 24:10-51, 29:1-30; Ex 2:15-21). But the story in John 4 disrupts the pattern. The woman is not single. Moreover, she's a Samaritan, and as the story reminds us, Jews and Samaritans have a long history of conflict, division, and animosity.

Instead of romance, this story is about religious tensions and rivalry, with overtones of what we might today describe as racism. The Samaritan woman confronts Jesus with the most important questions of the divide between their two peoples: Where should God be worshiped, in the Jewish temple in Jerusalem or the Samaritan temple on Mt. Gerizim? Whose father is Jacob and, therefore, who should rightly possess this very well beside them? Who are the true people of God, the Jews or the Samaritans?

So, in John 4, Jesus returns to Galilee following Passover, the festival that celebrates God's salvation of Israel from enslavement in Egypt so that they can be God's holy people in God's holy land. On his way home, Jesus sits down by a well that symbolizes this heritage, and he meets a woman who thinks this very same space symbolizes her own heritage. And they have a long, serious, focused conversation on the division between the Samaritans and Jews.

This conversation is remarkable. Often in John's Gospel, what begins as a dialogue quickly turns into a monologue from Jesus (as happens with Nicodemus in Jn 3:2-21, and the disciples in Jn 4:31-38). But at Jacob's well, the Samaritan woman is a real partner in the discussion. Her responses and questions indicate her awareness of history, theology, and current events. She is insightful.

In response, Jesus clearly announces the changing identity of the people of God—no longer Jew or Samaritan, but something else. And he clearly announces his own identity as Messiah and "I am." The woman in turn models the response to Jesus that John's Gospel expects (compare Jn 1:6-8; 1:32-34; 9:1-38; 20:30-31). Over the course of the conversation, she goes from identifying Jesus as a Jew, to recognizing him as a prophet, to realizing that he may just be the Messiah. She then testifies to his identity in her hometown.

> "I am" statements litter John's Gospel. Sometimes, they are used to explain specific elements of Jesus' identity (the bread of life, the light of the world, etc.). But sometimes, they are references to God's name in Exodus 3:14. Jesus' announcement to the Samaritan woman in John 4:26 is the first of these.

As Jesus' metaphor in John 4:35-38 anticipates, the nameless Samaritan woman's testimony leads to a great harvest. Her neighbors listen to her! Because of her words, they follow her back to the well to meet Jesus for themselves. They believe in Jesus on account of the woman's testimony as well as Jesus' own words (Jn 4:39-42). While Jesus' disciples are off buying food, this woman, a Samaritan and relative stranger to Jesus, does the work of God. She is an apostle.

But this isn't the way the Samaritan woman's story is usually told in the church. Instead, pastors and teachers focus their attention on one part of the exchange: John 4:16-18.

THE SAMARITAN WOMAN AND THE CHURCH

[The Samaritan woman] was an outcast and looked down upon
by her own people. This is evidenced by the fact that she came alone
to draw water from the community well when, during biblical times,
drawing water and chatting at the well was the social highpoint of a
woman's day. However, this woman was ostracized and marked as
immoral, an unmarried woman living openly with the sixth in a
series of men. The story of the woman at the well teaches
us that God loves us in spite of our bankrupt lives.

Got Questions Ministries, "What Can We Learn
from the Woman at the Well?"

Early in the third century, Tertullian, a Christian theologian in Carthage, described the Samaritan woman as a prostitute.[1] In an otherwise positive portrayal of the woman's intelligence and apostolic zeal, John Chrysostom told his congregation in fourth-century Antioch that the woman was guilty of wicked, shameful sin.[2] For John Calvin a millennium later, the woman's gender and marital history overwhelmed her story. He derided her as an adulterer who forced her husbands to divorce her.[3] Nineteenth-century revivalist Dwight L. Moody used John 4 to preach God's power to save even a "fallen woman" (that is, a prostitute) like the Samaritan woman.[4]

---

[1]Tertullian, *On Modesty* 11.1.
[2]John Chrysostom, *Homilies on John* 31-34.
[3]John Calvin, *The Gospel According to St. John 1–10*, trans. T. H. L. Parker, Calvin's Commentaries (1961; repr., Grand Rapids, MI: Eerdmans, 1978), 90.
[4]Dwight Lyman Moody, "Salvation for Sinners," in *"The Gospel Awakening." Comprising the Sermons and Addresses, Prayer-Meeting Talks and Bible Readings of the Great Revival Meetings*

There are disruptions to this interpretation. Chrysostom's representation
of the woman as an apostle is echoed by Marie Dentière in the sixteenth
century and Virginia Broughton in the twentieth century, for instance.[5] But
the emphatic accusations of adultery and prostitution resound across the
centuries to our own day, as the quotation above from Got Questions
Ministries indicates. The history of interpretation of John 4:4-42 in the
church reflects a consistent association of the Samaritan woman with
sexual sin, and a consequent minimization of her presence and contribution to the narrative.

There is a theological purpose to the characterization of the woman as a
shocking sinner, as this sermon preached by Charles Spurgeon shows:

> I think that I hear one ask, "Do you mean to say that that woman was saved?"
> Yes, I expect to meet her in Heaven. Among the fair daughters of the New
> Jerusalem, the woman that was waiting at the well will surely be found! "But
> she was such a shocking character," says one. She was a shocking character—I
> hope that there is not any woman here half as bad as she was, though there
> may be, and there may even be some worse than she was—but she was saved
> and so will you be, if you go the same way that she went.[6]

The Samaritan woman's story exemplifies the grace of God. Interpreters celebrate John 4:4-42 as a story of hope for all sinners, even those women who
sin in the same way the Samaritan woman did.

In addition, interpreters use the story to encourage particular evangelistic
practices. Jesus transgresses boundaries—Jew and Samaritan, male and
female, respected rabbi and (as one interpreter says) "that kind of woman"—
to share the good news of salvation.[7] He then convicts the woman of her
sexual sin because the condemnation of sin is a necessary step in salvation.

Conducted by Moody and Sankey, 20th ed., ed. L. T. Remlap (Chicago: Fairbanks and Palmer,
1885), 530-31.

[5]Marie Dentière, *Epistle to Marguerite de Navarre* and *Preface to a Sermon by John Calvin*, in *Marie
Dentière: Epistle to Marguerite de Navarre and Preface to a Sermon by John Calvin*, trans. and ed.
Mary B. McKinley, The Other Voice in Early Modern Europe (Chicago: University of Chicago
Press, 2004), 55; Virginia W. Broughton, *Women's Work: As Gleaned from the Women of the Bible*,
in *Virginia Broughton: The Life and Writings of a National Baptist Missionary*, ed. Tomeiko Ashford
Carter (Knoxville: University of Tennessee Press, 2010), 17.

[6]Charles Spurgeon, "Sychar's Sinner Saved," *Spurgeon's Sermons*, vol. 38, *Christians Classics Ethereal
Library*, https://ccel.org/ccel/spurgeon/sermons38/sermons38.xli.html.

[7]Liz Curtis Higgs, *Bad Girls of the Bible and What We Can Learn from Them* (Colorado Springs:
Waterbrook, 1999), 92.

In these ways, Jesus' interaction with the Samaritan woman provides a model for evangelists to follow.[8]

This version of the Samaritan woman's encounter with Jesus is quite different from the one I told at the beginning of the chapter. As you may have guessed, I think the common interpretation of this story in the church significantly misrepresents it. Sin is an important theme in John, and Jesus warns people against continuing in sin.[9] But sin is not mentioned in John 4:4-42. Neither is forgiveness. Jesus does not tell the woman to repent or change her life, and there's no indication that she does (or even, as we'll see in the second part of this book, that she could).

The insistent insertion of sin into the Samaritan woman's story has several problems. First, when sin becomes the lens for viewing the woman, a particular interpretation of her marital history overrides the rest of the story. The woman's intelligence, her insight, and the power of her words are diminished (and sometimes disappear altogether). The sexualization of the woman reduces her to an archetypal femme fatale. Instead of a model for discipleship and leadership in the Christian community, her story becomes a warning of the dangers of women's sexuality.

Second, this representation of the woman as sexual sinner separates her from Jesus' messages in John 4:4-42. Interpreters sometimes explore the story's contributions to understandings of God and worship without much attention to the woman.[10] Others question the woman's ability to understand what Jesus says.[11] However, the Samaritan woman is a real conversation partner in John 4:4-42. Her responses to Jesus drive the story forward. Notably, she introduces the question of the proper place for worship that sparks Jesus' message. To reduce the woman to a sinner in need of salvation minimizes her significant contribution in this narrative.

This minimization represents a third major problem with the prevailing interpretation of John 4:4-42. The characterization of the Samaritan woman

---

[8]For instance, John Calvin, *St. John 1–10*, 94; Scott Hoezee, "John 4:1-38: 'Welling Up,'" sermon preached at Calvin Christian Reformed Church, http://yardley.cs.calvin.edu/hoezee/2002/john4.html.

[9]Note Jn 5:14, 8:11, 8:24, 9:41, 15:22-24, 16:8-11.

[10]Tertullian, *On Prayer* 28; Cyril, *Catechetical Lectures* 16.11.

[11]Thomas Aquinas, *Commentary on the Gospel of John* 581; John Piper, "Not in This or That Mount, but in Spirit and Truth" (message given June 28, 2009), *Desiring God*, www.desiringgod.org/messages/not-in-this-or-that-mount-but-in-spirit-and-truth.

as an adulterer or prostitute exemplifies the dehumanizing, reductive sexualization of women in the theology and practice of the church. This pattern of interpretation endlessly repeats: Deborah and Jael, Bathsheba, Mary Magdalene, the woman who anoints Jesus in Luke 7:36-50. These women (among many others) are categorized and defined on the basis of gender and sexuality.[12]

As a consequence, their active participation in the story of Israel and the early church is diminished or lost entirely. The standard interpretations of biblical women impede their identification as leaders. This in turn limits the identification of these women as models for leadership in the church. Men cannot learn from their stories, and women are left without opportunity for active participation in the church or recognition for their contributions to the church.

Moreover, the reductive sexualization of women in the Bible teaches a message about women in the church: they are interesting or worthy of attention only with respect to sexuality. Women become objects of male desire and (consequently) stumbling blocks that cause men to fall into temptation and sin. The sexualization of women in theological tradition places the burden of sexual sin on women, at the same time making women available to men's gaze, desire, and action. As the history of the church shows all too clearly, this combination of minimization, limitation, and sexualization creates space for the victimization of women.

> Because this book focuses on the story of the Samaritan woman, and because so many of the recent allegations of sexual assault and rape have come from women, I have chosen to limit my discussion to the particular issues of women (including adolescent girls). But women are not the only ones to experience sexual abuse. Young children and men are also assaulted, and while the majority of assailants are men, women are also abusers. This book is focused on one element of the crisis of abuse, but the argument has implications for other vulnerable peoples and other biblical stories.

The history of interpretation of John 4:4-42 is revealing. It opens a window into Christian understandings of sex and sexuality. It displays the church's

---

[12]See further Sandra Glahn, ed., *Vindicating the Vixens: Revisiting Sexualized, Vilified, and Marginalized Women of the Bible* (Grand Rapids, MI: Kregel Academic, 2017).

minimization of women in the Bible and marginalization of women in Christian communities. These messages can have devastating consequences for the church.

BIBLICAL INTERPRETATION AND WOMEN IN THE CHURCH

*The problem of the metaphor's unintended effects remains. It is not enough
for many readers and hearers to be told, upon hearing such shocking and
brutal language, that the rape or torture just portrayed was (no worries!)
"just" a metaphor—particularly when the real brutality suffered by some
parishioners instantly upstages whatever the biblical point may have been.*

JOHN L. THOMPSON, *READING THE BIBLE WITH THE DEAD*

John L. Thompson's comments concern the imagery of the prophets: unfaithful wives, vivid portrayals of prostitution, and horrifying depictions of sexual violence directed against women. He pushes us to consider the effects of this imagery on readers.[13] How do we interpret texts like these? Especially, how do we interpret texts like these when we know that at least one in six women in the United States has been sexually assaulted? When, among Black women, that number is one in four, and among Indigenous women, one in three? When, from ages sixteen to nineteen, girls are four times more likely than anyone else to be raped or assaulted?[14]

> In addition to physical assault and violence, 65 percent of women globally report incidents of unwanted touching, leering, comments, explicit photos, and solicitations. Compared with rape, these daily experiences may seem unimportant. But these less-physical forms of assault are part of a web of violence against women. When harassment becomes normative, so do more physical forms of assault.[15]

---

[13]Rachael Denhollander, *What Is a Girl Worth?* (Carol Stream, IL: Tyndale Momentum, 2019), 89-90, addresses this same issue from the survivor's perspective.

[14]These statistics come from the Rape, Abuse, and Incest National Network (www.rainn.org /statistics) and the National Resource Center on Domestic Violence (https://vawnet.org/sc /gender-based-violence-and-intersecting-challenges-impacting-native-american-alaskan -village-1). While these statistics are specific to the United States, international data suggests similar trends around the world (with significant variation between countries and regions).

[15]See Pamela Cooper-White, *Cry of Tamar: Violence Against Women and the Church's Response*, 2nd ed. (Minneapolis: Fortress, 2012), 65.

8   *The Samaritan Woman's Story*

The way the church reads, interprets, and teaches the Bible matters. It matters for victims and survivors of sexual violence. It matters for perpetrators of sexual violence. How we use the Bible has consequences for the values, relationships, and messages of Christian communities. To misrepresent or omit traditionally feminine imagery or stories about women limits our understanding of God, God's people, and God's kingdom.

Take, for instance, biblical representations of God. Many metaphors come from nature (God is a rock or a fire). Others reflect masculine images like fathers, kings, or shepherds. But the Bible also portrays God as a woman giving birth, a mother bear avenging her cubs, and a woman cleaning her whole house to find a lost coin (Is 42:14; Hos 13:8; Lk 15:8-10). If we ignore these representations of God, we stunt our own knowledge of God. In the process, we also make it more difficult to recognize the image of God in women.[16]

Deborah the prophet spoke God's word to Israel, and all the people respected her judgment (Judg 4–5). Women traveled with Jesus along with the twelve (male) disciples (Lk 8:1-3). Paul recognized Phoebe as a leader of the church (Rom 16:1-2). When we claim that Deborah only led because no good men were available, ignore the presence of women among Jesus' closest disciples, and demote Phoebe from deacon and patron to servant, we effectively marginalize women in the story of God's people. These interpretations weaken the church by preventing women from using their gifts of speaking, teaching, and leadership.[17]

Sometimes, all too often, the stories we choose to read together and the messages we proclaim don't just limit our understanding of God or dilute our practices of faith. Sometimes the ways we read the Bible endanger women. The creation of woman in Genesis 2:18-25 and her transgression and its consequences in Genesis 3:1-16 are used to teach the inferiority of women, their greater inclination to sin, and their necessary subjugation to any and all male authority. The instructions to wives in 1 Peter 3:1-6 are used to

---

[16]See further Elizabeth A. Johnson, *She Who Is: The Mystery of God in Feminist Theological Discourse* (1992; repr., New York: Crossroad, 2018), 3-6, 34-42, 79-107.

[17]Lucy Peppiatt, *Rediscovering Scripture's Vision for Women: Fresh Perspectives on Disputed Texts* (Downers Grove, IL: IVP Academic, 2019), explores these ideas more thoroughly. See esp. pages 25-26, 114, 128-29.

discourage women in abusive relationships from seeking help or leaving an abusive partner.[18]

Likewise, the intersection of women, sex, and sin has serious consequences. Dinah bears the responsibility for her assault because she left her father's home to visit the Canaanite women (Gen 34). This interpretation sends a message about rape. It is the woman's fault: What was she wearing? Where was she? How was she behaving? She deserves what she gets for leaving the safety of her father's house and placing temptation in a man's way.[19]

Bathsheba bathes naked in what she knows to be the sight of the king. She seduces David, a man after God's own heart, into the sin of adultery (2 Sam 11). This interpretation ignores the power imbalances highlighted in the narrative. It blurs the distinction between adultery and assault. It also warns godly men against the danger of sexual, seductive, power-hungry women.[20]

The sin of the woman who washes Jesus' feet with her tears is defined as prostitution (what other kind of sin could a woman commit?). This woman is identified with the woman who anointed Jesus before his burial, who is then named as Mary the sister of Martha, who (on the basis of a shared name) is identified with Mary Magdalene. By this chain of interpretive moves, the "apostle to the apostles" becomes a reformed prostitute. The collapsing of four people into one minimizes women's contribution to Jesus' ministry. It also reduces four complex stories to a single, simple message centered in women's problematic sexuality and immorality.[21]

These interpretations are imposed on the biblical text. They ignore narrative clues that suggest a different message—Dinah's brothers' understanding of what has happened to her in Genesis 34:31; Nathan's

---

[18]See Amanda W. Benckhuysen, *The Gospel According to Eve: A History of Women's Interpretation* (Downers Grove, IL: IVP Academic, 2019), 11, 49-50 (and throughout); Peppiatt, *Scripture's Vision*, 44-54; Caryn A. Reeder, "1 Peter 3:1-6: Biblical Authority and Battered Wives," *Bulletin for Biblical Research* 25 (2015): 519-39.

[19]John L. Thompson, *Reading the Bible with the Dead: What You Can Learn from the History of Exegesis That You Can't Learn from Exegesis Alone* (Grand Rapids, MI: Eerdmans, 2007), 188-92; Mary DeMuth, *We Too: How the Church Can Respond Redemptively to the Sexual Abuse Crisis* (Eugene, OR: Harvest House, 2019), 34-36.

[20]See Sarah Bowler, "Bathsheba: Vixen or Victim?" in Glahn, *Vixens*, 81-100; Ruth Everhart, *The #MeToo Reckoning: Facing the Church's Complicity in Sexual Abuse and Misconduct* (Downers Grove, IL: InterVarsity Press, 2020), 100, 113-24.

[21]The three anointing stories appear in Lk 7:36-50; Mk 14:3-9 (paralleled in Mt 26:6-13); and Jn 12:1-8. See further Karla Zazueta, "Mary Magdalene: Repainting Her Portrait of Misconceptions," in Glahn, *Vixens*, 255-72.

condemnation of David's abuse of power in 2 Samuel 12:1-7; the broad meaning of "sinner" in Luke's Gospel. These interpretations also miss the responsibility men bear for their own sexual morality.

As Linda Klein notes, women in contemporary churches are often told they are "stumbling stones" to the men around them. Their bodies, clothing, and behavior make men fall into sexual sin.[22] In other words, women endanger men. The solution is to control women's presence in the church with, for instance, dress codes, restrictions on leadership, and the "Billy Graham rule" (which limits the time and space men share with women other than their own wives).

> In March 2021, a young White man shot eight people who worked at massage parlors in Atlanta, Georgia (one man and seven women, six of whom were of Asian descent). The shooter, who was active in his church, allegedly attributed the violence to sex addiction. He killed eight people in order to remove the source of temptation—a shocking, disturbing outworking of the identification of women as "stumbling stones." Responding to this violence, Rachael Denhollander warns that Christian teachings on sexuality "can be life and death," particularly for minoritized communities (as discussed further below).[23]

However, in Mark 9:42-48 the stumbling stone refers to the abuse of a vulnerable person. Here and in Matthew 5:27-30, Jesus demands that men who objectify women (or anyone else), seeking to satisfy their own sexual desires, police themselves to the extent of maiming their own bodies.[24] Paul's prohibition of the use of prostitutes in 1 Corinthians 6:15-16 protects these enslaved men and women from abuse by Christian men.[25] Instructions to a church leader in 1 Timothy 5:1-2 demand sexual integrity in all relationships

---

[22]Linda Kay Klein, *Pure: Inside the Evangelical Movement That Shamed a Generation of Young Women and How I Broke Free* (New York: Touchstone, 2018), 3.

[23]Rachael Denhollander, @R_Denhollander, Twitter thread, March 17, 2021, https://twitter .com/R_Denhollander/status /1372220091048333320.

[24]Marie Fortune, *Sexual Violence: The Sin Revisited* (Cleveland: Pilgrim Press, 2005), 101-2, addresses Mt 5:27-30 as representative of sexual violence.

[25]Though this protection may not be the primary purpose of Paul's exhortation, it is a consequence.

with the people of the church, putting the responsibility for ethical behavior entirely on the leader.

> These New Testament texts address men, reflecting the patriarchal cultural norms of the first century. But the warnings and instructions apply to all people. No one should take advantage of someone else, not by the way they look at, speak to, or treat the other person.

To restrict the Bible's women to their (sexualized) bodies and physical desires, to interpret women's words and actions as the deliberate seduction of men: These messages misrepresent the biblical text. They define women as sexual objects. They limit women's contributions to God's kingdom to sex. These messages make women's bodies available to men, and also make the women complicit in any action the men might take. Harassment, assault, and rape are reduced to mutual sin. And women are blamed for the "sin" regardless of their age, social position relative to the man, fear, or shame.

READING THE BIBLE AFTER #CHURCHTOO

*I wonder if the stranger who raped Melissa grew up hearing
Scripture interpreted to make women rape-able.*

Ruth Everhart, *The #MeToo Reckoning*

The reductive sexualization of the women in the Bible has dangerous consequences for women of all ages in our churches. It contributes to the creation of an environment within which sexual abuse can develop and flourish. As with Everhart's story of Melissa, raped in a hallway during a Christmas Eve worship service, the stories of sexual assault that have been told as part of the #ChurchToo movement make the danger clear.

In October 2017, Jodi Kantor and Megan Twohey published nearly thirty years of accusations of sexual misconduct by Harvey Weinstein. The publicity of Weinstein's case—and the speed with which he lost his credibility and his freedom—encouraged many women and some men to share their own experiences under the hashtag #MeToo (originally proposed by activist Tarana Burke in 2006). A wildfire of allegations grew against actors, directors, politicians, and more.[26]

#MeToo also inspired victims and survivors of sexual abuse, harassment, and wrongdoing perpetrated by Christian leaders to tell their stories. One of these women, Emily Joy Allison, tweeted her experience of being groomed by a youth leader in her church when she was only fifteen years old. Allison's friend, Hannah Paasch, added the hashtag #ChurchToo, and within a day the first story had been augmented by many more.[27]

Of course, these allegations are only the latest in a long history. Beginning in the second century, church leaders expressed concern for the safety of unmarried women dedicated to service in the church if men saw and desired them.[28] Reports of harassment, exploitation, and rape among anchorites, monastic communities, and churches appear in sources from the Middle East and across Europe, up to and beyond the Reformation.[29]

More recently, from the 1980s on, survivors and investigative journalists have revealed the systemic abuse of children, women in religious orders, and others within the Catholic Church around the world. Protestants are also implicated, as witnessed by the abuses in various American contexts: seminary professor John Howard Yoder; pastors Bill Hybels, Jack Hyles, and Andy Savage, among others; a number of churches associated with the Southern

---

[26]Jodi Kantor and Megan Twohey, "Harvey Weinstein Paid Off Sexual Harassment Accusers for Decades," *New York Times*, October 5, 2017, www.nytimes.com/2017/10/05/us/harvey -weinstein-harassment-allegations.html; and *She Said: Breaking the Sexual Harassment Story That Helped Ignite a Movement* (New York: Penguin, 2019).

[27]Emily Joy Allison (@emilyjoypoetry), Twitter thread, November 20, 2017, https://twitter.com /emilyjoypoetry/status/932789409551929345; see also Hannah Paasch, "Sexual Abuse Happens in #ChurchToo," *HuffPost*, December 4, 2017, www.huffpost.com/entry/sexual-abuse-church too_n_5a205b30e4b03350e0b53131. Emily Joy Allison has related a fuller version of her story and her experience of making her story public in *#ChurchToo: How Purity Culture Upholds Abuse and How to Find Healing* (Minneapolis: Broadleaf, 2021), 6-18.

[28]Tertullian, *On the Veiling of Virgins* 14.2; John Chrysostom, *Homilies on 1 Timothy* 8; John Calvin, *Genesis*, trans. John King, 2 vols. (1847; repr., Edinburgh: Banner of Truth Trust, 1975), 2:218. This is a generous interpretation of these authors (who each put the burden of assault on the women rather than on the men who desire them), but they did at least show awareness of the danger of assault for women.

[29]See, for instance, *Life of Maria the Harlot* 3 in *Harlots of the Desert: A Study of Repentance in Early Monastic Sources*, by Benedicta Ward, Cistercian Studies 106 (Kalamazoo: Cistercian Publications, 1987), 92-101; Fructuosus of Braga, *Rule for the Monastery of Compludo* 17; Dentière, *Epistle*, 70-71; Jeanne de Jussie, *The Short Chronicle: A Poor Clare's Account of the Reformation of Geneva*, trans. and ed. by Carrie S. Klaus, The Other Voice in Early Modern Europe (Chicago: University of Chicago Press, 2006), 62.

Baptist Convention, the African Methodist Episcopal Church, the Presbyterian Church USA, the United Methodist Church, and tragically, many more.[30]

Unfortunately, until recently few people understood that these incidents of abuse in the church were part of a pattern rather than isolated or disconnected cases. The silencing of victims and survivors to protect institutional reputation further obscured the crisis of sexual abuse. #MeToo and #ChurchToo amplify survivors' stories, forcing us to recognize the extent and severity of the crisis.[31]

In social media posts, articles, and books, survivors are able to tell their own experiences unmediated by institutional perspectives. The #MeToo and #ChurchToo movements make the prevalence of the experience of harassment and assault across a variety of church contexts clear, relatable, and hard to ignore: "I interned at a church in college. A male pastor that made it clear to me that women cannot be pastors came up behind me and started playing with my hair. #churchtoo."[32]

The contributions to #ChurchToo humanize the statistics of sexual assault in the church. In a 2008 survey, 2 to 4 percent of women in the United States reported sexual advances from religious leaders. Eight percent of women in this survey knew of a situation of misconduct on the part of a pastor, priest, rabbi, or other leader in their own worshiping community. In two other surveys, 39 percent of clergy self-reported their assault of a congregant, and a shocking 76 percent knew of a case in another church.[33]

As alarming as they are, these numbers are likely lower than they should be due to the silence of victims, survivors, and institutions. Some estimates

---

[30]These allegations are reviewed by Wietse de Boer, "The Catholic Church and Sexual Abuse, Then and Now," *Origins* 12, no. 6 (2019), http://origins.osu.edu/article/catholic-church-sexual-abuse -pope-confession-priests-nuns; Denhollander, *What Is a Girl*, 140-42; Everhart, *#MeToo*; Kristen Kobes Du Mez, *Jesus and John Wayne: How White Evangelicals Corrupted a Faith and Fractured a Nation* (New York: Liveright, 2020), 273-88; Allison, *#ChurchToo*.

[31]Cf. Kantor and Twohey, *She Said*, 181-82.

[32]Laura (@hannlaub), Tweet, November 21, 2017, 12:04 p.m., https://twitter.com/hannlaub/status /933063647823265792.

[33]Mark Chaves and Diana Garland, "The Prevalence of Clergy Sexual Advances Toward Adults in Their Congregations," *Journal for the Scientific Study of Religion* 48 (2009): 817-24; Diana Garland, "The Prevalence of Clergy Sexual Misconduct with Adults: A Research Study Executive Summary," *Clergy Sexual Misconduct*, https://www.baylor.edu/clergysexualmisconduct/index .php?id=67406; Cooper-White, *Cry of Tamar*, 149-51.

suggest 60 to 70 percent of assaults are never reported.[34] The paralyzing effects of fear, shame, and the awareness that very few cases are successfully prosecuted contribute to this particular statistic. Underreporting is one of the many reasons that the #MeToo and #ChurchToo movements are so important for empowering victims and survivors.

"Following the #churchtoo hash with interest. Many #metoo stories at the hands of the church. And me? I was made to sign a purity contract at age 11. And witnessed a man confess from the pulpit having sex w/a child. Praised for his bravery. No further action."[35] As Elizabeth Halford's experience suggests, allegations of harassment and assault are not easy for a church community to hear. Victims and survivors repeatedly report having their allegations silenced or covered over. Analysts and activists explain this sort of response as an indication that many Christians don't understand the legal definitions of assault, how it happens and why, or how it affects victims and survivors. Suppressing allegations protects the church as an institution at the expense of the safety and healing of its members.[36]

Sometimes, criminal acts are redefined as mutual sin or an inappropriate relationship. A pastor or other church leader might confess to falling prey to temptation or to having an affair. The identification of sexual harassment or assault as "sin" makes it a matter for the church to address without the involvement of law enforcement. When leaders or congregants confess their "sin," they are forgiven by their churches—even, as in Elizabeth Halford's story, applauded for their honesty and transparency.[37]

Sexual violence is sin, as Marie Fortune insists. It is not natural, godly, ethical, or good. It violates the humanity and integrity of another person.[38] However, when perpetrators or church communities identify assault as "sin," they usually mean mutual, nonviolent, noncoercive choices and actions taken by both participants. In essence, this approach makes the victim guilty of the sin of being assaulted.

---

[34]Cooper-White, *Cry of Tamar*, 107.
[35]Elizabeth Halford (@TheAlphaBetty), Tweet, November 21, 2017, 3:56 p.m., https://twitter.com/TheAlphaBetty/status/933091785915621376.
[36]See Anne Marie Miller, *Healing Together: A Guide to Supporting Sexual Abuse Survivors* (Grand Rapids, MI: Zondervan Reflective, 2019), 34-42, 73; Everhart, *#MeToo*, 35, 53.
[37]See also DeMuth, *We Too*, 20-23; Everhart, *#MeToo*, 136-40.
[38]Fortune, *Sexual Violence*, 1-4, 29-31, 66-69.

These reactions indicate the church's acceptance of abusers' false representation of abuse. As Mary DeMuth says, it is absolutely essential to recognize that sexual assault is not about sex, love, or relationship: "This is *not* about consensual affairs. This is about coercive control and abuse of power."[39]

Occasionally, pastors and other leaders are asked to leave a church. But without criminal charges or public awareness of the allegations, they are free to repeat the abuse. Often, no action is taken against an alleged perpetrator. Perpetrators have admitted that they choose to be involved with churches because they know people are inclined to trust, to be nice, and to forgive.[40] The way that church communities (fail to) handle allegations of abuse perpetuates the abuse.

At the same time Christian communities praise and forgive male leaders, they shame women and girls for their unwanted sexual experiences: "#churchtoo: when I was told that I shouldn't have gone over to his house by myself. Not that they were sorry. Not that his role would be changed. Just that I shouldn't have gone over there alone (wearing a dress) because it caused him to be 'overcome by lust.'"[41] Responses like this demonstrate the lack of awareness of issues of consent, power dynamics, and the trauma of assault. They also are the consequence of specific theological perspectives on sex, sin, and women.

The church has historically struggled to separate sex and sexuality from sin. In part, this connection develops from condemnations of certain categories of sexual intercourse in the Bible. Some New Testament texts seem to question the morality of any sexual intercourse (1 Cor 7:1-9, for instance). As we will see in chapter two, the ascetic inclinations of the early church compounded the definition of sex, whether with a legitimate spouse or someone else, as sin. The association of sex with sin has never entirely dissipated.

Sexuality also gets tied to gender in contradictory ways. Christian tradition has often depicted men as sexual actors and women as recipients.

---

[39]See DeMuth, *We Too*, 118; and also Everhart, *#MeToo*, 47-55.
[40]DeMuth, *We Too*, 54-55.
[41]Hannah (@hannahelisabeth), Tweet, November 21, 2017, 1:15 p.m., https://twitter.com/hanna helisabeth/status/933081493668286464. See also DeMuth, *We Too*, 126-29; Everhart, *#MeToo*, 140. Even when the case involves two legal adults, power imbalances in a clergy-parishioner relationship make consent impossible (see Cooper-White, *Cry of Tamar*, 152-54).

Men are created by God to have authority in the church, society, and family. As a consequence of their natural (manly) power, they also have an uncontrollable sex drive. This understanding effectively excuses men from acting on their desires. They are only doing what God created them to do, after all.[42]

Correspondingly, women are created by God as "helpmeets" (a term based on the King James translation of Gen 2:18). In terms of sexuality, they are taught to be submissive, subordinate recipients of male attention. As we will see, according to various Christian messages, women (sometimes limited to White women) do not have a natural sex drive. Their drive is rather to accept a man's invitation.[43]

The construction of women's identity around men's sexuality is, as many note, a significant factor in preventing girls and women from knowing that they can say no. Consent is murky in the midst of this gendered dichotomy between male and female.[44]

The reactions and responses of Christian communities to allegations of abuse show another competing view of women: like their mother Eve, women tempt men to sin by using makeup, wearing clothes, having bodies, being present. The same women who are defined as submissive recipients become seductresses as soon as a man acts on his natural sex drive. The shaming and blaming of victims and survivors of assault excuse perpetrators by, as Ruth Everhart says, making the victim into the perpetrator.[45]

> The racialization of sexual stereotypes exacerbates this concern for minoritized women in the United States. For instance, Tamura Lomax addresses the construction of Black women as insatiably sexual: "black women and girls are marked by hypersexuality and pursuance as an essential component of coming

---

[42]See Amy DeRogatis, *Saving Sex: Sexuality and Salvation in American Evangelicalism* (Oxford: Oxford University Press, 2015), 28-31, 61; Everhart, *#MeToo*, 140; Du Mez, *John Wayne*, 91-95, 170-79, 277.

[43]DeRogatis, *Saving Sex*, 112-13; Sara Moslener, *Virgin Nation: Sexual Purity and American Adolescence* (Oxford: Oxford University Press, 2015), 162-63; Du Mez, *John Wayne*, 91-92.

[44]Cooper-White, *Cry of Tamar*, 19; DeRogatis, *Saving Sex*, 31; D. L. Mayfield, "Focus on the Family," *Christ and Pop Culture* (blog), August 7, 2015, https://christandpopculture.com/focus-on-the -family/; Susan A. Ross, "Feminist Theology and the Clergy Sexual Abuse Crisis," *Theological Studies* 80 (2019): 632-52, esp. 639-42.

[45]Everhart, *#MeToo*, 140. See also DeRogatis, *Saving Sex*, 112-13; Miller, *Healing Together*, 36, 174; Du Mez, *John Wayne*, 277-78.

of age—regardless of sexual experience or consent."[46] The consequences of this racist construction are tragically clear in the statistics of rape and assault experienced by Black women. Similarly, the intersection of racialization and sexualization results in "mass objectification, exoticization, and fetishization" for women of Asian descent, factors underlying the mass shooting in Atlanta in March 2021.[47]

Christian teaching has repeatedly defined women as inferior to men in terms of physical strength, intellectual ability, emotional control, personal discipline, authority, and power. The #MeToo and #ChurchToo movements bear witness to the devastating consequences for women, children, and men. Male priests, pastors, youth leaders, Sunday School teachers, volunteers, and congregants are empowered to see girls and women as objects of desire to take and use. It's not their fault, according to their own communities, because women bear the responsibility for men's choices, behaviors, and actions. The reputation of the church or institution and the ministerial voice of the men are more valuable than women's bodies and souls.

THE SAMARITAN WOMAN AND #CHURCHTOO

The treatment of the Samaritan woman in the history of interpretation is
a textbook case of the trivialization, marginalization, and
even sexual demonization of biblical women, which reflects
and promotes the parallel treatment of real women in the church.

Sandra M. Schneiders, *Written That You May Believe*

This book falls into two major sections, each with its own brief introduction. In part one, I explore the history of interpretation of the Samaritan woman. The interpretation of John 4:4-42 from Tertullian to today offers a window

---

[46]Tamura Lomax, *Jezebel Unhinged: Loosing the Black Female Body in Religion & Culture* (Durham: Duke University Press, 2018), xii.

[47]See the Asian American Christian Collaborative's "AACC Statement on the Atlanta Massacre and Ongoing Anti-Asian Hate," www.asianamericanchristiancollaborative.com/atlantastatement; and Nancy Wang Yuen, "Atlanta Spa Shooting Suspect's 'Bad Day' Defense, and America's Sexualized Racism Problem," *Think* (blog), NBC News, 18 March 2021, www.nbcnews.com /think/opinion/atlanta-spa-shooting-suspect-s-bad-day-defense-america-s-ncna1261362.

into the history of the sexual objectification of women in the church. As Sandra Schneiders says, the way the church tells this story (and others like it) has clearly contributed to the formation of troubling, dangerous perspectives on women, perspectives that cannot be separated from the abuses perpetrated against women. I will delve more deeply into these connections in chapter four.

While the focus through part one will remain on the majority interpretation, we will also listen to dissenting perspectives, men and women (okay, mostly women) who remind us of the Samaritan woman's agency, intelligence, and participation in the work of the gospel. A growing number of biblical scholars and pastors today agree with this minority report. In part two of this book, I follow these examples to propose a reinterpretation of John 4:4-42 focusing on the woman's contribution to Jesus' revelation of the new identity of the people of God.

Read in this way, the Samaritan woman's story challenges the church to value women as preachers, teachers, and equal participants in the kingdom of God. As I suggest in the conclusion, the work of analyzing the history of interpretation and exploring a reinterpretation of John 4:4-42 in this book offers guidance for reading the Bible after #ChurchToo. It is possible to resist the tendency to sexualize and minimize women in the church. Replacing the reductive sexualization of women in biblical texts with more constructive habits of interpretation is a necessary element in a Christian response to the crisis of sexual assault.

Part One

READING THE SAMARITAN WOMAN'S STORY WITH THE CHURCH

A woman was used to carry the first gospel message to Samaria; she so advertised Jesus, that a large crowd came out to hear him at Jacob's well.

VIRGINIA BROUGHTON, *WOMEN'S WORK*

As [Jesus] rested, a Samaritan woman came to the well to draw water. We do not know her name; we do, however, know her reputation. She was the dirty, leathery faced town whore.

MARK DRISCOLL, *THE RADICAL REFORMISSION*

CHRISTIAN INTERPRETATIONS OF JOHN 4:4-42 frequently focus on the significance of Jesus' words for doctrines of God and church practices like baptism and worship. The woman herself may be mentioned only as the recipient of Jesus' teachings. Interpreters who pay attention to the woman face a problem. In John 4, Jesus shares deep theological truths with someone whom interpreters most often characterize as poor, uneducated, shockingly immoral, and limited by the constraints of gender. And yet this person is also a successful evangelist.

The quotations above demonstrate two different solutions to the problem of the Samaritan woman. Virginia Broughton, a Black American missionary and Bible teacher in the late nineteenth and early twentieth century, focused on the woman's preaching. In this approach, the end of the story becomes the lens for its interpretation. Mark Driscoll, a White American megachurch pastor in the twenty-first century, focused on what he identified as the woman's life of sexual sin. For Driscoll, the brief report of her many marriages in the middle of the story determines the interpretation of the whole.

As we'll see in this section of the book, Broughton's interpretation has significant echoes through the centuries, but only a few. Driscoll's approach, though stated with his customary crassness, represents the majority interpretation of John 4:4-42 in the church from the second century to today. The Samaritan woman has come to symbolize the dangers of female sexuality and the problem of women's speech.

How did we get to this point? The next three chapters survey the interpretation of John 4:4-42 from the second century to today. This review is necessarily limited to representative approaches from a vast array of commentaries, sermons, devotionals, and more. I have chosen to focus on pastoral approaches that connect the Samaritan woman with the life of the church.

> More comprehensive surveys are available in Craig S. Farmer, "Changing Images of the Samaritan Woman in Early Reformed Commentaries on John," *Church History* 65 (1996): 365-75; Janeth Norfleete Day, *The Woman at the Well: Interpretation of John 4:1-42 in Retrospect and Prospect* (Biblical Interpretation Series 61; Leiden: Brill, 2002); and Frances Gench, *Back to the Well: Women's*

Encounters with Jesus in the Gospels (Louisville: Westminster John Knox, 2004), 109-35. These surveys have their own limits. They do not include the interpretations offered by women before the twentieth century, or pastoral (non-academic) interpretations after the Reformation.

I argue in these chapters that interpretations of John 4:4-42 reflect and contribute to Christian perspectives on women's identity within the family, church, and society. The history of the interpretation of the Samaritan woman is also a history of the sexualization and marginalization of women, factors that have contributed to the crisis of sexual assault in the church. Consequently, I will contextualize interpreters' explanations of the story within their understandings of gender, sex, and sexuality more generally. These perspectives also clarify the significance of the Samaritan woman's significance for women and men in the church.

In chapter two, we'll explore several interpretations of the Samaritan woman from the early church. Scholars often praise John Chrysostom and other early interpreters for their descriptions of the woman as a respectful, intelligent apostle.[1] However, as we will see, the broader context of theological understandings of women, sex, and sin complicates these interpreters' praise. The characterization of the Samaritan woman as a sexual sinner and the problematic, reductive sexualization of women in the church find support in early Christian interpretation.

In chapter three, we'll follow these threads forward into the Protestant Reformation. John Calvin's interpretation of the Samaritan woman made her a symbol of the human story of sin and salvation. He also minimized her witness to Jesus. Calvin's focus on the woman's sin remained central into the social reforms and revivals of the nineteenth century. Clara Lucas Balfour and Dwight L. Moody both identified the Samaritan woman as a prostitute in need of salvation.

In chapter four, these threads pull together in interpretations of the Samaritan woman in the contemporary church in America. John Piper's

---

[1]Craig S. Farmer, "Changing Images of the Samaritan Woman in Early Reformed Commentaries on John," *Church History* 65 (1996): 365-70; Janeth Norfleete Day, *The Woman at the Well: Interpretation of John 4:1-42 in Retrospect and Prospect*, Biblical Interpretation Series 61 (Leiden: Brill, 2002), 11-14.

sermons on John 4:4-42 reflect the increasingly harsh characterization of the Samaritan woman as sexual sinner in the church today. Such portrayals are accompanied by a renewed emphasis on gender hierarchies, the sanctification of marital sex, and the rise of purity culture.

These interpretations also coincide with the current crisis of sexual assault in Christian churches and communities. The intersection of the sexualization of the Samaritan woman with #ChurchToo indicates the need to listen to other voices and explore different interpretations of John 4:4-42. We will begin this work in this section by listening to interpreters who, like Virginia Broughton, identify the Samaritan woman as a model disciple and teacher: John Chrysostom in the fourth century, Marie Dentière in the sixteenth century, Barbara Essex in the twenty-first century. Their approaches to the story will be the starting point for the second part of this book.

2

GENDERED SEXUALITY

The Samaritan Woman in Early Christianity

*Just as your own Lord Jesus Christ revealed himself to the
Samaritan prostitute at the well, won't you look upon me?*

LIFE OF ST. PELAGIA 7 (AT)

THE INTERPRETATIONS OF THE Samaritan woman's story in the very
early church include a range of perspectives. Some commentators found an
intelligent, thoughtful woman who modeled Christian learning and evangelization. The legends of her life included missionary journeys to Carthage
and Rome, and her eventual imprisonment and (in some accounts) martyrdom for preaching the gospel of Jesus.[1]

But, as in the *Life of St. Pelagia* quoted above, the earliest interpretations of John 4:4-42 also insistently emphasized the woman's sexuality.
This fifth-century story commemorated an actress who became a
Christian and lived the rest of her life as an ascetic cross-dressing monk.
In Pelagia's day, actresses were associated with sexual immorality (one
version of the *Life* clearly identified her as a prostitute).[2] The Samaritan
woman's example offered precedent for such a woman to speak with a
bishop of the church.

---

[1]Eva Catafyglotu Topping, *Saints and Sisterhood: The Lives of Forty-Eight Holy Women* (Minneapolis:
Light and Life, 1990), 138-41, summarizes the legends of the Samaritan woman's life.
[2]The Latin version identifies the Samaritan woman as a prostitute. In the Syriac version, Pelagia
is the prostitute.

These different approaches to the Samaritan woman reflect the complexity of early Christian perspectives on sexuality and gender. Bodies, physical pleasure, and sexual intercourse were all subject to a certain amount of suspicion on the parts of theologians, preachers, and monks. The suspicion spilled over to women more generally. The Samaritan woman encapsulated these fears. How should the church understand a woman with an expansive (and therefore questionable) marital history, who nonetheless spoke with Jesus and preached to her community?

In this chapter, I will explore three responses to the problem of John 4:4-42. I will begin with Tertullian who, at the turn of the third century, gives an early reflection on the woman's character. Origen, Tertullian's slightly younger contemporary, made the woman a symbol of people who are misled by unorthodox teachings. I will conclude a century later with John Chrysostom. He offered complex, rich reflections on John 4:4-42, but even he could not escape a troubling association of women, sex, and sin.

ADULTERY AND PROSTITUTION: TERTULLIAN ON JOHN 4:4-42

> *To the Samaritan woman, now during her sixth marriage*
> *not only an adulteress but also a prostitute—and yet the Lord*
> *displayed who he was to her, which he did not easily do.*
>
> TERTULLIAN, *ON MODESTY* 11.1 (AT)

Tertullian, a minister, theologian, and apologist, accused the Samaritan woman of adultery and prostitution in his essays *On Modesty* 11.1 and *On Monogamy* 8.9. He may have thought the woman sold her body for sex, but not necessarily. Tertullian defined marriage as an eternal bond. Consequently, to remarry following divorce or the death of a spouse was adultery. The Samaritan woman's multiple marriages, then, would condemn her of sexual sin whether or not she was faithful to her (current) husband.

Tertullian lived in a relatively wealthy, privileged Roman family in Carthage, in North Africa, from about 150 to 212 CE. At some point (probably during his adult life), Tertullian became a Christian. He held a leadership position in the church as a presbyter, and he wrote extensively on different issues of doctrine and Christian life in a pagan society.[3]

Because Tertullian primarily used biblical texts to develop and support his arguments and ideas, he did not thoroughly analyze or explain John 4:4-42. His brief references are important, however, for two reasons. First, they represent the interpretation of the Samaritan woman's story in the very early church. Second, Tertullian wrote extensively on men, women, and sexuality. His characterization of the Samaritan woman reflects and reinforces his warnings concerning the dangers of women and sex to the Christian man.

Many of Tertullian's perspectives seem strange and even problematic from a modern standpoint. As we'll see, some of his positions were debated in his own time. But Tertullian's critiques of sexuality and women's identity had lasting influence in the early church, and they still echo in the church today. Considering Tertullian's definitions of sex, sexuality, and sexual sin gives us an important starting point for understanding Christian perspectives on gender and sexuality, and how these issues intersect in interpretations of the Samaritan woman.

Tertullian's Samaritan woman. Tertullian drew on John 4:4-42 in multiple essays, but he only mentioned the Samaritan woman in a few places. He noted that Jesus revealed his identity to the woman in *Against Praxeas* 21. He quoted her words to explain the Samaritans' heretical beliefs in *Against Marcion* 4.35. In two other essays, Tertullian critiqued the woman's sexual history. He wrote *On Monogamy* and *On Modesty* in response to what he saw as a weakening of the standards of sexual morality in the church. In both, he used the Samaritan woman's story to emphasize the significance of sexual sin.

As the title suggests, *On Monogamy* is a lengthy argument in favor of monogamy. Tertullian defined "monogamy" as one marriage per person, per lifetime. Based on Matthew 19:3-9, he understood marriage to be an eternal commitment. This interpretation led him to conclude that, in contrast to common practice, Christians should not remarry following divorce or the

---

[3]Learn more about Tertullian in J. Patout Burns and Robin M. Jensen, *Christianity in Roman Africa: The Development of Its Practices and Beliefs* (Grand Rapids, MI: Eerdmans, 2014).

death of a spouse.[4] He identified the Samaritan woman (with her six marriages) as a warning against remarriage.

According to Tertullian's interpretation of John 4:18, Jesus denied that the woman's sixth marriage was legitimate precisely in order to teach his followers that multiple marriages are adultery. Tertullian argued that Christianity demanded bodily holiness. Jesus modeled this holiness by his own celibacy and faithfulness to his spouse, the church.[5] The Samaritan woman, then, became an anti-Christ for Tertullian, the precise opposite of the standard set by Jesus.

In *On Modesty*, Tertullian emphasized the woman's extraordinary sin. He wrote this essay to refute a bishop's decision to forgive Christians who had committed sexual sins, restoring them to full participation in the church following their repentance.[6] In challenging this change in church practice, Tertullian defined adultery and fornication as sins against a person's own body (which belongs to God). They were among the most serious sins a person could commit, on the same level as murder and idolatry in the Ten Commandments. Such sins could only be granted forgiveness within the church at the person's baptism.[7]

Baptism was a serious matter in the early church. People who wanted to be baptized first had to learn the Scriptures, the faith of the church, and spiritual disciplines under the guidance of pastors and teachers. For Tertullian, baptism represented the complete renunciation of sin (including sexual sins). It empowered Christians to live as Jesus did, in holiness, purity, and sexual continence. He discouraged people from seeking baptism until they had demonstrated their ability to maintain a disciplined Christian life.[8]

Some sins could be forgiven after baptism: anger, lying, physical violence. But serious sins like idolatry, murder, and adultery raised questions about

---

[4]Tertullian, *Monogamy* 9.3-9, 10.7-12 (and also *Exhortation to Chastity* 11.1-2; *To His Wife* 1.4.3-8, 1.7.1-5). See further Burns and Jensen, "Forms of Christian Life: Marriage, Virginity, and Widowhood," ch. 9 in *Christianity in Roman Africa*; Outi Lehtipuu, "To Remarry or Not to Remarry? 1 Timothy 5:14 in Early Christian Ascetic Discourse," *Studia Theologica* 71 (2017): 29-50, esp. 35-38.

[5]Tertullian, *Monogamy* 8.8-10.

[6]Tertullian, *Modesty* 1.6-8.

[7]Tertullian, *Modesty* 5.1-6, 16.9-10, 22.13-14. See also Geoffrey D. Dunn, *Tertullian*, Early Church Fathers (London: Routledge, 2004), 55-56.

[8]Tertullian, *Baptism* 4-8, 18; *Modesty* 6.16-18. See also Burns and Jensen, "Becoming a Christian: The Ritual of Baptism," ch. 5 in *Christianity in Roman Africa*.

Christian commitment. A person who committed sexual sin after baptism must be cast out of the church so they could not share in the body and blood of Christ or in Christian fellowship. They should surely repent in the hope that God would mercifully forgive them, but the church did not have that right or power.[9]

"But wait," Tertullian imagined a critic asking, "didn't Jesus forgive the Samaritan woman, who committed sexual sins?" In raising this potential objection, Tertullian characterized the woman as an adulterer and prostitute.[10] These accusations depended on Tertullian's understanding of remarriage as sexual sin. However, he also classified the Samaritan woman with the woman who washed Jesus' feet with her hair (Lk 7:36-50), whom he interpreted as a prostitute. For Tertullian, the Samaritan woman's multiple marriages equated to prostitution.

Jesus revealed his identity to the Samaritan woman, an almost unique occurrence in John's Gospel. However, this did not mean that Christians who committed sexual sin belonged in the church. After all, Tertullian reasoned, the woman was not a Christian when she met Jesus.[11] He did not comment on what may have happened to the woman following her conversation with Jesus. But if her acceptance of Jesus' living water represented her conversion, then she must have changed her life entirely, pursuing sanctification through celibacy.[12] For Tertullian, if she continued in her life of adultery and prostitution, she was no Christian.

Marriage, sex, and sin. Tertullian's interpretation of the Samaritan woman's story reflects his complex, complicated perspectives on marriage, women, and sexual sin. Some of his perspectives represent ideas that continue to influence Christian theologies and practices today. It will be useful, therefore, to explore Tertullian's broader thought to understand both his interpretation of John 4 and the roots of the reductive sexualization of women in the church.

---

[9]See Tertullian, *Modesty* 7.15-16, 19.23-24; and Carly Daniel-Hughes, "'We Are Called to Monogamy': Marriage, Virginity, and the Resurrection of the Fleshly Body in Tertullian of Carthage," in *Coming Back to Life: The Permeability of Past and Present, Mortality and Immortality, Death and Life in the Ancient Mediterranean*, ed. Frederick S. Tappenden and Carly Daniel-Hughes (Montreal: McGill University Library, 2017), 239-64 (here 247).

[10]Tertullian, *Modesty* 11.1.

[11]Tertullian, *Modesty* 11.1-3.

[12]Comparably, Tertullian connects worship, prayer, sanctification, and sexual morality with Jn 4:23 (without mentioning the Samaritan woman) in *Prayer* 28.

As we've seen, Tertullian understood marriage to be an eternal commitment. In this life, marriage maintained the social hierarchy of male rule and female subordination, and it was a useful tool for preventing sexual immorality.[13] But marriage was not entirely good. Tertullian traced a progressive shift away from marriage in the biblical narrative, culminating in the preference of Jesus and Paul for singleness.[14]

Tertullian also understood Matthew 22:30 to mean that sex and sexual desire will not be part of marriage in the resurrection. Marriage and sexual intercourse were, therefore, less than perfect and holy. Furthermore, if it is good not to touch a woman (1 Cor 7:1), then it must be wrong to touch a woman. How "good" could marriage be, if the alternative is to suffer divine punishment (1 Cor 7:9)?[15]

As these arguments suggest, Tertullian was deeply suspicious of the act of sexual intercourse. The only difference between lawful, permissible intercourse in a marriage and adultery was the legal status of the woman. The act of intercourse itself was the same. For Tertullian, this association tainted intercourse between spouses with sin.[16] Though marriage was a legitimate outlet for sexual desire, the tool to prevent sin was itself implicated in sin.

Carly Daniel-Hughes explains that, for Tertullian, sexual desire and pleasure disrupted and weakened a person's body and spirit. Sex made a disciplined Christian life more difficult to attain.[17] Citing the New Prophecy teachings of Priscilla, Tertullian identified sexual renunciation as an

---

[13]Tertullian, *Exhortation* 1.1-2, 3.5; *Monogamy* 1.3-4, 3.3-7, 3.10; *Wife* 1.3; etc. See also Mathew Kuefler, *The Manly Eunuch: Masculinity, Gender Ambiguity, and Christian Ideology in Late Antiquity* (Chicago: University of Chicago Press, 2001), 187-94; Daniels-Hughes, "Monogamy," 258-61.

[14]Tertullian, *Exhortation* 6.1-2; *Monogamy* 5.6-7.

[15]Tertullian, *Exhortation* 3.7-10; *Monogamy* 3.2-6, 10.7-8. He attributes 1 Cor 7:1 to Paul himself, though Paul is quoting (and refuting) the Corinthians here.

[16]Tertullian, *Exhortation* 9.1-4; *Veiling* 2.4; and *Wife* 2.3. See further David G. Hunter, "The Reception and Interpretation of Paul in Late Antiquity: 1 Corinthians 7 and the Ascetic Debates," in *The Reception and Interpretation of the Bible in Late Antiquity*, ed. Lorenzo DiTommaso and Lucian Turcescu, Bible in Ancient Christianity 6 (Leiden: Brill, 2008), 163-91, esp. 173-74; Dyan Elliott, *The Bride of Christ Goes to Hell: Metaphor and Embodiment in the Lives of Pious Women, 200-1500*, The Middle Ages (Philadelphia: University of Pennsylvania Press, 2012), 16-19. See further J. Patout Burns and Robin M. Jensen, "Forms of Christian Life: Marriage, Virginity, and Widowhood," ch. 9 in *Roman Africa*.

[17]Daniel-Hughes, "'Monogamy," 246-47. See also Catherine Conybeare, "Tertullian on Flesh, Spirit, and Wives," in *Severan Culture*, ed. Simon Swain, Stephen Harrison, and Jaś Elsner (Cambridge: Cambridge University Press, 2007), 430-39, esp. 432-34.

essential aspect of sanctification. The person who overcame the dangers of desire and intercourse could focus on prayer, the study of the Scriptures, and worship. This person was empowered in the Christian battle against demons (perceived to be a significant danger in the early Christian world).[18]

New Prophecy, also called Montanism, was an eschatological, charismatic renewal movement founded by Priscilla, Maximilla, and Montanus in the late second century. It was eventually declared heretical, but in Tertullian's day it was an accepted part of the church. Some scholars connect Tertullian's increasingly harsh comments on marriage and sex with his adherence to New Prophecy, though his perspectives remained fundamentally consistent through his works.[19]

I have been saying "a person," but for Tertullian, this person was male. Privileged Roman men like Tertullian defined masculinity as the exercise of power over the self and others. A man's self-control was visible in emotional restraint, rejection of luxuries, and the ability to reason. He exercised control over his dependents: his wife, children, slaves, and others for whom he was legally responsible.[20]

Freeborn women could be masculine to a certain degree through their own self-control, the exercise of authority over others, and courage. Tertullian praised women martyrs for their manliness in enduring martyrdom, for instance.[21] However, the ultimate display of masculinity was reserved for wealthy, powerful men.

The broader cultural understanding of masculinity shaped Tertullian's own views in two important ways. First, Tertullian associated the spirit with masculinity, and the body (or flesh) with femininity. While the body was weak and prone to sin, the spirit was the source of self-control, discipline, and reason—all masculine attributes. Consequently, masculine discipline allowed Christian men to control their bodily urges.[22] Tertullian argued that

---

[18]Tertullian, *Exhortation* 1.1-2, 10.1-5; *Modesty* 16.12, 17.1; *Monogamy* 3.2-3, 3.7-9, 8.1.

[19]See further Dunn, *Tertullian*, 6-7.

[20]See Conybeare, "Tertullian," 430-39; Caryn A. Reeder, *Gendering War and Peace in the Gospel of Luke* (Cambridge: Cambridge University Press, 2019), 27-29.

[21]Tertullian, *On the Apparel of Women* 2.13.3-5.

[22]See Tertullian, *Exhortation* 1.1-2; *Modesty* 2.3; and *Monogamy* 7.3-4.

male virgins were more honorable than female virgins precisely because of their masculine self-control.[23]

> The masculinity of sexual restraint in Tertullian's essays contrasts with Roman men's extensive sexual freedom. A man had access to his wife, his slaves, enslaved prostitutes, and entertainers at parties or in the theater. None of this was considered adultery under the laws of the time nor immoral by social standards. As long as a man was not overly indulgent with his sexual liaisons, they were unlikely to attract much attention or interest.
>
> By contrast, Tertullian argued that overly permissive sexual morality emasculated men (*Modesty* 2.3). The self-discipline of sexual renunciation, therefore, made Christian men more masculine than their non-Christian neighbors.[24]

Second, Tertullian's assertion of the superiority of male virgins developed from the connection of masculinity with sexuality. Reflecting the importance of power, masculinity was expressed in initiating sex and acting as the penetrator in a sexual encounter. Women were passive recipients of men's advances.[25] For Tertullian, the distinctive sexual roles of men and women made sexual desire a man's problem, so self-control was both a masculine virtue and men's responsibility.

Tertullian's perspectives on gender, marriage, and sexuality were clearly informed by his social and cultural contexts in the Roman Empire.[26] In the patriarchal, patrilineal structures of his day, men had priority in terms of legal standing and authority. The intersection of legal and social power with definitions of masculinity helps explain Tertullian's understanding of Christian discipline and sexual morality. However, these contexts raise

---

[23]Tertullian, *Veiling* 10.2-4. Daniel-Hughes, "Monogamy," 256-58, and Benjamin H. Dunning, *Specters of Paul: Sexual Difference in Early Christian Thought* (Philadelphia: University of Pennsylvania Press, 2011), 140-47, explore the intersections of self-control, virginity, and gender in Tertullian.

[24]Peter Brown, *The Body and Society: Men, Women, and Sexual Renunciation in Early Christianity*, Lectures on the History of Religions (New York: Columbia University Press, 1988), 19-24, discusses Tertullian's perspectives against the background of Stoic philosophy. See also Kuefler, *Manly Eunuch*, 170-85.

[25]Tertullian, *Exhortation* 9.2; *Modesty* 4.2-4; *Monogamy* 3.2; *Veiling* 2.4. See also Reeder, *War and Peace*, 29.

[26]See further P. Brown, *Body*, 76-82.

questions for his interpretation of the Samaritan woman. If men were sexual actors with the capability to exercise personal discipline with respect to sexuality, why did he accuse the woman herself of sexual sins?

Tertullian's view of women. Tertullian praised the courage of Christian women who withstood arrest, torture, and public execution. He supported women's right to prophesy (an important aspect of the New Prophecy movement). He recognized numerous important contributions Christian women made to the church: visiting prisoners, welcoming strangers, caring for the poor. In his vision of an ideal Christian marriage, wives and husbands taught and encouraged each other as they lived out their faith together.[27] On the basis of these ideas, some scholars argue that Tertullian had a generally positive view of women.[28]

However, for Tertullian female martyrs were explicitly manlike in their courage and strength. This description reflects his association of women with the body (or flesh), which symbolized weakness and lack of discipline. Just as the body needed the control of the manly spirit, women needed to be under the control of men in the household and church. Tertullian's women were "subjected to men in everything."[29]

Women's subordination had consequences for their lives. Tertullian assumed wives obeyed their husbands, even if their husbands' commands contradicted the wives' own practice of the Christian faith. From puberty on, women had to cover themselves with a veil in public to mark their subjection to men. While Tertullian allowed women prophets to speak, they had to wait until worship ended. He denied any woman the right to speak during worship or to teach, conduct a Eucharist, or baptize other Christians.[30]

Tertullian's perspectives on women reflected his social and cultural contexts and also his own theological understanding. He identified women with their ancestor, Eve, the devil's instrument to attack the first man. Like her,

---

[27]Tertullian, *Against Marcion* 5.8.11; *The Soul* 9.4; *Wife* 2.4, 2.8.

[28]For instance, Daniel L. Hoffman, *The Status of Women and Gnosticism in Irenaeus and Tertullian,* Studies in Women and Religion 36 (Lewiston, NY: Edwin Mellen, 1995), 153-79; Barbara Finlay, "Was Tertullian a Misogynist? A Reconsideration," *Journal of the Historical Society* 3 (2003): 503-25.

[29]Tertullian, *Veiling* 10.1 (author's translation). See further Conybeare, "Tertullian," 435-39; Daniel-Hughes, "Monogamy," 255-56.

[30]Tertullian, *Apparel* 2.13.3; *Baptism* 17.4-5; *Veiling* 9.1-2, 10.1; *Wife* 2.3-4. These perspectives contrast with women's leadership in New Prophecy in some locations; see Finlay, "Tertullian," 516-17.

all women endangered the men around them: sons, brothers, fathers, fellow Christians. The danger here is sex. Tertullian warned that simply to see a woman made a man experience sexual desire and (however inadvertently) fall prey to the sins of adultery and fornication. Women were, therefore, swords to kill men.[31]

The sword was sharpened by women's fine clothing, elaborate hairstyles, and jewelry. For Tertullian, women (at least the privileged, wealthy women he wrote about) were passive recipients of men's sexual attention. Consequently, their fundamental sin was the desire to be desired by men. Women adorned themselves in order to attract and please men, and they were repaid by the men with sexual intercourse.[32] Since Tertullian identified sexual desire and pleasure with sin, women's attention to their personal appearance was also sin.[33]

> Perceptions of sexuality depended on an individual's social and economic status. Wealthy, privileged women were expected to maintain strict standards of sexual chastity. Because women's sexuality affected their family's social honor, they were also subjected to masculine control over their exercise of sexuality.
>
> By contrast, because slaves' bodies belonged to their owners, enslaved people did not have the right to consent to (or refuse) sex. They were unable to be sexually chaste. Because of their contact with strangers, women who worked in bars or shops also lacked the right of chastity. The association of poor or enslaved women with a constant state of sexual immorality marked sexual desire and pleasure as dishonorable. Tertullian reflected this broader cultural understanding in his association of sexual desire and pleasure with non-Christian women (*Apparel* 2.1.3, *Wife* 2.3).

There is a significant inconsistency in Tertullian's treatment of men and women's different disciplines of sexual morality. He defined self-control as

---

[31]Tertullian, *Apparel* 1.1.1-3, 2.2.4; *Modesty* 6.6-7; *Veiling* 7.2-3, 16.3. See also P. Brown, *Body*, 81-82; Finlay, "Tertullian," 508-11; Elliott, *Bride*, 20-22.

[32]Tertullian, *Apparel* 1.2.1-2, 1.4.2, 2.1.1-3; *Veiling* 2.3-4, 14.2-5.

[33]Tertullian also warned men against attentiveness to their appearance. See *Apparel* 2.1.1-3, 2.5.3-4, 2.8.1-2; *Wife* 2.3; Finlay, "Tertullian," 512.

a masculine virtue, which Christian men practiced by controlling their own sexual desires. But despite men's capability to control themselves, Tertullian also thought that women endangered men by appearing in their sight. Tertullian therefore made women responsible for protecting men's self-control by hiding their own bodies with veils, unattractive penitential clothing, and limited attention to their physical appearance—his version of an early church dress code for women.[34]

These measures to desexualize women's bodies were, ironically, made necessary by Tertullian's initial step of sexualizing women's bodies. Even if the man was disciplined, he would have an involuntary physical response to the appearance of a woman, whether the man wanted to or not and whether the woman's intention was to seduce or not. The connection between women, the body (or flesh), and sexual desire in Tertullian's essays inextricably linked women with sin.

The Samaritan woman as a symbol of women's problematic sexuality. Tertullian created a tension between marriage and procreation as Christian practices, and the inherent sinfulness of sexual desire, pleasure, and intercourse. He solved this tension by emphasizing control. Marriage became a space for the practice of both sexual renunciation and the subjection of women to men's authority. But regardless of control, Tertullian warned that the mere sight of a woman led a man to desire her. Since sexual desire and pleasure were immoral, women became symbolic of sexual sin. Tertullian gave women a significant responsibility for both endangering and protecting men's sexual morality.

Tertullian's teachings on sexual morality add significance to his references to the Samaritan woman. Three of his four brief references to the woman are negative. She represented the heretical errors of the Samaritans and sexual sin: multiple marriage, adultery, and prostitution. Tertullian explained her interaction with the virgin monogamist Jesus by reminding readers of her non-Christian, pre-conversion identity. But the result was a significant disconnect between these three references to the woman's story and his repeated use of Jesus' own words in John 4:4-42 to explain Christian practices of baptism and prayer.

---

[34]Tertullian, *Apparel* 2.2.5-6, 2.3.3, 2.5.1; *Veiling* 16.3-4. See also Dunn, *Tertullian*, 53-54.

Tertullian's essays preserve one of the earliest interpretations of the Samaritan woman. His emphasis on the woman's sexuality in *On Modesty* and *On Monogamy* leaves us with a problem, however. How can a woman mired in sexual sin also be Jesus' conversation partner and an evangelist to her community? The sexualization of the Samaritan woman reappeared in Origen's commentary on John and in John Chrysostom's sermons. Both interpreters attempted in different ways to reconcile the woman's gender and sexuality with her active role in John 4:4-42.

ORIGEN: THE SAMARITAN WOMAN AS ALLEGORY

> *She received the living water so that . . . she was able to see the*
> *truth like the angels do, beyond human understanding.*
>
> ORIGEN, *COMMENTARY ON JOHN* 13.41
> (AT)

Origen, a slightly younger contemporary of Tertullian, grew up in a Christian family in Alexandria, Egypt, and eventually ended up in Caesarea, Palestine.[35] Both men bobbed about in the same Roman Mediterranean cultural soup. Consequently, they shared some perspectives on gender and sexuality. Their church contexts were different in significant ways, however, which made Origen's approach to the Samaritan woman distinctive from Tertullian's interpretation. For Origen, the Samaritan woman and her marriages represented a Christian's development from simple understanding, to heresy, to the truth.

Origen on sexuality and gender. Origen understood sexual intercourse as a natural physical desire. But he also identified the original (pre-fall) and final (post-resurrection) state of humanity as ungendered virginity.[36] The human desire for sex sits uncomfortably between these two ends. Origen consequently shared Tertullian's suspicions of the dangerous alliance of sex with sin.[37] More strongly than Tertullian, Origen encouraged

---

[35]Joseph W. Trigg, *Origen*, Early Church Fathers (London: Routledge, 1998), surveys Origen's life, thought, and works.

[36]Origen, *Commentary on Song of Songs* 3.9; see further P. Brown, *Body*, 168; Kuefler, *Manly Eunuch*, 225.

[37]Origen, *Commentary on John* 1.5-7; *Fragments from Commentary on 1 Corinthians* 6:13-14; *First Principles* 3.2.2; *Homilies on Genesis* 3.6. See P. Brown, *Body*, 164-68, 170-71; Hunter, "Reception," 176-78; Elliott, *Bride*, 38.

complete abstinence from sex by teaching the superiority of lifelong virginity over marriage.

Origen himself never married—quite the opposite, if we believe the rumors that he chose to be castrated! Origen worked as a teacher for new Christians. According to Eusebius's *Church History*, Origen's castration was the consequence of a too-literal reading of Matthew 19:12 combined with his concern to avoid accusations of sexual immorality with women students.[38]

Whether or not the story is true is debated. Later in his life, at least, Origen interpreted Matthew 19:12 in terms of self-control empowered by divine grace. Chastity represented masculine strength. Like Tertullian, Origen attributed the need for marriage to human weakness. He also warned that women's beauty could emasculate the strength of chastity.[39]

In Origen's works, masculinity symbolizes reason and moral virtue, while femininity represents the body (or flesh), sin, and a lack of self-control.[40] The symbolism corresponds with Origen's representation of women as lesser creations than men. They could overcome their feminine weakness through salvation and the disciplined pursuit of virtue.[41] But women's weakness made them more inclined to sin. Origen interpreted Jesus' prohibition of divorce as a call for husbands to bear the burden of their wives' sinfulness. As for Tertullian, marriage (even if it was second-best to virginity) provided space for maintaining the social order of male superiority and rule over women.[42]

Origen taught women the Christian faith, and wealthy women supported him financially and socially. Nonetheless, he argued that women's inferiority limited their participation in the Christian community. They could, like Tertullian's women, serve the church by offering hospitality. Older women should teach younger women to be obedient, chaste, modest wives. But women should not teach men. Even if a woman was a prophet, even if her

---

[38]Eusebius, *Church History* 6.8.2-3. P. Brown, *Body*, 168-69, suggests Origen's castration may represent the rejection of masculinity entirely, a sort of embodiment of virginity.

[39]Origen, *Fr. 1 Cor.* 6:13-14; *Commentary on Matthew* 14.25, 15.4; *Homilies on Exodus* 2.1; *Homilies on Numbers* 20.1.3; *Princ.* 3.2.2. See further Jennifer Knust, "Marriage as a Social Good: Origen of Alexandria and John Chrysostom, Revisited," *Marriage, Families & Spirituality* 26 (2020): 7-25, esp. 11-12.

[40]Origen, *Hom. Gen.* 1.15-16, 4.4, 5.2; *Hom. Exod.* 2.1-2. See further Elliott, *Bride*, 38.

[41]Origen, *Homilies on Judges* 5.2; *Homilies on Luke* 8.1.

[42]Origen, *Comm. Matt.* 14.16, 14.24; *Hom. Gen.* 6.1; *Hom. Exod.* 8.5.

message was good and holy, she could not speak in the context of a church gathering.[43]

Given the similarities between Tertullian and Origen's representations of sexuality and women in the Christian community, we might expect a similarly harsh critique of the Samaritan woman. But instead, Origen praised her as an eager seeker for the truth. He recognized her faith and fervent witness to Jesus in her community as a model for Christians to follow. Origen developed this interpretation of John 4:4-42 through the use of allegory.

Origen's Samaritan woman. The church in Alexandria was famous for its use of allegory as a tool to interpret Scripture. In an allegorical approach, various elements of a biblical text—a well, livestock, husbands—are interpreted as symbols of deeper spiritual realities.[44] The extensive use of symbolism in John's Gospel invites this kind of interpretation. In John 4:4-42, water and food both represent more than literal water and literal food. If that is the case, perhaps other elements of the story also have symbolic significance.

In his commentary on the Gospel of John, Origen identified Jacob's well as a symbol of Scripture. The woman represented all people who do not (yet) know the truth of Jesus, and therefore do not drink from the well with understanding.[45] According to Origen, the woman's marital history in John 4:16-18 told the story of a seeker's life. The five husbands are the five senses through which all people begin to understand the world. The Samaritan woman moved beyond the physical realities in search of a deeper spiritual truth, but unfortunately her sixth husband, her teacher, misled her into unorthodox beliefs.[46]

> For Origen, the unorthodox were Gnostic Christians. Gnostic Christianity combined elements of Greek philosophy and religious traditions with Christian faith.

---

[43]Origen, *Comm. Jo.* 32.132; *Commentary on Romans* 10.17, 20; *Fr. 1 Cor.* 74. See Korinna Zamfir, "Women Teaching—Spiritually Washing the Feet of the Saints? The Early Christian Reception of 1 Timothy 2:11-12," *Annali di Storia dell'Esegesi* 32 (2015): 353-79, esp. 359-61; and (with a more generous interpretation) Ilaria L. E. Ramelli, "Colleagues of Apostles, Presbyters, and Bishops: Women *Syzygoi* in Ancient Christian Communities," in *Patterns of Women's Leadership in Early Christianity*, ed. Joan E. Taylor and Ilaria L. E. Ramelli (Oxford: Oxford University Press, 2021), 26-58, esp. 53-57.
[44]On Origen's use of allegory, see Trigg, *Origen*, 33-35.
[45]In addition to his commentary on John, see Origen, *Hom. Gen.* 7.5-6, 10.2-3.
[46]Origen, *Comm. Jo.* 13.6, 31, 38-39, 51-52. See further Knust, "Marriage," 10-11.

It was a popular movement in the early church, but in the second century many Christian leaders saw it as heresy.

Origen wrote his commentary on John as a response to a Gnostic Christian named Heracleon. According to Origen's summary of Heracleon's (now lost) commentary, Heracleon identified the woman's husbands as actual men with whom she fornicated. The woman was a social outcast on account of her sexual sin. Origen's denial of the woman's sexual sin rebutted Heracleon's interpretation (*Comm. Jo.* 13.68-74, 92).

Through her conversation with Jesus, the woman denied her illegitimate sixth husband. She asked Jesus, her true husband, for his gift of living water, and she received the ability to understand the truth. Jesus therefore sent her as an apostle to her unorthodox neighbors.[47]

This allegorical interpretation removed the problem of sexuality from the story. For Origen, the woman was not an adulterer or prostitute, but a seeker. She experienced a complete conversion, resulting in her rejection of her previous heretical teachers in favor of Jesus. Moreover, her unorthodox neighbors came to faith in the truth (Jesus) because of her witness. Origen encouraged his readers to follow the woman's example of evangelism.[48]

Origen's understanding of women as weaker, lesser creations is also represented in his commentary. His interpretation of the Samaritan woman as a symbol of those who are misled by false teachers associates women with heresy. This connection is explicit in Origen's explanation of the disciples' reaction in John 4:27: they were surprised that Jesus was speaking with a woman who was, by virtue of her gender, easily deceived. Origen used the disciples' surprise to remind readers that God cares for the lowly and protects the weak, including this woman.[49]

Origen's identification of the woman as an apostle to her people, then, does not result in comprehensive support for women's right to witness to Jesus or teach the truth in the church. But the contrast between his commendation of the woman as an apostle and Tertullian's condemnation of her

---

[47]Origen, *Comm. Jo.* 13.41, 48-52, 101.
[48]Origen, *Comm. Jo.* 13.173-174, 340.
[49]Origen, *Comm. Jo.* 13.167-169.

sexual sin is nonetheless remarkable. By interpreting the woman as a symbol, Origen removed the issue of sexual sin entirely. It's an ingenious solution to the problem of the woman's role in the story.

AN APOSTLE AND SINNER: JOHN CHRYSOSTOM'S SERMONS ON THE SAMARITAN WOMAN

> *She did apostolic work by announcing the good news to all,*
> *calling them to Jesus, and bringing a whole city out to him.*
>
> JOHN CHRYSOSTOM, *HOMILIES ON JOHN* 32.1
> (AT)

Adultery, prostitution, evangelism, faith: John Chrysostom's sermons on the story of the Samaritan woman hold the different elements introduced by Tertullian and Origen in tension. Chrysostom identified the woman's marital history as wicked, shameful sin. But at the same time, he recognized the woman's thoughtful, wise responses to Jesus and her proclamations to her community. He encouraged his congregation to imitate her by listening, learning, and living in obedience to Christian discipline.

> John Chrysostom lived a century after Tertullian and Origen (347–407 CE). He followed a strict, ascetic spiritual discipline as a young Christian before being ordained as a deacon and priest in his hometown, Antioch of Syria. His pastoral reputation earned his appointment as bishop of Constantinople later in his life, though his experience there was troubled by political intrigue and opposition.[50]

Because Chrysostom's sermons present the Samaritan woman as a model disciple, scholars often praise his work as a contrast to the more common denigration of the woman's character.[51] However, Chrysostom's general teachings on marriage, sexuality, and women complicate this assessment. As we will see, Chrysostom's Samaritan woman is a nearly singular exception to his expectations for women in the church and home.

---

[50]Wendy Mayer and Pauline Allen, *John Chrysostom*, Early Church Fathers (London: Routledge, 2000), introduce Chrysostom's life and ministry.
[51]See Farmer, "Changing Images," 366-67; Day, *Woman at the Well*, 12-13.

Sex, sin, and the Christian marriage. The Christians of Antioch participated fully in the rich cultural and religious life of their city. They attended sacred festivals and theatrical performances, purchased magical amulets for protection, and displayed their wealth in their clothing and home furnishings. But Chrysostom warned that temples, synagogues, and theaters were full of demons, and expensive furniture and jewelry gave the devil a foothold in the home.[52]

To equip his congregants for the spiritual warfare of life in a non-Christian city, Chrysostom challenged them to live simply, giving generously to the poor. He encouraged them to develop a distinctive Christian identity through separation and disengagement from the rest of society. He envisioned the Christian household as a place for the practice of ascetic spiritual disciplines, including with respect to sexual desire and intercourse.[53]

Chrysostom shared some of Tertullian and Origen's suspicions of sex, even within a legitimate marriage.[54] In contrast to the more permissive cultural context of the Roman Empire, Chrysostom expected husbands as well as wives to be virgins at their first marriage. His definition of adultery to include the man's marital status restricted men from using prostitutes, entertainers, and enslaved women for sex. And he affirmed wives' authority over their husbands' bodies (1 Cor 7:4).[55]

When and with whom a man had sex was only part of the issue for Chrysostom. He warned that simply to see a woman, even if she was only selling vegetables, caused involuntary, uncontrollable responses in a man's body. Sexually explicit theatrical performances increased the danger. Chrysostom thought that demonic power imprinted the sight of women performers on a man's soul. Whether desire was acted upon or not, it resulted in spiritual fornication.[56]

---

[52]Chrysostom, *Baptismal Instructions* 1.2, 20-22; *Homilies on Ephesians* 22-24; *Homilies on Colossians* 12; Dayna S. Kalleres, *City of Demons: Violence, Ritual, and Christian Practice in Late Antiquity* (Oakland: University of California Press, 2015), 25-93.

[53]See further P. Brown, *Body*, 312-15; Mayer and Allen, *John Chrysostom*, 28-36; Chris L. de Wet, *Preaching Bondage: John Chrysostom and the Discourse of Slavery in Early Christianity* (Oakland: University of California Press, 2015), 85, 94-97.

[54]Chrysostom, *Homilies on 1 Corinthians* 19, 37; *Letter to Theodore* 1.3; *On Marriage*; *On Virginity* 10.3, 11.1, 14.5-6, etc. Chrysostom rejected celibate marriage, however see Knust, "Marriage," 22.

[55]Chrysostom, *Hom. 1 Cor.* 19.2; *Homilies on 1 Timothy* 9; *Hom. Eph.* 20. See also P. Brown, *Body*, 306-9; De Wet, *Bondage*, 149-51, 222-31.

[56]Chrysostom, *Against the Games and Theaters*; *Hom. 1 Cor.* 18; *Hom. Col.* 12; *Homilies on Matthew* 7. See also P. Brown, *Body*, 315-17; Kalleres, *Demons*, 63-65; De Wet, *Bondage*, 244-45.

The sight of women, therefore, could destroy a man's marriage. Chrysostom discouraged men from entering spaces where they might see women's bodies on display. He warned Christian women against enhancing their appearance in ways that could cause a man to sin.[57] In addition, he limited the opportunity for interactions between men and women by separating them spatially.

In the cultural context of the Roman Empire, public space was the realm of men, while (privileged) women's space was the home. Chrysostom thought men were emasculated by too much time spent in women's space. Likewise, privileged women were corrupted by contact with the kinds of women who inhabited public space (especially prostitutes, entertainers, and other slaves). He encouraged women to remain within the protected space of the home.[58]

> The division between public and private was not what we might mean by these terms. The home was the site of household productivity, business, and public engagement. Wives had authority over this work (Chrysostom, *How to Choose a Wife*).
>
> The home was not secluded space, then, but it was restricted space. Women inside the household were protected against the harassment, violence, and accusations of immorality faced by women in the streets and public spaces of a city. Chrysostom hinted at this reality in *Against the Games and Theaters* and *Baptismal Instructions* 1.37.[59]

Like Tertullian and Origen, Chrysostom identified women as weaker than men, more prone to sinful behaviors, and uncontrolled. The sin of Eden was, in part, the upending of the natural order when the man listened to his wife, who listened to the serpent. Chrysostom was consequently very concerned with maintaining the gender hierarchy. Women needed to be under male authority.[60]

---

[57]See Chrysostom, *Games and Theaters*; *Bapt.* 1.35-38, 43; *Hom. 1 Tim.* 8; *Virginity* 62-63.

[58]Chrysostom, *Hom. Col.* 12; *Against Cohabitation* 9-11; *How to Choose a Wife*.

[59]See also De Wet, *Bondage*, 117-18.

[60]See Chrysostom, *Hom. 1 Cor.* 26; *Hom. 1 Tim.* 9; *Hom. Eph.* 20; *Hom. Gen.* 16-17; and also Zamfir, "Teaching," 362-63; Knust, "Marriage," 22-23.

A (privileged) family should lock a daughter away in interior rooms, strictly limiting her engagement even with other family members. When a young girl married, she would consequently know little of the world. Her (much older) husband could mold her into an obedient, compliant "partner" in household life. Chrysostom recognized wives' valuable contribution to the household.[61] But he also warned husbands to be prepared for a lifetime of instructing, forgiving, and reforming their wives. Women's inferiority and susceptibility to sin were burdens for husbands to bear.[62]

The subjection of women in the household carried over to the church. In sermons on 1 Corinthians 11:2-16 and 14:34-35, Chrysostom identified head coverings and silence as symbols of women's subjection. He described women's speech as idle, pointless, and futile, reflecting their inferior, un-developed intellects. Women's words deceived men.[63] For this reason, he did not allow women to ask questions, let alone teach or lead in the church.

Despite the limitations Chrysostom placed on women, he relied on the financial and social support of women patrons. As bishop in Constantinople, he ministered alongside Olympias, the leader of a group of ascetic women.[64] He also recognized the authority of women in biblical texts. Phoebe, Priscilla, Mary, and Junia in Romans 16, for instance, taught the gospel (including to men), traveled as the male apostles did, and courageously faced the dangers of persecution. These women were manly in their ability to reason and understand.[65]

On the basis of Romans 16, Chrysostom exhorted the women of his con-gregation to adorn themselves with virtue, study Scripture, and offer hospi-tality to visiting Christians. Women could only teach, however, in the space of the household, and their instruction was limited to their children, to unbelieving or sinful husbands, and to believing husbands who were not as wise as their wives.[66] If the husbands were ashamed to be taught by their wives (as they should be), Chrysostom said in another sermon, they should

---

[61]Chrysostom, *Hom. Col.* 12; *Hom. Eph.* 20; *How to Choose*; *Marriage*. De Wet, *Bondage*, 123-26, explores the tension between women's authority in the household and men's authority over women.

[62]These points are especially emphasized in Chrysostom, *Hom. Eph.* 20; *How to Choose*.

[63]Chrysostom, *Hom. 1 Tim.* 9; *Hom. Eph.* 20; *Hom. Gen.* 16-17. See also Zamfir, "Teaching," 363.

[64]See Mayer and Allen, *Chrysostom*, 42-50.

[65]Chrysostom, *Hom. Rom.* 30-31.

[66]Chrysostom, *Hom. Rom.* 30-31. See further Zamfir, "Teaching," 365-66.

reform their sinful behavior and take back their proper authority over the household.[67]

Chrysostom's perspectives on women in the household and church are more positive in some ways than Tertullian's. But the limitations on women's presence and participation in Christian community remain. Social order and peace depended on the subjection of women in the household and church. Women who disrupted this expectation were demonized, literally in the case of performers and prostitutes, and implicitly in the case of women who assumed authority over their husbands. Chrysostom's Samaritan woman fits within this construction of Christian society.

John Chrysostom's Samaritan woman. The Samaritan woman met and spoke with Jesus in public, in men's space. She was a many-times-over wife, and while Chrysostom did not condemn remarriage, he discouraged it.[68] Finally, the Samaritan woman preached to the men and women of her village. As his four sermons on her story suggest, the Samaritan woman upended Chrysostom's carefully constructed social categories. His interpretation rests uneasily between praise for the woman and insistence on the limitations of her gender and marital history.

First, the praise. Chrysostom interpreted the woman's questions and responses to Jesus as signs of her wisdom and discernment. He contrasted her success as an evangelist with the (male) apostles who, at this point in the Gospel of John, hadn't done much.[69] He repeatedly challenged the men and women of his congregation to follow the Samaritan woman's example.[70]

This characterization of the woman stands out from Chrysostom's definition of women as unable to reason, intellectually childish, and overly concerned with unimportant matters. His surprisingly positive portrayal has several explanations. First, Chrysostom recognized the importance of John 4:39-42 as a lens for interpreting the entire story. The woman's success as a witness to Jesus meant she must have understood him. Second, Chrysostom appreciated the narratival pairing of the woman with Nicodemus in John 3–4. Neither of them understood Jesus' metaphors

---

[67]Chrysostom, *Hom. Matt.* 7.
[68]See Chrysostom, *Hom. Eph.* 20; Lehtipuu, "To Remarry," 39-41.
[69]Chrysostom, *Hom. Jo.* 31.4, 32.1-2, 33.2, 34.1.
[70]Chrysostom, *Hom. Jo.* 31.5, 32.3, 34.1, 34.3.

immediately. But unlike Nicodemus, the Samaritan woman persisted in seeking understanding, and she responded with faith.

Chrysostom's emphasis on this comparison highlights a third reason for his praise: the Samaritan woman was not a Jew. Chrysostom represented "the Jews" in John's Gospel as enemies of Jesus who refused to understand or accept him. He contrasted the woman with "the Jews" on each point. In this way, he made her into a representative of the Gentile mission that resulted from the Jewish rejection of Jesus.[71]

> Chrysostom's representation of "the Jews" reflected the rhetoric of the Gospel of John, but it is also an example of early Christian anti-Semitism. Chrysostom used problematic representations of Jews and Judaism as part of his pastoral effort to develop a distinctive Christian identity for the church of Antioch.[72]

Gender formed part of Chrysostom's critique of Nicodemus and "the Jews." Nicodemus displayed an unmanly lack of reason surpassed by the Samaritan woman's masculine understanding and action.[73] In this sense, the Samaritan woman was one of the biblical women who led (only) when men failed in understanding or discipline. As erring husbands should be shamed by their wives' instruction, Nicodemus and "the Jews" should be shamed by the Samaritan woman's superior masculinity.

So should Chrysostom's congregation. He deliberately used the Samaritan woman to shame their inattentiveness to his sermons and unwillingness to seriously study the Bible at home.[74] The work of women as teachers, preachers, or evangelists represented an implicit critique of male weakness, unbelief, and sin. Neither the women of Romans 16 nor the Samaritan woman normalized or justified women's vocal participation in the church.

Despite his praise for the Samaritan woman's intellect, Chrysostom also described her as poor, uneducated, and low in status. The length of Jesus' conversation with her was the consequence of her slowness to understand. Her

---

[71]Chrysostom, *Hom. Jo.* 31.2, 32.1.

[72]See further Chrysostom, *Discourses Against Judaizing Christians*, and Isabella Sandwell, *Religious Identity in Late Antiquity: Greeks, Jews and Christians in Antioch* (Cambridge: Cambridge University Press, 2007), especially 82-90.

[73]Chrysostom, *Hom. Jo.* 32.1.

[74]Chrysostom, *Hom. Jo.* 31.5, 32.3.

ainful, wicked marital history further tarnished her character. The disciples were right to wonder at Jesus' condescension in speaking with such a woman.[75]

The shifting representations of the Samaritan woman through Chrysostom's sermons are consistent with his treatment of the other women in John's Gospel. His sermons on John 2:3-5 wavered between respect for Mary as a parent and critique of her misguided attempt to solve the wine shortage. Mary and Martha in John 11 were limited in their understanding and faith by their gender. Chrysostom used their grief for their brother to warn the women in his congregation against public displays of mourning that, he complained, verged on fornication.[76]

Finally, in two sermons on John 20, Chrysostom recognized Mary Magdalene's importance as the person who told the (male) disciples about the empty tomb. But, while the men understood the resurrection as soon as they saw the empty tomb, Mary needed angels and the appearance of Jesus himself to realize the truth. Chrysostom further marginalized Mary by his insistence that it was no disgrace or shame for men to learn of the empty tomb from a woman. Moreover, Jesus had to appear to the disciples in person, because who would believe a woman?[77]

Within this context, John Chrysostom's interpretation of the Samaritan woman was remarkably more positive. But his broad praise for the woman across his four sermons on John 4:4-42 was limited by the contrast between her as a Samaritan and "the Jews" (a group that includes the other women of John). She was, in the end, an "insignificant example," a woman of little importance in the story of Jesus.[78]

This was the surprise of the story. Educated, powerful men like Nicodemus failed to understand Jesus, but this silly, ignorant woman was persistent (and masculine) enough to develop understanding and faith. Chrysostom's sermons leave us with an ambiguous, contradictory characterization of the woman. By maintaining the tension between her gender and marital history and her role as Jesus' conversation partner and apostle, Chrysostom preserved his own understanding of the gender hierarchy that ordered the world.

---

[75]Chrysostom, *Hom. Jo.* 32.1-3, 33.2-3, 34.1.

[76]Chrysostom, *Hom. Jo.* 21-22, 62.

[77]Chrysostom, *Hom. Jo.* 85-86.

[78]Chrysostom, *Hom. Jo.* 34.1 (author's translation).

TRACING THE THREADS

For Tertullian, the Samaritan woman represented the dangers of sexual sin. For Origen, she symbolized the journey of a spiritual seeker from heterodoxy to orthodoxy. And John Chrysostom used the poor, uneducated, morally questionable woman to shame his congregation into studying the Scriptures and listening to pastoral instruction. Despite Chrysostom's praise for the Samaritan woman's wisdom, her story did not open space for other women to speak, teach, or preach in the church.

Table 2.1. John 4 according to Tertullian, Origen, and John Chrysostom

Interpreter	Explanation of the Woman's Character and Participation in the Story	Significance of the Story for the Church
Tertullian, *On Monogamy* and *On Modesty* (between 200 and 220?)	The woman is guilty of adultery and prostitution on account of her multiple marriages. Jesus spoke to her and revealed his identity to her (only) because she was not yet a Christian. Tertullian classified the Samaritan woman with the "prostitute" of Luke 7:36-50.	The Christian life demands bodily holiness, including monogamy (defined as marrying only once) and sexual chastity. The Samaritan woman is an example of what not to do.
Origen, *Commentary on John* (between 230 and 250?)	The woman's story is an allegory of the human search for understanding through reliance on the five senses, the danger of heretical teachers, and the truth (Jesus). Despite her womanly low status and weakness, Jesus sends her as an apostle to her people.	The woman models Christian faith and evangelism. However, the story associates women with false teaching. It does not authorize women's leadership in the church.
John Chrysostom, *Homilies on John* (circa 390)	The woman's conversation with Jesus shows her intelligence and discernment, and she is a successful evangelist. However, she is also poor, slow to understand, and guilty of sexual sin. Chrysostom contrasts the woman with Nicodemus and, more broadly, "the Jews" in John's Gospel.	The woman's example should shame Christians into serious study of the Bible. She also models evangelistic practice. However, the woman's evangelization is unique to her; her story does not authorize women's leadership in the church.

This interpretation of John 4:4-42 ran alongside the identification of women as dangerous objects of male desire. According to Tertullian, Origen, and John Chrysostom, the very sight of a woman, whether she was a prostitute, a fishmonger, or a virgin dedicated to the service of the church, caused a man to fall into lust and (spiritual) fornication.

They assumed women's active (and sinful) desire to be desired. In combination with the minimization of women's vocal, active participation in the church, the reductive sexualization of women could well have affected women's physical safety. I started this chapter with the *Life of Pelagia*, a story that gave Pelagia herself ownership over her life and sexuality. In another early Christian narrative about a reformed prostitute, the woman was the victim of assault.

The *Life of Maria the Harlot* recorded what we would today identify as the grooming of a woman ascetic. A visiting monk spent a year seducing Maria through a window until she finally gave in and climbed out to meet him. This was no Rapunzel-esque love story, though: "At once [the monk] defiled and polluted her by intercourse out of wicked iniquity and lust."[79]

Like many victims of sexual assault, Maria was overcome with shame. She wished for death, but as a second-best alternative, she fled her life of monastic seclusion to work as a prostitute in the city. This sort of behavior is now recognized as a common reaction to assault.[80] Maria was an early #ChurchToo victim.

Despite Tertullian and Chrysostom's claims, even women who secluded themselves entirely from the sight of men were not safe from men's lust. Maria's story demonstrates the consequences of the identification of women as weak, sinful, silent objects of male desire. As we'll see in the next chapter, these consequences continued to plague women in the sixteenth and nineteenth centuries.

---

[79] *Life of Maria the Harlot* 3 in *Harlots of the Desert: A Study of Repentance in Early Monastic Sources*, by Benedicta Ward, Cistercian Studies 106 (Kalamazoo: Cistercian Publications, 1987), 92-101.

[80] See Anne Marie Miller, *Healing Together: A Guide to Supporting Sexual Abuse Survivors* (Grand Rapids, MI: Zondervan Reflective, 2019), 173-74.

3

SIN AND SPEECH

The Samaritan Woman in Protestant Perspective

What woman was a greater preacher than the Samaritan
woman, who was not ashamed to preach Jesus and his word,
confessing him openly before everyone, as soon as she heard
Jesus say that we must adore God in spirit and truth?

MARIE DENTIÈRE, *EPISTLE TO MARGUERITE DE NAVARRE*

IN GENEVA IN 1539, Marie Dentière published a defense of Protestant theology and practice. She composed her book in the form of a letter encouraging the queen of France, Marguerite de Navarre, to use her political power to protect the Reformers. As a woman addressing a woman, Dentière also argued for the responsibility of women to educate themselves and for their right to teach and preach in the church.[1]

Marie Dentière, Margeurite de Navarre, Argula von Grumbach, Katharina von Bora Luther, Katharina Schütz Zell, Jeanne de Jussie, Margarethe Prüss, Caritas Pirckheimer: in the sixteenth century, women across Europe participated actively in the Protestant and Catholic Reformations. They published books,

---

[1]Mary B. McKinley, volume editor's introduction to *Marie Dentière: Epistle to Marguerite de Navarre and Preface to a Sermon by John Calvin*, trans. and ed. Mary B. McKinley, The Other Voice in Early Modern Europe (Chicago: University of Chicago Press, 2004), 1-23, and Kirsi Stjerna, *Women and the Reformation* (Oxford: Blackwell, 2009), 133-47, introduce Dentière's life and writings.

counseled clergy, and argued theology with (and against) men. These women
deeply influenced Christian practice, worship, and teaching.[2]

By publishing her book, Dentière enacted her own right as an educated
woman to teach the church. She recognized that many people would object,
so she included a "Defense of Women" in the preface to her book. This
"Defense" surveyed the women of the Bible, including the Samaritan woman,
as support for women's leadership in the church.

Dentière connected the Samaritan woman with Mary Magdalene, the
first witness of the resurrection, who was commanded to preach by Jesus.
More than any other biblical woman, these two proved that women have the
right to teach and preach in the church. Dentière also interpreted John 4:23
as a (Protestant-esque) critique of (Catholic) ceremony. The separation of
worship from ritual made the Samaritan woman a proto-Reformer and a
model for Dentière herself.[3]

Dentière particularly denounced Catholic tradition for defining women
only as objects to provide men with pleasure. As such, women were not allowed to study the Bible for themselves.[4] These connected critiques take on
a particular edge alongside another issue she raised: the sexual exploitation
of women by parish priests.[5] Her solution to the objectification and abuse
of women was access to Scripture, which, she argued, enabled women's education and authority.

Consequently, Dentière replaced women's subordination to male authority with women's love and men's respect. The spiritual equality of women

---

[2]See Stjerna, *Women and the Reformation.*

[3]Marie Dentière, *Epistle to Marguerite de Navarre,* in *Marie Dentière: Epistle to Marguerite de Navarre and Preface to a Sermon by John Calvin,* trans. and ed. Mary B. McKinley, The Other Voice in Early Modern Europe (Chicago: University of Chicago Press, 2004), 54-55, 59. See further R. Gerald Hobbs, "The Biblical Canon of Early Evangelical Feminists," *Reformation & Renaissance Review* 18 (2016): 216-32, esp. 219-25.

[4]Dentière, *Epistle,* 53-54, 61, 76, 79.

[5]Dentière, *Epistle,* 70-71. The accusation represents a common Protestant critique of Catholicism. See also John Calvin, *Sermons on 1 Timothy* 40, in *Sermons on 1 Timothy,* trans. Robert White (Carlisle, PA: Banner of Truth, 2018). Catholics at the time made similar accusations as in, for instance, Jeanne de Jussie, *The Short Chronicle: A Poor Clare's Account of the Reformation of Geneva,* trans. and ed. by Carrie S. Klaus, The Other Voice in Early Modern Europe (Chicago: University of Chicago Press, 2006), 62. See further Wietse de Boer, *The Conquest of the Soul: Confession, Discipline, and Public Order in Counter-Reformation Milan,* Studies in Medieval and Reformation Thought 84 (Leiden: Brill, 2001), 97-104.

in God's kingdom meant practical equality in the family and equal participation in the church.[6] Dentière embodied this message through her life as she ministered along with her husbands (both pastors) and preached in the convents and streets of Geneva.[7]

Dentière's Samaritan woman represented women's capacity to speak and teach publicly as spiritual and intellectual equals to men. Unfortunately, her book was suppressed by the city council of Geneva. Moreover, despite her clearly stated support for John Calvin, he once denigrated her as a troublesome, meddling woman.[8] Her book's influence would have been questionable even without these barriers. Despite women's involvement in the theological and pastoral work of the early Reformation, the (male) pastors and teachers of the Protestant church firmly located women in the household. They made marriage and motherhood into spiritually significant vocations. But they also limited women to these two vocations.[9]

Instead of a powerful preacher and model for women's ministry in the church, then, the majority interpretation of the Samaritan woman from the Reformation onward focused on her utter, complete sin. Her story was (and is still) used to show that anyone—even such a vile sinner as this woman—can experience God's mercy.[10]

Although the Samaritan woman became an archetypal sinner in this approach, her gender remained central. Her story therefore had specific significance for the lives of women in the church. This chapter explores the intersection of the Samaritan woman's story with Protestant perspectives on women, sex, and sin represented by Dentière's contemporary, John Calvin, and in the late nineteenth century by the evangelical reformer Clara Lucas Balfour and revivalist Dwight L. Moody.

---

[6]Dentière, *Epistle*, 51, 53-54, 56, 79-80.

[7]See Calvin, Letter 173, in *Letters of John Calvin*, ed. Jules Bonnet, trans. David Constable, 4 vols. (Philadelphia: Presbyterian Board of Publication, 1858), 3:70-72; Jussie, *Short Chronicle*, 151-52; McKinley, *Marie Dentière*, 4-5, 16.

[8]Calvin, Letter 173. See also McKinley, *Marie Dentière*, 13-16, 19-20; Stjerna, *Women*, 143-46.

[9]See Stjerna, *Women*, 33-34; Beth Allison Barr, *The Making of Biblical Womanhood: How the Subjugation of Women Became Gospel Truth* (Grand Rapids, MI: Brazos, 2021), 103-10.

[10]A point emphasized by Craig S. Farmer, "Changing Images of the Samaritan Woman in Early Reformed Commentaries on John," *Church History* 65 (1996): 373, 375.

JOHN CALVIN. THE DANGER OF A WOMAN'S WORDS

[The woman] would have acted recklessly if she had assumed
the office of a teacher; but when she was desiring nothing more
than to stir up her fellow-citizens to hear Christ speak, we will
not say that she forgot herself and went too far; for she was only
being, as it were, a trumpet or a bell to invite others to Christ.

JOHN CALVIN, THE GOSPEL ACCORDING TO ST. JOHN

The tension between the Samaritan woman's gender and sexuality and her work
as an evangelist overwhelms John Calvin's commentary on John 4:4-42. Calvin
praised the woman for accepting Jesus' rebuke of her sin, focusing rightly on
the Messiah, and zealously sharing her new faith. But he also critiqued her for
mocking and insulting Jesus. Her life of sin made her unworthy to speak to
Jesus at all. Finally, as the quote above indicates, he disparaged her preaching.

Calvin was instrumental in developing the ideas of the first generation of
Reformers into clear doctrines and practices for the Protestant church, local
government, and civil law. His proposals affected the daily lives of ordinary
Christians in sixteenth century Geneva in significant ways, with expectations for regular attendance at worship services; Bible study in the home;
harmonious relationships between husbands and wives; formal education
for children; social support for the poor and ill; fashion, entertainment, and
public decorum; and more.[11]

> For Calvin, Christian identity should influence every facet of life. This perspec-
> tive blurred the lines between private and public, and between secular and sa-
> cred. Calvin saw the government of the church (the Consistory) and the city (the
> Council) as partners in administering and enforcing God's moral law. So, for
> instance, premarital sex was punished by public reproof of both persons before
> the Consistory and imprisonment by the Council.[12]

---

[11]T. H. L. Parker, *Calvin: An Introduction to His Thought*, Outstanding Christian Thinkers (1995;
repr., London: Continuum, 2002), and Paul Helm, *Calvin: A Guide for the Perplexed* (New York:
Bloomsbury, 2008), introduce Calvin's life, theology, and social vision.

[12]See Helm, *Calvin*, 127-28, and Suzannah Lipscomb, "Subjection and Companionship: The
French Reformed Marriage," *Reformation & Renaissance Review* 6 (2004): 349-60.

Calvin insisted on the spiritual equality of women with men. He praised the companionship possible in marriage, and he recognized the contributions women made to household life by teaching children and supporting their husbands.[13] Citing 1 Timothy 5:9-10, he also gave women the specific work of caring for the poor and ill in the church.[14] Calvin himself relied on wealthy women for the financial support of seminary education and the protection of Protestant communities in Catholic-majority regions.

Spiritual equality, however, did not translate into functional equality in church or society.[15] For Calvin, the distinctive order and purpose of the creation of the woman in Genesis 2 made women subordinate to men. On the basis of 1 Corinthians 11:2-16 and 1 Timothy 2:11-15, he argued that women did not reflect the image of God as fully as men. Women were consequently subjected to male rule in the family, church, and society.[16]

Gender disqualified women from any responsibility that would give them authority over men. They should not participate in theological debates, teach in the church, or lead in any way. Women's silent subordination in the church, society, and household signified their acceptance of what Calvin defined as a divinely ordered gender hierarchy.[17]

---

[13]See John Calvin, *Genesis*, trans. John King, 2 vols. (1847; repr., Edinburgh: Banner of Truth Trust, 1975), 1:128-31; *The First Epistle of Paul the Apostle to the Corinthians*, trans. John W. Fraser, Calvin's Commentaries (1960; repr., Grand Rapids, MI: Eerdmans, 1979), 229-30; *The Second Epistle of Paul the Apostle to the Corinthians and the Epistles to Timothy, Titus, and Philemon*, trans. T. A. Smail, Calvin's Commentaries (1964; repr., Grand Rapids, MI: Eerdmans, 1979), 217, 229.

[14]Calvin, *Institutes of the Christian Religion* 4.3.9, 4.13.18, 8th ed., trans. John Allen, 2 vols (Grand Rapids, MI: Eerdmans, 1949). See also *The Epistles of Paul the Apostle to the Romans and to the Thessalonians*, trans. Ross MacKenzie, Calvin's Commentaries (Grand Rapids, MI: Eerdmans, 1960), 320-22.

[15]Note that Jane Dempsey Douglass, *Women, Freedom, and Calvin* (Philadelphia: Westminster, 1985), 45-65, sees potential for progressiveness in Calvin's perspectives on women.

[16]Calvin, *First Epistle to the Corinthians*, 229-34, 306-7; *Genesis*, 1:128-34, 171-72; *Institutes* 4.15.20-22, 4.20.29; *Second Epistle to the Corinthians*, 216-19; *Sermons on 1 Timothy* 18; etc. See further John L. Thompson, "*Creata ad Imaginem Dei, Licet Secundo Gradu*: Woman as the Image of God According to John Calvin," *Harvard Theological Review* 81 (1988): 125-43; Nico Vorster, "John Calvin on the Status and Role of Women in Church and Society," *Journal of Theological Studies* 68 (2017): 178-211, esp. 186-91.

[17]John Calvin, *The Epistle of Paul the Apostle to the Hebrews and the First and Second Epistles of St. Peter*, trans. William B. Johnston, Calvin's Commentaries (1963; repr., Grand Rapids, MI: Eerdmans, 1979), 281-82; *First Epistle to the Corinthians*, 230-31, 306-7; *Second Epistle to the Corinthians*, 216-17; *Sermons on 1 Timothy* 17. See also John Lee Thompson, *John Calvin and the Daughters of Sarah: Women in Regular and Exceptional Roles in the Exegesis of Calvin, his Predecessors, and his Contemporaries*, Travaux d'Humanisme et Renaissance 259 (Geneva: Librairie Droz, 1992).

As with John Chrysostom, the Samaritan woman's public discourse with Jesus and her neighbors seems to challenge these assumptions. Calvin's commentary on John 4:4-42 explained away the problem of the woman's words by situating her within a particular historical moment, making her a symbol of a sinner's undeserved salvation, and minimizing her role in spreading the news of Jesus in her community.

The Samaritan woman as archetypal sinner. As a pastor and teacher, Calvin wrote for the church. The Protestant Reformers centered the Bible as the authority for Christian faith and life. In his commentary on John's Gospel, Calvin guided ordinary Christians to understand this authority for themselves and use its messages in their lives.[18]

Like Marie Dentière a decade earlier (though probably independently of her work), Calvin connected the Samaritans and the Jews with the Catholic Church through the issue of worship in John 4:20-23. The story therefore became a lesson in rejecting liturgical ceremony and reliance on church tradition.[19] Calvin did not, however, share Dentière's appreciation for the Samaritan woman herself. He represented the woman's words and character increasingly negatively through his commentary.

Already in his comments on John 4:10, well before the reference to the woman's marital history in John 4:16-18, Calvin condemned her sexual immorality. He interpreted her marital history in John 4:18 as Jesus' revelation of her sin (repeated in his comments on Jn 4:29). Finally, Calvin assumed the woman's five legitimate husbands all divorced her on account of her behavior.[20]

Calvin defined a good wife as a woman who accepted her subjection to her husband's authority.[21] By this standard, his representation of the Samaritan woman condemned her for rejecting subjugation to her husbands. He characterized her as a truly terrible person, someone so lost in the sins of adultery, immorality, and rebellion that she was almost dead.[22]

---

[18]Note Calvin, *Institutes* 1.6.2, 1.9.2, and throughout; John Calvin, *The Gospel According to St. John 1–10*, trans. T. H. L. Parker, Calvin's Commentaries (1961; repr., Grand Rapids, MI: Eerdmans, 1978), 5-6. See further John L. Thompson, "Calvin as a Biblical Interpreter," in *The Cambridge Companion to John Calvin*, ed. Donald K. McKim (Cambridge: Cambridge University Press, 2004), 58-73.

[19]Calvin, *St. John 1–10*, 92, 95-101. J. Thompson, *John Calvin*, 42-43, notes that it is unlikely Dentière influenced Calvin.

[20]Calvin, *St. John 1–10*, 90, 94, 104.

[21]See Lipscomb, "Subjection and Companionship," 352-53; Vorster, "John Calvin," 193-97.

[22]Calvin, *St. John 1–10*, 94.

The Samaritan woman's continual sin led her into prostitution. It's not clear if Calvin thought she earned a living by sex work, or if he interpreted her (supposed) repeated adultery as prostitution.[23] In either case, he consistently used sexually charged descriptions for the Samaritan woman: she was a wanton, wicked, adulterous, infamous prostitute.[24]

For Calvin, adultery, premarital sex, and any sexual act outside of marriage were among the worst sins a person could commit.[25] He identified marriage as the solution to the problem of fornication. He argued that sexual intercourse in marriage could be good and holy. But Calvin also shared some of the early church's suspicions of sexual desire and pleasure. Sex turned humans into animals. Marital intercourse, then, should be bound by chastity, propriety, and decency, with no indulgence of lust.[26]

These perspectives on sex, sin, and marriage had certain consequences. Calvin discouraged men and women from dressing or behaving in ways that might attract attention or arouse desire in another person. He compared fashionably dressed women to prostitutes whose clothing (and behavior) advertised their sexual availability.[27] He also emphasized the dangers of youthful desire.

> Commenting on Genesis 34, Calvin blamed Dinah's sexual assault on her. She should not have left the safety of her home to go out where a man could see her and desire her. God protects (only?) chaste, obedient virgin girls (*Genesis*, 2:218; *Harmony*, 3:92).

---

[23]Prostitution overlapped with adultery in the cases heard before the Consistory under Calvin's leadership. See Robert M. Kingdon, *Adultery and Divorce in Calvin's Geneva* (Cambridge: Harvard University Press, 1995), 101-11, 134-36; John Witte and Robert M. Kingdon, *Sex, Marriage, and Family in John Calvin's Geneva*, vol. 1, *Courtship, Engagement, and Marriage* (Grand Rapids, MI: Eerdmans, 2005), 303.

[24]Calvin, *St. John 1–10*, 90, 94, 104.

[25]See John Calvin, *Commentaries on the Four Last Books of Moses, Arranged in the Form of a Harmony*, vol. 3 of 4, trans. Charles William Bingham (Edinburgh: Calvin Translation Society, 1853), 68-69, 75-76, 79, 91-92; *First Epistle to the Corinthians*, 131-32; Witte and Kingdon, *Sex, Marriage, and Family*, 1:43-47, 71-73, 415-17; and Jeffrey R. Watt, *The Consistory and Social Discipline in Calvin's Geneva*, Perspectives on Early Modern Europe (Rochester: University of Rochester Press, 2020), 101-15.

[26]Calvin, *Harmony*, 3:77, 84, 95-96, 108-9; *First Epistle to the Corinthians*, 137-41, 159. See further Witte and Kingdon, *Sex, Marriage, and Family*, 1:39.

[27]Calvin, *Inst.* 2.8.44; *Harmony*, 3:109; and for women specifically, *Hebrews*, 280-82; *Second Epistle to the Corinthians*, 215-16; *Sermons on 1 Timothy* 17.

Calvin recognized the dangers of deception and violence for women [*Genesis*, 2:219; *Harmony*, 3:79, 83]. In several Consistory cases, women were not blamed or punished following assault, though the male assailants were executed. In other cases, however, women who accused men of rape were themselves investigated and even punished for lewd behavior and fornication.[28]

Because of the dangers of female sexuality, fathers should carefully guard their daughters against unchastity before marriage. Husbands should protect their wives from their own desires too. A woman who either had sex before marriage or committed adultery could not be trusted.[29] On all these counts, the active sexual life Calvin gave to the Samaritan woman marked her as the worst kind of sinner.

The seriousness of sex and marriage helps explain Calvin's interpretation of the Samaritan woman, but his condemnation extended beyond her sexual and marital depravity. He claimed that she mocked and shamed Jesus with her response to his request for water (Jn 4:9). She pretended that Jesus was speaking about literal water (even though she clearly knew he was speaking figuratively), and she condemned his egotistical assumption of superiority over Jacob (Jn 4:11-12). Her mockery continued in John 4:15 with the implication that Jesus couldn't do what his words suggested.[30]

This characterization of the woman reflects Calvin's understanding of the human state. All humans were born, lived, and died under the weight of Adam's sin, and as a result all humans were ignorant of God, utterly incapable of anything good, and entirely committed to evil. No one was capable of knowing or worshiping God. Even to recognize the human state required divine revelation. And, of course, no one could fix the problem of sin for themselves.[31]

Calvin's Samaritan woman was a representative example of this theological narrative.[32] Like any human, she could do no good, and so Calvin interpreted every word she spoke through the lens of sin. For someone like this, only the sting of divine judgment could incite her to accept the grace

[28]See Kingdon, *Adultery*, 120-22, 125-26; Watt, *Consistory*, 109-11.
[29]Calvin, *Harmony*, 3:75-76, 79, 84, 91-92; *First Epistle to the Corinthians*, 144, 165-67.
[30]Calvin, *St. John 1–10*, 92-94.
[31]For instance, Calvin, *Institutes* 1.1.1-2, 2.1.1, 3.17.8; *Genesis*, 1:151-55. See also Parker, *Calvin*, 40-56.
[32]Note Calvin, *St. John 1–10*, 90-93, 103, 107; Farmer, "Changing Images," 375.

of God. This was why, Calvin explained, Jesus brought up her marital history in the first place.[33]

Even if a woman was not a prostitute like the Samaritan woman, and even if a man had not committed a "terrible crime," everyone sinned in some way, and therefore no one deserved God's grace. For Calvin, Jesus' actions in John 4:4-42 demonstrated the availability of the gift of salvation for all. Equally, the Samaritan woman's immediate acceptance of Jesus' judgment provided a model of repentance, obedience, and acceptance of the teachers God provides.[34] For Calvin, the Samaritan woman symbolized both the weight of sin, and the grace of undeserved salvation.

The woman's words. Origen, Chrysostom, and Dentière all emphasized the Samaritan woman's wisdom in her conversation with Jesus and her evangelization among her neighbors. Calvin also praised her zeal to invite others to meet Jesus, even publicizing her own sin in the process. Her neighbors recognized Jesus as a prophet on account of her witness. Her testimony had power.[35]

Calvin's interpretation of John 4:4-42 through the themes of sin and salvation made it relevant to all women and men. He encouraged all people to identify with the woman because they were, like her, utterly undeserving of God's grace. Despite his praise for the woman and the general applicability of her story, though, Calvin also gendered the story in particular ways.

The representation of the Samaritan woman as a disobedient, adulterous wife made her sin and, therefore, her story uniquely female. Calvin's consistent disparagement of the woman's words throughout the commentary reinforced this message. In contrast to Chrysostom and Dentière, Calvin's Samaritan woman was no apostle.

I've already noted the representation of the woman's initial responses to Jesus as insulting, contemptuous mockery. Calvin's explanation of her efforts to evangelize in her community raised additional critiques. He wondered if the newness of her faith and incompleteness of her understanding made her words unsound. While he rejected this potential interpretation, his mention of false teaching introduces a suspicion of her message. His identification of

---

[33]Calvin, *St. John 1–10*, 93-94.
[34]Calvin, *St. John 1–10*, 90, 94-95, 102.
[35]Calvin, *St. John 1–10*, 103-4, 109.

women's speech in general as "usually untrustworthy" stressed this suspicion, as did his reference to her apparent lie that Jesus told her all she had ever done (Jn 4:29).[36]

Women's speech was problematic for Calvin. He identified talkativeness in general as a female failing, and he attributed rumors and superstitions to "old women." From Eve onwards, women used their words to mislead others.[37] Calvin's expectation that women should be silent and refrain from teaching (or other expressions of authority) in church and society reflects both the hierarchy of creation and the danger of women's speech.[38]

The Samaritan woman, already an example of Eve's sin in her rejection of her subordination to her husbands, was made even more dangerous by her words. Calvin therefore minimized the woman's witness in several ways. He described her as overly chatty, so much so that Jesus had to condemn her sin to shut her up. He denied that the Samaritan woman taught anyone anything since she was "unqualified" to preach or teach. She was only "a trumpet or a bell" to alert her neighbors to Jesus' presence.[39] Presumably, an actual trumpet or bell would have worked just as well.

The woman's words were inferior, weak testimony that could not bring anyone to faith. Calvin interpreted the Samaritans' belief "because of the woman's word" in John 4:39 as indicating only their willingness to listen. Consequently, instead of encouraging his readers to imitate the woman by preaching to their neighbors, he upheld Jesus, the true evangelist and teacher, as the model to follow.[40]

Like Chrysostom, Calvin also minimized the words of Mary, Martha, and Mary Magdalene. He argued that Jesus' mother and Martha both spoke out of turn, and the women at the tomb were weak, foolish, and overly emotional.[41] Calvin concluded that the only reason Jesus used women to

---

[36]Calvin, *St. John 1–10*, 104, 109-10.

[37]John Calvin, *Antidote to the Council of Trent*, in *John Calvin: Selections from His Writings*, ed. John Dillenberger, American Academy of Religion Aids for the Study of Religion 2 (Atlanta: Scholars Press, 1975), 143; *Genesis*, 1:151-55, 164, 171-72; *First Epistle to the Corinthians*, 306-7; *Second Epistle to the Corinthians*, 217-218, 259; *Sermons on 1 Timothy* 18.

[38]See further Vorster, "John Calvin," 198-200.

[39]Calvin, *St. John 1–10*, 104. See also Farmer, "Changing Images," 375.

[40]Calvin, *St. John 1–10*, 104, 109-10.

[41]Note Calvin, *St. John 1–10*, 46; John Calvin, *The Gospel According to St. John 11–21 and the First Epistle of John*, trans. T. H. L. Parker, Calvin's Commentaries (1959; repr., Grand Rapids, MI: Eerdmans, 1978), 7-8, 11, 191, 196.

announce the resurrection was to shame the (male) disciples. In fact, this purpose would have been accomplished equally well by sending an ox or donkey to the disciples.[42] Trumpets and bells and livestock: Calvin's dehumanization of the biblical women who speak removed the potential power of their words. As he said, these women were not apostles.[43]

The Samaritan woman in the Protestant Reformation. Marie Dentière saw the Samaritan woman as an example of the power of women's words. But for Calvin, the woman's gender and personal history made her words suspect. Instead of evidence of women's right to participate in the ministry of the church, the Samaritan woman—a slut; an unhappy, poor, and common woman; a prostitute—exemplified the undeservedness of God's grace.[44]

For Calvin, the woman's story served as a powerful reminder that all people can be saved. This message was echoed by other men who wrote and preached on the story in the sixteenth century, and it persisted well beyond the sixteenth century. We'll explore its contemporary representations in the next chapter. But before we get to our own day, we've got one last historical stop: the nineteenth century social reformers and revivalists.

THE PROSTITUTE AT THE WELL: JOHN 4:4-42
IN NINETEENTH-CENTURY REFORM AND REVIVAL

The interpretations of John 4:4-42 by Clara Lucas Balfour and Dwight Lyman Moody include messages we've already heard, but they also reflect the social and theological upheavals of the Industrial Revolution. Before exploring Balfour and Moody's Samaritan woman, I will briefly survey these changes and their consequences for men and women in the church.

In the eighteenth and nineteenth centuries in England and America, the Industrial Revolution moved household-based productivity to factories. Workers left rural areas for cities, with all the pleasures and temptations of urban life: gin, opium, gambling, and prostitution. The wealthy

---

[42]Calvin, *St. John 11–21*, 199. Comparably, Calvin thought Deborah's leadership in Judg 4–5 shamed and punished the unworthiness of the men of her day. A stone or a "fool" would have worked as well (*Sermons on 1 Timothy* 19). See also J. Thompson, "*Creata*," 135-38; Vorster, "John Calvin," 200-202.

[43]Calvin, *St. John 11-21*, 200.

[44]Calvin, *St. John 1–10*, 90, 102-3.

got wealthier, and the poor struggled to survive without the social safety nets of rural life.[45]

These shifts affected family life. In impoverished families, men, women, and children all worked outside the home in factories. For women, poverty combined with urbanization sometimes resulted in sex work. From the perspective of the privileged, poverty corresponded to degradation and immorality. Wealthier families also changed as women and children lost their ability to contribute to the household economy. They became dependent on the paycheck of the adult male in the family, who worked entirely outside the home.[46]

In middle- and upper-class families, women's economic contribution to the household was replaced by piety. Women took responsibility for maintaining a family's faith through devotions, prayers, spiritual instruction for children, and (gentle) moral influence on their husbands. These women became the guardians of social morality through participation in women's societies, reform organizations, and political activism.[47]

The association of piety with femininity challenged men's long-held spiritual authority. The church, religion, and morality became women's realm. Women (at least, wealthy White women) were no longer irrevocably stained by Eve's sin. Rather, they were "angels in the home."[48] However, women's superiority depended on their morality (including their sexual morality). Women who demonstrated immorality in their actions or lifestyles threatened the status of all women.[49]

---

[45]E.g., Callum G. Brown, *The Death of Christian Britain: Understanding Secularisation 1800–2000*, Christianity and Society in the Modern World (Abingdon: Routledge, 2001), 59; Marion Ann Taylor and Heather E. Weir, *Let Her Speak for Herself: Nineteenth-Century Women Writing on Women in Genesis* (Waco: Baylor University Press, 2006), 2-4.

[46]See Margaret Lamberts Bendroth, *Fundamentalism and Gender: 1875 to the Present* (New Haven: Yale University Press, 1993), 15-16; Brown, *Christian Britain*, 89-90; Stephanie Coontz, *Marriage, a History: From Obedience to Intimacy or How Love Conquered Marriage* (New York: Viking, 2005), 154-69; Barr, *Biblical Womanhood*, 161-64.

[47]See Bendroth, *Fundamentalism*, 22; Barbara J. MacHaffie, *Her Story: Women in Christian Tradition*, 2nd ed. (Minneapolis: Fortress, 2006), 163-70; Sara Moslener, *Virgin Nation: Sexual Purity and American Adolescence* (Oxford: Oxford University Press, 2015), 16-19.

[48]Bendroth, *Fundamentalism*, 17-18; Brown, *Christian Britain*, 58-63, 88; MacHaffie, *Her Story*, 160-63; Barr, *Biblical Womanhood*, 165-67.

[49]Brown, *Christian Britain*, 64; Coontz, *Marriage*, 169; MacHaffie, *Her Story*, 161.

Poor women, Black women, and non-European women in general did not share the superior piety and morality of White, privileged women. For instance, in nineteenth century America, the hypersexualization of Black women and girls as "unconditionally promiscuous" contributed to sexual violence against them.[50]

Racism did not begin in the nineteenth century, of course, but the racialization of intellectual capability, morality, gender, and sexuality is a significant context for Christian theology and practice in this period. From this point forward, I will draw attention to racial identity, stereotypes, and racism as components of interpretations of the Samaritan woman's story, the sexualization of women, and women's participation in the church.

Clara Lucas Balfour and Dwight Lyman Moody participated in two different responses to the social changes of the nineteenth century: social reform and evangelical revival. Balfour, a White woman active in the temperance movement and welfare reform in England, often incorporated a strong moral, spiritual, or theological component in her lectures and published works. Her primary focus, however, remained on social reform.[51] Moody, a White American revivalist, interpreted the same social problems through the lens of sin and salvation. His ministry and his evangelistic sermons exhorted his listeners to repent of the sins of alcohol, gambling, and promiscuity and to allow Christ to change their lives.[52]

Like Calvin, Balfour and Moody explored the Samaritan woman's story as an example of the dangers of sexual sin and the hope of salvation. While both classified the woman as a prostitute, however, they drew different messages for the women of their intended audiences. These differences, reflecting their contrasting focuses, complicate the interpretation of the story for the church.

---

[50]See Estelle B. Freedman, *Redefining Rape: Sexual Violence in the Era of Suffrage and Segregation* (Cambridge: Harvard University Press, 2013), and Tamura Lomax, *Jezebel Unhinged: Loosing the Black Female Body in Religion & Culture* (Durham: Duke University Press, 2018), 15-31.

[51]On Balfour's life and work, see Kristin G. Doern, "Balfour, Clara Lucas," in *Oxford Dictionary of National Biography*, ed. David Cannadine (Oxford: Oxford University Press, 2004), 3:514-15.

[52]The essays in Timothy George, ed., *Mr. Moody and the Evangelical Tradition* (London: T&T Clark, 2004), provide a helpful introduction to Moody's life, message, and ministry.

AN INTELLIGENT WOMAN. CLARA LUCAS BALFOUR'S SAMARITAN WOMAN

In the midst of all her degradation, the heart of this woman was not
utterly seared; she had felt the bitterness of remorse—the struggle
with convictions; she knew too much of good to be happy in evil,—she
possessed a mind "Not all degraded, Even by the crimes through
which it waded." Hence her restless, inquiring, arguing spirit.

CLARA LUCAS BALFOUR, WOMEN OF SCRIPTURE

In *The Women of Scripture*, published in 1847, Clara Lucas Balfour classified the Samaritan woman with the woman who washed Jesus' feet with
her tears and hair (Lk 7:36-50), whom she identified as a prostitute. She
accused the Samaritan woman of utter moral degradation and the corruption of womanly domesticity.[53] For Balfour, John 4 was about sex and
sin (though, being a proper Victorian, Balfour hid this meaning behind
the rhetoric of "degradation").

Balfour wrote *The Women of Scripture* for wealthier White women, the
wives and mothers responsible for the spiritual instruction of their families
and for broader social reform.[54] Following the Victorian construction of
womanhood, she identified women as eminently gifted in morality, spirituality, and faith. She also challenged certain ideas. Women were generally
considered to be too emotional to be reasonable or intelligent. They were
accused of having a childishly faulty, uncontrolled mind. Balfour, however,
insisted on intelligence as a defining characteristic of women.[55]

> Though the church and academy limited women's right to interpret the Bible as
> a whole or to address serious matters of theology, women's stories and practi-
> cal advice for women's lives were seen as appropriate work for women

---

[53]Clara Lucas Balfour, *Women of Scripture* (London: Houlston and Stoneman, 1847),
309-11, 315.

[54]Note Balfour, *Women*, 15, 76, 213, 222, 368, etc.

[55]See Balfour, *Women*, iii-iv, 12-13, 347-49, and throughout; and also MacHaffie, *Her Story*, 160-63;
Christiana de Groot, "Deborah: A Lightning Rod for Nineteenth-Century Women's Issues," in
Faith and Feminism in Nineteenth-Century Religious Communities, ed. Michaela Sohn-Kronthaler
and Ruth Albrecht, The Bible and Women: An Encyclopedia of Exegesis and Cultural History
8.2 (Atlanta: SBL Press, 2019), 63-98, esp. 71-72.

interpreters. Many nineteenth-century women authors wrote about biblical women for women's moral instruction.[56]

Women's intelligence intersected with their morality and virtue. Like Dentière, Balfour connected sin and the stereotypical failings of women to their lack of education. Education, therefore, enabled women to fulfill their responsibilities as partners for their husbands and teachers for their children.[57] The stories of Miriam, Deborah, Esther, Priscilla, and Phoebe—smart women who participated in the work of God in the world—also demonstrated the importance of women's intelligence for social engagement.

Balfour exhorted her audience to seek education so that their benevolence, charity, and piety could influence (and redeem) the home and society.[58] But women who failed to maintain their moral superiority—women like the Samaritan woman or the woman of Luke 7:36-50—undermined the redemption of society. For Balfour, then, Jesus' interaction with these two women offered an example of ministry to such women for her audience to follow.

Balfour's Samaritan woman. Balfour's interpretation of John 4:4-42 moves between the woman's domestic degradation, the historical context of the divide between Jews and Samaritans, and acknowledgment of the woman's expressions of and reputation for intelligence. Like Chrysostom, for Balfour the Samaritan woman was complex, ambiguous, and problematic. Nonetheless, the story had important lessons for her audience.

Balfour excused what she interpreted as the Samaritan woman's initial rudeness to Jesus with reference to the prejudice between their two peoples. While the woman proved her intelligence through her contributions to the conversation, she remained somewhat contemptuous of Jesus until he condemned her sinful life.[59] As a woman, she should have been a model of pious domesticity, but she was instead mired in "degrading domestic affairs."[60]

---

[56]See Rebecca Styler, "A Scripture of Their Own: Nineteenth-Century Bible Biography and Feminist Bible Criticism," *Christianity and Literature* 57 (2007): 65-85, especially 65-68.

[57]Balfour, *Women*, 4-5, 32-33, 347-49, etc.

[58]Note Balfour, *Women*, 176-79, 357, 364-68.

[59]Balfour, *Women*, 306-7, 309.

[60]Balfour, *Women*, 310-11.

Doopite the Samaritan woman's initial rejection of Jesus, his manner and appearance attracted her interest. Balfour quoted a romantic, almost eroticized, poem in praise of Jesus' physical appearance and "perfected manhood" to explain this change of heart (Balfour, *Women*, 308). This fascinating reversal of the more common sexualization of the woman herself reflects the sentimentality of Victorian spirituality.

Balfour did not address the precise nature of the Samaritan woman's degradation, though the association with the "prostitute" of Luke 7:36-50 certainly implicated the Samaritan woman in sexual sin. Uniquely among the interpretations we have surveyed, however, Balfour warned her readers against judging this woman by their own standards of morality. Her situation may be due to the extensive rights of divorce for men in her day. Moreover, she may have been victimized by a man, the true sinner and the more proper object of feminine anger.[61]

This warning reflects Balfour's problematic, colonialist assumption of Western cultural and moral superiority, particularly with respect to sexuality.[62] But it also pointedly reminded readers of men's necessary involvement in women's sexual sin, whether in ancient Samaria or nineteenth-century England. Balfour's inclusion of the Samaritan woman's men in her interpretation of the story opens space to question the reductive sexualization of the woman in the work of Tertullian and John Calvin.

Despite her acknowledgment of historical circumstance, Balfour did not excuse the Samaritan woman's complicity in her situation: "The way in which our Lord alludes to the domestic character of this woman marks his sense of its revolting nature." Jesus did not, however, condemn the woman. His compassionate instruction provided a lesson and model for Balfour's readers. They, too, should refrain from judging women like the Samaritan woman, instead working to restore them to morality.[63]

Balfour represented the woman's responses to Jesus in John 4:16-20 as a mix of confusion, deflection, and redirection.[64] But the woman did

---

[61]Balfour, *Women*, 303-5, 311.
[62]Note esp. Balfour, *Women*, 2-12, 179.
[63]Balfour, *Women*, 311, 314. See also Styler, "A Scripture of Their Own," 76.
[64]Balfour, *Women*, 309-10.

eventually recognize Jesus' identity, and she responded with true, sincere faith. She was the most effective of the earliest evangelists—many people were saved through the woman's work.[65]

> Balfour's interpretation of the Samaritan woman reflects a trend in the use of John 4:4-42 by women social activists in the nineteenth and early twentieth centuries. Like Marie Dentière, these women identified the Samaritan woman as an exemplar of women's speech and leadership.[66]

The Samaritan woman's conversational skills, questions, and witness to her community evidenced her intelligence, as did her neighbors' respect (since no one would listen to a fool).[67] Given Balfour's association of education with morality, her emphasis on the woman's wisdom is somewhat surprising. Less surprisingly, she argued that the woman's intelligence only made her sin the worse.[68] But added to the reminder of men's responsibility in women's sexual misconduct, Balfour's attention to the Samaritan woman's intelligence and evangelistic influence challenges the vilification of the woman in Christian interpretation.

Balfour's own engagement in social reform is reflected in her distinction between the sin and the sinner, her insistence on male culpability in women's sexual sin, and the recognition that a woman who has a degrading personal situation can at the same time be virtuously intelligent. In the end, Balfour encouraged her readers to imitate Jesus, not the Samaritan woman. But the woman did offer another example, alongside Phoebe, Priscilla, and other New Testament women, of the importance of women's active engagement in the church.

---

[65]Balfour, *Women*, 313-314.
[66]See Harriet Livermore, *Scriptural Evidence in Favour of Female Testimony in Meetings for Christian Worship* (Portsmouth, NH: R. Foster, 1824), 81-82; Phoebe Palmer, *The Promise of the Father* (1859; repr. Eugene: Wipf & Stock, 2015), 11-12; and Virginia W. Broughton, *Women's Work: As Gleaned from the Women of the Bible*, in *Virginia Broughton: The Life and Writings of a National Baptist Missionary*, ed. Tomeiko Ashford Carter (Knoxville: University of Tennessee Press, 2010), 17.
[67]Balfour, *Women*, 310-11, 313.
[68]Balfour, *Women*, 311.

DWIGHT L. MOODY: PREACHING TO THE PROSTITUTES

> *While [Christ] is sitting on the curb-stone of the well, a poor fallen*
> *woman of Samaria comes along for water. You know the people*
> *in those days used to come out in the morning or evening to get*
> *their water, not in the blaze of the noon-day sun. No doubt she*
> *was ashamed to come out there to meet the pure and virtuous at*
> *the well, and that was the reason why she stole out at that hour.*
>
> DWIGHT L. MOODY, "SALVATION FOR SINNERS"

Like Balfour, Dwight L. Moody identified the Samaritan woman with sexual sin. Both also drew attention to the woman's testimony to Jesus. As an evangelist, however, Moody focused his interpretation on repentance, conversion, and sanctification. His representation of the Samaritan woman was thoroughly negative. She exemplified a life of sin that endangered men, and from which men and all women like her must be saved.

When Moody looked around late nineteenth century cities like Boston and Chicago, he saw sin everywhere. It was clearly visible in the abuse of alcohol, gambling, and prostitution in impoverished neighborhoods. Moody also insisted on the complete sinfulness of seminary presidents, businessmen, and moral, respectable White people (the wealthy, in other words). He illustrated this point by contrasting the Samaritan woman with Nicodemus. Everyone could agree the Samaritan woman needed to repent and change her life. But Jesus told Nicodemus he, too, must be born again.[69]

During months-long revival meetings from New York to Chicago, Moody called his (primarily White) audiences to confess Christ and allow the power of Christ to save, reform, and strengthen them for the unending battle against sin and Satan.[70] This power was available to men and women. But Moody described its effects in distinctly gendered terms: "If we boldly took

---

[69]Dwight Lyman Moody, *Moody: His Words, Work, and Workers*, ed. W. H. Daniels (New York: Nelson & Phillips, 1877), 411-12. Note that Moody's sermons were transcribed by journalists to be printed in newspapers; they were later collected for publication.

[70]See, for instance, Moody, *Moody: His Words*, 275, 345, 387-88, 395; Dwight Lyman Moody, *"The Gospel Awakening." Comprising the Sermons and Addresses, Prayer-Meeting Talks and Bible Readings of the Great Revival Meetings Conducted by Moody and Sankey*, 20th ed., ed. L. T. Remlap (Chicago: Fairbanks and Palmer, 1885), 118-19, 530-31, 656, 672.

up our cross and bore it manfully, the world would soon see the influence of these meetings."[71]

The portrayal of Christianity as masculine countered the perceived feminization of the church through the nineteenth century. As women took responsibility for morality and religion, the church itself became associated with women (and, as we see with Balfour, women became instrumental in church movements and social reform). Early fundamentalists like Moody wanted to reclaim Christianity for men.[72] The masculine imagery of war, power, and strength reflected this intent.

Moody addressed his revival sermons to the young men who spent their days gambling, the older men who were enslaved to alcohol, and the businessmen who were too, well, busy for religion. His sermons centered on men's work, leisure activities, and familial expectations.[73]

It is not clear if Moody's audiences included Black men. He welcomed Black people as equals in Christian faith, but there are very few explicit references to Black concerns in post-emancipation America in the edited transcripts of his sermons. Moody consistently used *black* as a synonym for sin, evil, and impurity. He illustrated the impossibility of saving yourself from sin with the inability of Black men to wash themselves white.[74]

Similarly, while women were certainly present at his revivals, Moody rarely directly addressed them in his sermons. He did, however, refer to women's moral and religious influences on little boys and grown men. His emotive illustrations of mothers praying for their prodigal sons tugged directly on Victorian heartstrings.[75]

Moody relied on women as colleagues. He gave Emmeline Dryer the responsibility of founding, organizing, and running an educational institution to train

---

[71]Dwight Lyman Moody, *Glad Tidings Comprising Sermons and Prayer-Meeting Talks Delivered at the N. Y. Hippodrome*, ed. H. H. Birkins (New York: The Tribune Association, 1876), 186. See also *"Gospel Awakening,"* 78, 319.

[72]See Bendroth, *Fundamentalism*, 6-7, 13-24; Moslener, *Virgin Nation*, 21-24.

[73]For instance, Moody, *Moody: His Words*, 86, 117, 330-33; Dwight Lyman Moody, *Dwight Lyman Moody's Life Work and Gospel Sermons*, ed. Richard S. Rhodes (Chicago: Rhodes and McClure, 1907), 69-71, 93-94, 382-83.

[74]Moody, *"Gospel Awakening,"* 116, 188, 258, etc. See further Thomas E. Corts, "D. L. Moody: Payment on Account," in George, *Mr. Moody*, 51-73, esp. 64-65.

[75]See Moody, *Moody: His Words*, 14, 126-37, 182-83; *Moody's Life Work*, ii-iii, 32-35; etc.

evangelists and missionaries. Frances Willard preached to women and taught people interested in conversion for three hours a day at Moody's revivals.[76]

Moody certainly recognized that women needed salvation. But, in contrast to his constant references to the specific sins of (White) men, representations of women as sinners are uncommon in his sermons. The one consistent sin he associated with women was nonmarital sex, and even this sin was problematic primarily because of its consequences for men: "How many men come into these inquiry rooms bound hand and foot with this infamous vice! They are in the power of some harlot, and she says: 'If you desert me I will expose you.' [. . .] Many a man has been brought down to hell by that sin."[77]

Moody condemned women who worked in prostitution as the "devil's servants." They ensnared young men, in the process destroying their own womanly virtue, the lives of their customers, and their customers' families.[78] Apparently, this message caught the attention of a prostitute during his revival in Chicago in 1876.

This self-identified "sinful girl" sent Moody a letter critiquing his failure to preach salvation to the prostitutes—the "victims of man's lust"—in addition to the young men who were so ensnared.[79] In response, he invited Chicago's prostitutes to attend the next evening's meeting, when he preached a sermon about three Gospel prostitutes: the woman of Luke 7:36-50, the woman of John 8:3-11, and the Samaritan woman.

Moody's Samaritan woman. Moody began his sermon with a reminder that Jesus' purpose was to save all sinners, including the tax collectors, abusive husbands, and "fallen women" of Chicago.[80] He spoke directly to any prostitute who may have accepted his invitation to the meeting. He addressed both the severity of women's sexual sin and the potential for repentance and regeneration. These two emphases frame Moody's

---

[76]See further Bendroth, *Fundamentalism*, 14-18, 25-29; D. W. Bebbington, "Moody as Transatlantic Evangelical," in *Mr. Moody*, ed. George, 75-92, especially 81, 89.

[77]Moody, *Moody: His Words*, 418.

[78]For instance, Moody, *Moody: His Words*, 275, 333, 418; *Moody's Life Work*, 45, 151-52.

[79]The letter is reproduced in Moody, *Moody: His Words*, 433-34 (though its accuracy or historicity is unclear).

[80]Moody, "*Gospel Awakening*," 527-28.

interpretation of the stories of Jesus' interactions with "fallen women" in Luke 7:36-50, John 4:4-42, and John 8:3-11.

Moody's definition of the woman who washed Jesus' feet with her tears and hair as a prostitute followed the popular interpretation of her story. His inclusion of John 8:3-11 identified that woman's adultery as prostitution. In contrast to the biblical definition of adultery around the marital status of the woman, Moody assumed this woman was unmarried. He gave her a tragic backstory: a stepmother who kicked her out of the home; an alcoholic father who introduced her to moral corruption. But (as with Balfour's Samaritan woman) this narrative did not excuse the woman's sin. Moody identified her as the "blackest" and "vilest" of the three women.[81]

In this context, Moody's interpretation of John 4:4-42 clearly identified the Samaritan woman as a prostitute who sold her body. He twice referred to her as a "fallen woman." He also claimed that she went to the well at noon to avoid the company of the morally upright women of the village. Her initial reactions to Jesus showed her disinterest, perhaps, Moody suggested, like any prostitutes who attended his revival meeting out of idle curiosity. Much as Moody did in his sermon, Jesus addressed the Samaritan woman's sin to get her attention and her confession.[82]

Jesus' conversation with the woman convinced her that he was the Messiah. Moody vividly described her subsequent evangelism. She started shouting her news as soon as she was through the city gates, and immediately everyone ran out to the well to meet Jesus. Moody identified "the poor fallen woman" as the sower who, in Jesus' metaphor, prepared the fields for the harvest. He credited her testimony as no less important than Jesus' in bringing about the faith of her neighbors.[83]

> In another sermon, Moody identified the Samaritan woman as a better Christian than Nicodemus (though not as good as the believer of John 7:37-38, whose faith flooded the world).[84]

[81]Moody, "*Gospel Awakening*," 531-32.
[82]Moody, "*Gospel Awakening*," 530.
[83]Moody, "*Gospel Awakening*," 531.
[84]Moody, *Moody: His Words*, 397-98.

Keeping his intended audience and his own evangelistic purpose firmly in view throughout his sermon, Moody stressed Jesus' welcome for all three women. Jesus did not reject, shame, or judge them. He instead forgave. Moody suggested that none of these women were named in the Gospels so that no one, meeting them in heaven, would be able to judge or shame them on the basis of their pasts. They were completely redeemed.[85]

Redemption demanded change. Moody did not speculate on the lives of the three women beyond their encounter with Jesus. Instead, he told the stories of prostitutes who had been saved through his revivals. These women, he said, immediately left their professions through the help of their own families and other Christians.[86] He exhorted the "fallen women" at the Chicago revival to do the same. They should not even return to their brothels. According to one published version of this sermon, Moody said it was better for these women to die in poverty than buy their daily bread with the literal wages of sin.[87]

Moody's sermon to the "fallen women" reflected his understanding of the essential sinfulness of all people, the free availability of divine forgiveness, and the power of God to change the saved, even prostitutes. This message responded to one of the requests in the letter from the unnamed woman who worked as a prostitute in Chicago. Her letter also critiqued Moody's messages concerning prostitution. He blamed women for misleading men. But, the letter writer noted, the women were the real victims. Going further than Balfour did, she insisted on the injustice of condemning women for men's sins.[88]

Moody acknowledged this injustice and the economic realities that the women faced.[89] But as in his interpretation of John 8:3-11, the women's personal histories, economic deprivation, and social ostracism did not excuse their sin.[90] Neither did the involvement of male customers. Moody judged the women who worked as prostitutes to be impure, guilty of the worst of sins. He

---

[85]Moody, *"Gospel Awakening,"* 529-30.

[86]Moody, *"Gospel Awakening,"* 533-35. See also Bruce J. Evensen, *God's Man for the Gilded Age: D. L. Moody and the Rise of Modern Mass Evangelism* (Oxford: Oxford University Press, 2003), 147-49.

[87]Moody, *Moody: His Words*, 441-42. This striking claim is not in the transcription of the sermon in *"Gospel Awakening"* (though there is a similar sentiment, 535).

[88]Quoted in Moody, *Moody: His Words*, 433.

[89]Moody, *"Gospel Awakening,"* 532, 535-36; see also *Moody: His Words*, 147, 221.

[90]This point is explicit in Moody, *Moody's Life Work*, 152.

did not challenge the church, let alone society, to reform the social and economic structures that created, encouraged, and supported prostitution.

Moody's representation of the Samaritan woman as a prostitute recalls Tertullian, John Calvin, and his own demonization of such women as Satan's little helpers. His condemnation of women's sexuality, however, stands in tension with his acceptance of repentant prostitutes as fully redeemed. In contrast to the danger of women's words in Calvin's writings, Moody recognized the Samaritan woman as an evangelist. Coupled with the work of the women reformers in Moody's revivals, his own explorations of John 4:4-42 and the words of the unnamed woman from Chicago complicate the critique of women as (only or primarily) sexual temptresses.

TRACING THE THREADS

In 1639, Marie Dentière connected sexual assault with women's subjection to male authority, lack of education, and limitation from leadership in Christian communities. Her "Defense of Women" insisted on women's right to read the Bible, be educated, and take on pastoral roles in the church. Her Samaritan woman was an intelligent, thoughtful teacher and reformer who effectively ministered to her entire village. A church full of women like this would, presumably, protect women against the exploitation and violence Dentière saw in non-Reformed churches.

But this vision was not realized in Protestant tradition. Instead, the male Reformers and their spiritual descendants almost universally characterized the Samaritan woman as an archetypal sinner. As such, her story of salvation had significance for all Christians. But the contextualization of this interpretation within traditions that continued to represent women as sexual temptresses who bear the guilt of their own sexual sin meant the Samaritan woman's story had particular relevance for women. The vilification of the Samaritan woman as a prostitute who misleads and destroys men has, as we'll see in the next chapter, real consequences for women in the church.

Table 3.1. John 4 according to Marie Dentière, John Calvin, Clara Lucas Balfour, and Dwight Moody

Interpreter	Explanation of the Woman's Character and Participation in the Story	Significance of the Story for the Church
Marie Dentière, *Epistle to Marguerite de Navarre* (1539)	The woman is a proto-Reformer and preacher. Her conversation with Jesus represents a critique of religious ceremony and ritual. Dentière associates the Samaritan woman with Mary Magdalene, who was sent by Jesus to announce the resurrection to the other disciples.	The story supports the Protestant Reformation. The woman's participation in the story proves women's right to preach and teach in the church.
John Calvin, *The Gospel According to St. John* (1553)	The woman is sexually immoral, divorced by her husbands for disobedience and adultery, and guilty of prostitution. She is a social outcast who mocks Jesus. Her speech to her neighbors offers a powerful witness to Jesus, but she is not an apostle—she only alerts people to Jesus' presence (like a bell or trumpet).	The woman symbolizes the complete sinfulness of humanity. While the story more generally teaches the rejection of religious ritual, the woman serves only to represent God's undeserved gift of salvation.
Clara Lucas Balfour, *The Women of Scripture* (1847)	The woman is intelligent but contemptuous of Jesus. She is guilty of sexual sin, though her situation may be the consequence of her legal and social context. She is an effective preacher and evangelist. Balfour compares the Samaritan woman with the "prostitute" of Luke 7:36-50.	The story offers a warning against judging others for their sin, as well as encouragement for women to minister to sinful women like the Samaritan woman. It also represents the need for women's education.
Dwight L. Moody, "Salvation for Sinners" (1876)	The woman is a prostitute who is socially ostracized by her community. She is not interested in Jesus when the conversation begins. However, her conversion makes her an evangelist who saves her neighbors. Moody categorizes the woman with the "prostitutes" of Luke 7:36-50 and John 8:1-11. He also contrasts her with Nicodemus.	The story teaches the availability of salvation to prostitutes who repent and leave their lives of sin.

4

#CHURCHTOO

The Samaritan Woman Today

Oh, it gives me shivers just to think of it! The Lord
reaching out to someone who was in all ways a social reject.
Notice he didn't command her; he asked her. His words were
polite and forthright, the start of a lengthy conversation—the longest
found in Scripture between Jesus and anyone,
let alone a Samaritan.

Let alone a woman.

Let alone that *kind of woman.*

Liz Curtis Higgs, *Bad Girls of the Bible*

Liz Curtis Higgs is a prolific writer and speaker, minis-
tering to women (and men) through radio programs, Christian conferences,
and many books and articles and blog posts, as well as on staff at her United
Methodist church. Her accessible, extremely popular Bad Girls of the Bible
series includes three books, each with multiple editions, associated study
guides, videos, Pinterest boards, and more.

The biblical "bad girls" are women with stories of youthful rebellion, ad-
diction, poor marriages, or mundane sins of gossip, unkindness, and neglect.
These broad parameters are rather comprehensive. According to Higgs (who
is very frank about her own "bad girl" story), all women are bad girls who

want to be good girls.[1] The Samaritan woman's story shows that even (very) bad girls can be redeemed and changed.

Higgs categorized three biblical women as "Bad for a Season, but Not Forever": the Samaritan woman; Rahab, the prostitute of Jericho; and the woman, again identified as a prostitute, in Luke 7:36-50. Despite this association, Higgs insisted that the Samaritan woman was not a prostitute herself. However, as a fornicator who lived in sin with her boyfriend, she was guilty of serious sexual immorality.[2]

This representation of the woman carries consequences for her story. Higgs suggested the woman went to the well alone because she was ostracized on account of her immoral life. She was both "polite but gutsy" and "a pushy broad" in her conversation with Jesus. The woman deflected attention from her sin with her question about worship. Her testimony following her conversation with Jesus included confession of her sin (all that she had done).[3]

Higgs explained that the "men" of the town listened to the woman because they saw the effects of her conversion. However, like John Calvin, Higgs did not identify the woman herself as a preacher. She was the harvest in Jesus' analogy in John 4:35-38, but Jesus himself was the sower. The woman taught by means of the example of her changed life rather than with her words.[4]

> Like Clara Lucas Balfour, Higgs wrote for women specifically. She reassured her women readers that her husband, an educated Bible scholar, had carefully checked her work. Along with her informal style, her self-deprecation forms part of her rhetorical appeal to a lay audience. It also reflects the sometimes limited opportunities for women to teach in Christian contexts. These aspects of Higgs's book reinforce the implications of her Samaritan woman's nonverbal testimony to Jesus.

We have seen similar interpretive choices before. Higgs added her own perspective to the majority interpretation by, first, incorporating a romantic

---

[1]Liz Curtis Higgs, *Bad Girls of the Bible and What We Can Learn from Them* (Colorado Springs: Waterbrook, 1999), 3-4.
[2]Higgs, *Bad Girls*, 5-6, 95-96.
[3]Higgs, *Bad Girls*, 92-99.
[4]Higgs, *Bad Girls*, 99-101.

subplot into John 4:4-42. The Samaritan woman longed for a man's love. Higgs suggested the woman converted her boyfriend to Christian faith and then married him.[5] This fairy tale ending makes the Samaritan woman all the more relatable to a modern woman reader.

Second, Higgs emphasized the difficulty of life in a first-century context. After losing multiple husbands to war, injury, or disease, the Samaritan woman was forced to remarry again and again. Rather than a rebellious, adulterous wife, Higgs pictured an older woman imprisoned in her situation by poverty. And the well was a dangerous place. Higgs interpreted Jesus' question about the woman's husband as reassurance that Jesus did not want to abuse her.[6]

So Higgs leaves us with something of a conundrum: a woman who was a sinner of the worst sort, "that kind" of woman; a woman who was looking for love in all the wrong places; and at the same time a woman who was the victim of a male-centered, sex-centered society. Although Higgs showed sympathy to the Samaritan woman, the difficulty of her situation did not redeem the guilt of her lifestyle. As for Dwight Moody, this woman needed salvation from her sin, not her situation.

> Higgs is White, and the examples and stories in her book assume White American experience almost exclusively (see, for instance, *Bad Girls*, 9-21). Her work can be compared with another take on the Bible's "bad girls": Black pastor Barbara J. Essex's *More Bad Girls of the Bible*. While Essex recognized the human complexity of biblical women, she presented these women as activists who courageously disrupted the oppressive systems of the world. Her Samaritan woman was a theologian and the first missionary in the New Testament.
>
> Essex challenged readers to move beyond the church's obsession with the Samaritan woman's sexual history. Reflection questions ask readers to consider the sexual objectification of women, how they might stand in solidarity with today's "Samaritans," and what the woman's story teaches about witnessing to others. "The story of this bad girl, the Samaritan woman, is a cautionary tale

---

[5]Higgs, *Bad Girls*, 96, 102.
[6]Higgs, *Bad Girls*, 95-96.

> that has the power to bring folks to Christ on their own terms and in their own ways."[7]

Higgs pushed beyond the standard messaging of biblical women and women in the church, but she also accepted it. This contradiction is clear in her modern retelling of John 4:4-42. Her twentieth-century Samaritan woman was divorced by four of her five husbands, some of whom, Higgs implied, also abused her—as did her current lover. Working at a bar, the woman managed constant harassment from male patrons who blatantly sexualized her. Higgs gave her an internal monologue entirely focused on her marital and sexual history, at least until a stranger showed up and started serving everyone water.[8]

Both Higgs's Samaritan women were used and abused by the men around them. Both also internalized the social and sexual shame consequent upon this use and abuse, and Higgs left readers with the understanding that they were right to do so. The women bore responsibility for their lives and their sin. As, indeed, all women do: "we've all been Bad Girls. . . . *How can I see so much of myself in these sleazy women?*"[9]

Reading the Samaritan woman's story in the church today. Together, the versions of the Samaritan woman given by Higgs and Essex represent the three most common interpretations in the United States today, across different ethnic, racial, and denominational communities. In an informal survey of forty sermons, blog posts, Bible studies, and other interpretations published between 2000 and 2020, twenty-six adopted a version of the majority interpretation. Eight of the forty represented the Samaritan woman as a victim rather than a seductress, with only six moving beyond sexuality as an essential element of John 4:4-42.[10]

The emphasis on the sexuality of the Samaritan woman in the first two interpretations fits into a larger narrative of Christian responses to changing

---

[7] Barbara J. Essex, *More Bad Girls of the Bible* (Cleveland: Pilgrim Press, 2009), xiii-xvi, 95-102.

[8] Higgs, *Bad Girls*, 84-90.

[9] Higgs, *Bad Girls*, 4 (italics original).

[10] The survey included interpretations from men and women representing diverse backgrounds. The sources not discussed here are listed in the bibliography under "Additional Sources Consulted." I am very grateful to Aniel Morey for her assistance in researching and analyzing this material.

social, political, and religious landscapes. Consider all that happened between 1920 and 2020: women's suffrage, the civil rights movement, reliable birth control and the sexual revolution, the internet, the legalization of same-sex marriage, Black Lives Matter, the shift away from a gender binary. The church in the United States today sits in an increasingly complex, rapidly changing social web.

Churches and parachurch organizations have internalized certain social developments. The increased presence of sex in entertainment, advertising, and public discourse, for instance, reshaped Christian perspectives on sexuality. Today, a healthy sex life is likely to be celebrated as an important element of marriage. More problematically, the sexualization of women is also apparent in warnings concerning the bodies and clothing of women (and young girls), and proclamations of men's unending struggles with lust.[11]

Christian communities have also reacted against developments perceived as destabilizing to the gospel, the family, and (as Sara Moslener and Kristin Kobes Du Mez argue) national security.[12] Two such threats, second wave feminism and the increased presence of women in higher education and professional careers, were answered with an emphatic insistence on traditional gender hierarchies in the family, church, and society. Masculinity was defined around physical strength, activity, and assertiveness. The opposite qualities defined femininity: inferior strength (physically and mentally), passivity, subordination.[13]

Despite the integration of sexuality with spirituality, the sexual revolution, the sexualization of the media, and easy access to (and widespread acceptance of) pornography have also been identified as destabilizing dangers. In response, beginning in the 1980s churches and parachurch ministries developed purity movements. Organizations like True Love Waits and Generations of

---

[11]See Amy DeRogatis, *Saving Sex: Sexuality and Salvation in American Evangelicalism* (Oxford: Oxford University Press, 2015), 3, 42-43; Tamura Lomax, *Jezebel Unhinged: Loosing the Black Female Body in Religion & Culture* (Durham: Duke University Press, 2018), x-xii, 31-33; Kristen Kobes Du Mez, *Jesus and John Wayne: How White Evangelicals Corrupted a Faith and Fractured a Nation* (New York: Liveright, 2020), 88-92, 170.

[12]Sara Moslener, *Virgin Nation: Sexual Purity and American Adolescence* (Oxford: Oxford University Press, 2015), 1-5; Du Mez, *John Wayne*, 11-27.

[13]E.g., Margaret Lamberts Bendroth, *Fundamentalism and Gender: 1875 to the Present* (New Haven: Yale University Press, 1993), 55-59, 64-66, 81-82, 98-99; Du Mez, *John Wayne*, 11-13, 78-79, etc.; and Beth Allison Barr, *The Making of Biblical Womanhood: How the Subjugation of Women Became Gospel Truth* (Grand Rapids, MI: Brazos, 2021), 14-25.

Light emphasized girls' responsibility to guard their own virginity and protect boys and men from sexual sin.[14] This responsibility is significant, given the correspondence between sex and sin, and purity and salvation.[15]

> While Catholic, Orthodox, and Protestant churches can all be found at different places on the continuum from more traditional to less, some of the most vocal responses to social changes in gender and sexuality have come from primarily White evangelical churches and organizations. These communities' perspectives on gender, family, and sexuality reflect a particular middle-class, White American definition of Christian identity. Their perspectives have been disseminated nationally and globally through political influence, the media, conferences, consumer products, and more.[16]

These particular developments reinforce some of the contradictions I've noted in earlier Christian traditions. Women are sexual prizes for men and at the same time dangers to men's salvation. Women are exhorted to be modest, passive, and submissive and at the same time expected to refuse men's sexual aggression. In this chapter, I will explore this message in contemporary interpretations of John 4:4-42 from John Piper (adopting the majority interpretation), Mary DeMuth (identifying the Samaritan woman as victim), and a smattering of others. In between, I will also examine the consequences of this message for women revealed by #ChurchToo.

A SCANDALOUS WOMAN: JOHN PIPER ON JOHN 4:4-42

> *If people are spiritually asleep, you have to shock them, startle*
> *them, scandalize them, if you want them to hear what you*
> *say. Jesus was especially good at this. When he wants to*
> *teach us something about worship, he uses a whore.*
>
> JOHN PIPER, "GOD SEEKS PEOPLE TO WORSHIP HIM
> IN SPIRIT AND TRUTH"

---

[14]Moslener, *Virgin Nation*, 30-33, 162-63. See also DeRogatis, *Saving Sex*, 28-31, 39-40.
[15]Moslener, *Virgin Nation*, 124-25.
[16]Du Mez, *Jesus and John Wayne*, traces the development and influence of evangelical Christianity across the American government and society.

In a sermon preached at Bethlehem Baptist Church in Minneapolis in 1984, White pastor John Piper practiced the shock tactics he found in John 4:4-42 by describing the Samaritan woman as a "sensually-minded, unspiritual harlot," "enslaved to the flesh," and "hopelessly carnal." It amazed the disciples and Piper himself that Jesus even spoke to her. Reflecting a Calvinist view of human sinfulness and divine grace, Piper celebrated the enduring message of the story: if a woman like this could become a true worshiper of God, anyone can.

In this sermon, the Samaritan woman becomes an object lesson for the church. Like Higgs, Piper connected the woman to his modern audience. He compared her with drunk men at a baseball game and with himself, when he felt particularly unspiritual and sinful.[17] The Samaritan woman was the only woman mentioned in the sermon, though. In this respect, Piper's explicit, crude sexualization of the woman is troubling. Men may sin by drinking too much; male pastors may feel sinful at times. But women's sin is defined around sex.

The messages of his 1984 sermon and a sermon series on John 4:4-42 preached in 2009 both reflect (and reinforce) Piper's detailed, well-developed, practical theology of gender and sexuality. His work, which echoes the concerns of contemporary American evangelical Christianity, has influenced the church in the United States (and beyond) through his pastoral ministry; his website (*Desiring God*) and books; and his efforts with the Council on Biblical Manhood and Womanhood. His work therefore gives us the opportunity to understand particular contemporary perspectives on women in the church, family, and society. I will take time to explore Piper's perspectives on gender and sexuality before returning to his interpretation of the Samaritan woman.

John Piper on gender and sexuality. In response to the perceived threats of feminism, the sexualization of the media, and challenges to the family posed by sex education in public schools, Planned Parenthood, women in the military, and more, Piper champions gender complementarianism.[18] In

---

[17]John Piper, "God Seeks People to Worship Him in Spirit and Truth" (message given April 8, 1984), *Desiring God*, www.desiringgod.org/messages/god-seeks-people-to-worship-him-in -spirit-and-truth.

[18]While Piper uses the language of complementarian to describe his approach, Lucy Peppiatt, *Rediscovering Scripture's Vision for Women: Fresh Perspectives on Disputed Texts* (Downers Grove,

his perspective, men and women were created equally but differently. Men were created by God to "lead, provide for and protect" women, and women to "affirm, receive and nurture strength and leadership from worthy men."[19] For Piper, these essential differences determine appropriate behaviors, responsibilities, familial structures, and professional occupations for men and women.

A person's gender overrides all other concerns. So, for instance, Piper says a mature man should assert his masculinity by opening doors for or speaking gently to women colleagues. For her part, a mature woman gladly receives and affirms male leadership, even as she directs male subordinates at work or gives directions to a male driver. She experiences the freedom of submission to the leadership of her husband and other "worthy" men.[20]

Like Tertullian, Chrysostom, and Calvin, Piper makes gender fundamental to a person's participation in the church. Men lead and teach. Women may minister in different ways, but they must always be subordinate to male leadership. For a woman to teach men directly in any circumstance, whether in church or seminary, no matter how skilled or capable she might be, would disrupt the hierarchy of creation.[21]

The same hierarchy governs family life. A mature man takes responsibility for his family's spiritual practices, even, as emphasized in one "Ask Pastor John" episode, if his wife has a more developed spirituality. A father should also act as disciplinarian for the children. A mature woman expresses a "spirit of submission" to her husband, even if she is actively resisting his sinful behaviors.[22]

IL: IVP Academic, 2019), 6-7, argues that it is better described as hierarchical. I have adopted her language throughout this section.

[19]John Piper, "A Vision of Biblical Complementarity: Manhood and Womanhood Defined According to the Bible," in *Recovering Biblical Manhood and Womanhood: A Response to Evangelical Feminism*, ed. John Piper and Wayne Grudem (1991; repr., Wheaton, IL: Crossway, 2006), 31-59, here 35-36.

[20]Piper, "Biblical Complementarity," 36-52.

[21]Piper, "Biblical Complementarity," 53; see also John Piper, "Can a Woman Preach if Elders Affirm It?," February 16, 2015, *Ask Pastor John* (podcast), *Desiring God*, www.desiringgod.org /interviews/can-a-woman-preach-if-elders-affirm-it; "Is There a Place for Female Professors at Seminary?," January 22, 2018, *Ask Pastor John* (podcast), *Desiring God*, www.desiringgod.org /interviews/is-there-a-place-for-female-professors-at-seminary (spoiler alert: no, there's not).

[22]Piper, "Biblical Complementarity," 39-41, 47; John Piper, "My Wife Is More Spiritual—How Do I Lead Her?," *Ask Pastor John* (podcast), *Desiring God*, November 9, 2020, www.desiringgod.org /interviews/my-wife-is-more-spiritual-how-do-i-lead-her.

Piper both accepts the sanctification of sex in contemporary Christianity, and sharply critiques any sex outside of heterosexual marriage as sin.[23] He warns that premarital sex is a dangerous, devastating sin that leads a person away from God. In fact, sexual sin may so damage a man's soul that he cannot repent. This message intersects with an "Ask Pastor John" episode in which Piper told a male questioner that his girlfriend's desire to have sex with him expressed either her foolish ignorance or her cruel attempt to destroy him.[24]

The male-centric focus of these messages reflects the consequences of Piper's definitions of masculinity and femininity for sexuality. Since masculinity is active and aggressive, men are responsible for initiating sexual intercourse. Femininity is passive, responsive, and emotional. A wife may invite her husband to initiate sex, but only so that she can properly respond to his leadership.[25] Within this framework, the woman who wanted to have sex with her boyfriend was guilty of both sexual sin and rebellion against the gender hierarchy.

Piper insists on the equality of men and women in God's creation. At the same time, he explicitly claims that "God has given Christianity a masculine feel." After all, God is revealed in the Bible through mostly masculine metaphors, and Jesus was undeniably male. Biblical priests, the twelve disciples, and church and household authorities are men. For Piper, therefore, male leadership, courage, decisiveness, and sacrifice are essential to the flourishing of the church, and of men and women in the church.[26]

"God requires more of men in relation to women than he does women in relation to men."[27] Piper's consistent prioritization of masculinity over

---

[23]E.g., John Piper, "How Far Is Too Far Before Marriage?," *Ask Pastor John* (podcast), *Desiring God*, April 19, 2013, www.desiringgod.org/interviews/how-far-is-too-far-before-marriage.

[24]John Piper, "Why Save Sex for Marriage?," *Ask Pastor John* (podcast), *Desiring God*, October 7, 2014, www.desiringgod.org/interviews/why-save-sex-for-marriage; and "I Sought a Prostitute—Am I Doomed?," *Ask Pastor John* (podcast), *Desiring God*, November 2, 2020, www.desiringgod.org/interviews/i-sought-a-prostitute-am-i-doomed.

[25]Piper, "Biblical Complementarity," 40-41. See also De Rogatis, *Saving Sex*, 61; Du Mez, *John Wayne*, 178-79.

[26]John Piper, "'The Frank and Manly Mr. Ryle'—The Value of a Masculine Ministry" (message, Desiring God 2012 Conference for Pastors, January 31, 2012), *Desiring God*, www.desiringgod.org/messages/the-frank-and-manly-mr-ryle-the-value-of-a-masculine-ministry. See further Du Mez, *John Wayne*, 200.

[27]John Piper, "Do Men Owe Women a Special Kind of Care?," *Desiring God*, November 6, 2017, www.desiringgod.org/articles/do-men-owe-women-a-special-kind-of-care.

femininity and men over women undermines his assertion of the spiritual equality of men and women. How equal can women be in a "masculine" faith that worships a "masculine" God?[28] The imbalances established by Piper's gender hierarchy have significant implications for his interpretation of the Samaritan woman.

John Piper's Samaritan woman.

> *Jesus knows there is something in her life that makes it painful*
> *for her to come to the place where all the women gather and*
> *talk. So he means something like: "You don't like to come here?*
> *You feel conspicuous. Vulnerable. Perhaps, you should bring your*
> *husband with you. He could stand with you and protect you, and*
> *you could be proud of him like an elder at the city gates."*
>
> JOHN PIPER, "THE TRAGIC COST OF HER CAVERNOUS THIRST"

Piper's four sermons on John 4:4-42 in 2009 added complexity and nuance to the basic message of his 1984 sermon. He continued to emphasize the woman's sexuality, accusing her of adultery. Reflecting the language of twentieth-century purity movements, Piper described the woman as impure and unclean, a social outcast who experienced rejection by other local women. She was utterly lost to her sin, blinded (like Nicodemus) to Jesus' identity.[29]

Piper's portrayal of the Samaritan woman is consistent with his perspectives on the damaging nature of sexual sin. Her sin restricted her spiritual understanding. Piper represented her denial of a husband as manipulative (so Jesus was ironic when he said she told the truth). When Jesus convicted her of sin, the woman changed the subject to deflect his attention.[30]

As in Higgs's interpretation of John 4:4-42, Piper's Samaritan woman sought to fill her deepest desires through sex. Piper connected the woman's desire with the men and women in his congregation. All humans are seeking

---

[28]See also Peppiatt, *Scripture's Vision*, 6-7; Barr, *Biblical Womanhood*, 16-19.

[29]John Piper, "You Will Never Be Thirsty Again" (message given June 14, 2009), *Desiring God*, www .desiringgod.org/messages/you-will-never-be-thirsty-again.

[30]John Piper, "The Tragic Cost of Her Cavernous Thirst" (message given June 21, 2009), *Desiring God*, www.desiringgod.org/messages/the-tragic-cost-of-her-cavernous-thirst.

something.[31] But in conjunction with the sensational sexualization of the Samaritan woman, the use of a woman as a representative of this search sends a specific message: the desire for relationship or connection through sex is women's sin.[32]

Piper's sermon on John 4:20-26 again identified the Samaritan woman's questions and comments as obstructive attempts to shift Jesus' attention away from her own sin. He minimized her importance in the story by repeatedly emphasizing her interest in what he described as the inconsequential issue of the right location for worship.[33] According to this sermon, the woman provided only a narrative foil for Jesus' own words.

The first three sermons in the series present the significantly negative portrayal of the Samaritan woman characteristic of the majority interpretation. The fourth explicitly (and problematically) connects gender, sexuality, and violence with John 4:4-42.

Women, sex, and violence. Somewhat surprisingly, given his nearly comprehensive rejection of women's right or ability to teach in the church, in his final sermon Piper credited the Samaritans' conversion to the woman's verbal testimony to Jesus. Presumably he, like John Calvin, differentiated her testimony from teaching or leading.[34] In an article from 1984, Piper explicitly denied that the Samaritan woman's "evangelistic activity" disrupted his gender hierarchy of male leadership and female subordination.[35]

Piper inserted his gender hierarchy into his sermon on John 4:27-42. He explained the disciples' surprise in verse 27 as the result of cultural misogyny. From the disciples of the first century, he jumped to the "extreme pathological case" of George Sodini, who had killed three women at a gym a few days before Piper gave this sermon. He quoted extensively from Sodini's personal blog, choosing entries that displayed Sodini's frustration with his

---

[31]Piper, "Cavernous Thirst."

[32]See also John Piper, "Manhood and Womanhood: Conflict and Confusion After the Fall" (message given May 21, 1989), *Desiring God*, www.desiringgod.org/messages/manhood-and-womanhood-conflict-and-confusion-after-the-fall.

[33]John Piper, "Not in This or That Mount, but in Spirit and Truth" (message given June 28, 2009), *Desiring God*, www.desiringgod.org/messages/not-in-this-or-that-mount-but-in-spirit-and-truth.

[34]John Piper, "The Food of Christ Is to Give Eternal Life" (message given August 9, 2009), *Desiring God*, www.desiringgod.org/messages/the-food-of-christ-is-to-give-eternal-life.

[35]John Piper, "Did Jesus Teach That Women Are to Be Leaders?," *Desiring God*, January 10, 1984, www.desiringgod.org/articles/did-jesus-teach-that-women-were-to-be-leaders.

inability to find a woman to date or have sex with him: "I dress good, am clean-shaven, bathe, touch of cologne—yet 30 million women rejected me—over an 18 or 25-year period."[36]

> George Sodini can be identified as an *incel* (involuntary celibate). Incels are primarily White, heterosexual men who connect (often online) over the experience of rejection by women. They perceive their lack of relationship as the result of women's unjustified social power. A number of acts of mass violence have been carried out by incels to punish women and more sexually successful men.[37]

Piper defined misogyny as "the deep distrust, disrespect, and dislike of women." But as the quotations he chose from Sodini's blog indicate, this violence did not originate in a general hatred of women. Rather, Sodini felt that, as a man, he deserved sex from women. This perspective objectifies women. It marks women as less important, worthy, or valuable than men. Their only purpose is to satisfy men's desires.

These are Sodini's ideas, and Sodini's frustration. But Piper chose to quote Sodini's words in a sermon series in which he also condemned the Samaritan woman on account of her active sexuality. The association of the Samaritan woman with the murder of women in retribution for their failure to provide a man with sex is jarring. So too is the use Piper made of the Sodini story to celebrate the care and respect shown to women by Jesus and Christian men who adopt a hierarchical understanding of gender relations.

In connecting Sodini with the disciples in John 4:27, Piper clarified that he did not mean men in the first century abused women. However, they also did not commonly treat women well. Nor, he noted, do various cultures around the world, as evident in the 2009 film *The Stoning of Soraya M.* According to Piper, such behavior reflects the disruption of God's plan for human relationships.[38]

Piper reminded his congregation that men and women are spiritually equal, but they have different "roles." The sin of Adam and Eve in Genesis 3 distorted gender by pushing men and women toward the extremes—men

---

[36]Piper, "Eternal Life."
[37]See Roberta Liggett O'Malley, Karen Holt, and Thomas J. Holt, "An Exploration of the Involuntary Celibate (Incel) Subculture Online," *Journal of Interpersonal Violence*, September 24, 2020, https://doi.org/10.1177/0886260520959625.
[38]Piper, "Eternal Life."

toward either (unmanly) passivity or (über-manly) severity, and women toward either (unwomanly) aggression or (über-womanly) helplessness. Jesus restored the original plan for gender, allowing men to protect women and women to submit to men without fear.[39]

This claim explains Piper's interpretation of John 4:16 as Jesus' desire for the Samaritan woman to have a husband to protect her.[40] But the connection of John 4:4-42 with Piper's own gender hierarchy is tenuous (as the woman's vocal participation throughout the story indicates). It is also inconsistent. His Samaritan woman is utterly condemned by her sinful sexuality regardless of the negative views of women held in her society, and—importantly—regardless of the apparent refusal of any man to protect her.

Sodini's violence against women provides only a brief sermon illustration. Piper did not point out the problematic logic of Sodini's statements, or the physical and psychological endangerment of women when men view them primarily as sexual objects.[41] He also did not note the overlap of his own gender hierarchy with the assumptions expressed by Sodini.

For both Piper and Sodini, masculinity involves physical strength, assertiveness, and success in the workplace and home. Sodini's reference in one blog post to a man's need for a woman to support him resembles Piper's vision for mature women to "make men stronger and wiser" by their nurture. Both minimize women as the supporting cast to a male-centric society. In another journal entry, Sodini critiqued his mother for being too dominant, a claim that resonates eerily with Piper's understanding of the way sin distorts gender identity.[42]

Piper repeatedly claims that his gender hierarchy protects women from abuse. He has blamed proponents of gender equality for creating a world in which men abuse women because they are not taught their special, God-given responsibility of protecting women.[43] Abuse certainly does occur in churches that teach gender equality. But this assertion ignores the pervasive

---

[39]Piper, "Eternal Life."

[40]Piper, "Cavernous Thirst."

[41]See O'Malley, Holt, and Holt, "Involuntary Celibate," 7, 10.

[42]Piper, "Biblical Complementarity," 48-49, and "Eternal Life"; George Sodini, blog posts dated December 29 and 31, 2008, from "George Sodini's Blog; Full Text by Alleged Gym Shooter," *ABC News*, August 5, 2009, https://abcnews.go.com/US/story?id=8258001&page=1.

[43]E.g., Piper, "Eternal Life," "Masculine Ministry," and "Men Owe Women." Also, John Piper, "Sex-Abuse Allegations and the Egalitarian Myth," *Ask Pastor John* (podcast), *Desiring God*,

presence of abuse across the church (and broader society), including in communities that adopt a gender hierarchy—and among the Christian leaders who teach a gender hierarchy.[44]

A second problem with Piper's assertion is its circular logic. Men's protection of women is made necessary because men, already stronger than women by virtue of their masculinity, also hold authority over women. This contradiction is exposed by Piper's infamous advice for wives to accept abuse "for a season" because of their God-given responsibility of submission to their husbands.[45] (This advice was posted online just ten days after he gave his fourth and final sermon on John 4:4-42.) In Piper's own words, hierarchical definitions of gender do not protect women against abuse.[46]

A sermon on the curse of sin in Genesis 3:16, "Manhood and Womanhood: Conflict and Confusion After the Fall," illustrates this contradiction. Piper warned his congregation that women exploit men by using their own bodies to inflame men's lust. For their part, men's brute strength allows them to "rape and abuse and threaten and sit around and snap their fingers." The contrast of behaviors here is alarming, particularly in consideration of the amount of space given to each gendered sin—two sentences on men's violence in the space of two paragraphs on women's seductive power over men. (Notably, the only example Piper provided of women's exploitation of men comes from advertising, an industry known for its sexism and gender inequity.)[47]

March 16, 2018, www.desiringgod.org/interviews/sex-abuse-allegations-and-the-egalitarian-myth.

[44]See Susan A. Ross, "Feminist Theology and the Clergy Sexual Abuse Crisis," *Theological Studies* 80 (2019): 637-43; Tamie Davis, "Why Equality Is Not Enough When You've Been Abused," *Lausanne Global Analysis* 7, no. 4 (2018), https://lausanne.org/content/lga/2018-07/why-equality-is-not-enough-when-youve-been-abused; Mary DeMuth, *We Too: How the Church Can Respond Redemptively to the Sexual Abuse Crisis* (Eugene, OR: Harvest House, 2019), 66; Du Mez, *John Wayne*, 273-91; Ruth Everhart, *The #MeToo Reckoning: Facing the Church's Complicity in Sexual Abuse and Misconduct* (Downers Grove, IL: InterVarsity Press, 2020), 9-12; Barr, *Biblical Womanhood*, 201-8.

[45]John Piper, "What Should a Wife's Submission to Her Husband Look Like if He's an Abuser?" This "Ask Pastor John" episode from August 19, 2009, is no longer available at *Desiring God*, but a copy is posted at "John Piper: Does a Woman Submit to Abuse?," September 1, 2009, video, https://youtu.be/3OkUPc2NLrM.

[46]See further Moslener, *Virgin Nation*, 162-63; Du Mez, *John Wayne*, 170-79, 292-93.

[47]See also Glen Kreider, "Eve: The Mother of All Seducers?," in *Vindicating the Vixens: Revisiting Sexualized, Vilified, and Marginalized Women of the Bible*, ed. Sandra Glahn (Grand Rapids, MI: Kregel Academic, 2017), 129-46, especially 132-33.

Piper's characterization of the Samaritan woman minimizes her active, intelligent conversation with Jesus to make her into a caricature, the antitype of Piper's ideal woman. His insistence on Jesus' respect for women in John 4:4-42 does not affect his interpretation of the woman, or its implications for women in his audience.

In conjunction with his portrayal of the Samaritan woman, the use of an act of violence against women as a sermon illustration is deeply troubling. Incorporated without significant discussion, the violence shocks and appalls with no instructional value (which, given the violence of the story, would be difficult in any case).

The uneasy correspondence between Piper and Sodini's understandings of gender further problematizes the illustration. As I discussed in chapter one, Ruth Everhart tells the story of a woman who, during a Christmas Eve worship service, was raped in the hallway outside the sanctuary. Everhart wonders whether the rapist had heard Bible stories interpreted in ways that make women rape-able.[48] I wonder how many men listening to Piper's sermons on the Samaritan woman felt justified in their abusive treatment of women like this—or of any woman.

SEX, SIN, AND #CHURCHTOO

I've extensively engaged with Piper's sermons on John 4:4-42 because they demonstrate the minimization, subordination, and sexual objectification of women as part of Christian interpretations of the Bible. Mixed with hierarchical definitions of gender (whether theological or cultural), this type of interpretation creates the conditions for the abuse of women.[49] Piper's sermon illustration of violence against women, advice to abused wives, and warnings about women's ability to overpower men with their bodies demonstrate the danger.

Consider also the interpreters we met in chapters two and three. John Chrysostom expressed concern for the safety of women who were seen by men. Along with Tertullian and John Calvin, he warned women against displaying themselves to attract attention, and he encouraged fathers to

---

[48]Everhart, *#MeToo*, 119-23.
[49]See also Ross, "Feminist Theology," 633, 639-43; Du Mez, *John Wayne*, 273-78; Everhart, *#MeToo*, 8, 12, and throughout.

protect and control their daughters.[50] At the same time, Chrysostom identified sexual desire and intercourse with sin, and demonized women who
appeared in public in the theater or marketplace.[51]

Taken together, these messages reduce women to objects of sexual desire.
While interpreters consistently highlighted the threat to men's sexual mo-
rality, their warnings endangered women. Remember that in the *Life of
Maria the Harlot*, the monk seduced Maria before he had even seen her.
Marie Dentière's analysis is helpful here: the limitation of women's purpose
to pleasing men created the conditions for men to abuse women.[52] Maria's
assailant used her body to satisfy his own desire because, according to
Christian teachings, that was women's purpose.

The redefinition of womanhood around piety, morality, and sexual purity
in the nineteenth century gave (White, middle-class) women certain authority in the family, church, and society. But in this framework, women
with nonmarital sexual experience, impoverished women, and women of
color became the inversion of good, moral womanhood. These women
threatened the moral authority of all women. Consequently, while Clara
Balfour and Dwight Moody recognized the social conditions that might
force a woman into sexual immorality, they argued such conditions did not
excuse the Samaritan woman or her sisters from sin.[53]

The letter written by a prostitute to Moody exemplifies the tension here.
As the letter writer said, women did not necessarily become sex workers out
of personal choice. Rather, they had no other choices.[54] The implication
that, as in the *Life of Maria*, many women became prostitutes after being

[50]E.g., John Chrysostom, *Homilies on 1 Timothy* 8, *Homilies on Ephesians* 20, *On Marriage and Family Life*; Tertullian, *On the Apparel of Women* 1.2.1-2, *On the Veiling of Virgins* 2.3-4; John Calvin, *Genesis*, trans. John King, 2 vols. (1847; repr., Edinburgh: Banner of Truth Trust, 1975), 2:218, and *Commentaries on the Four Last Books of Moses, Arranged in the Form of a Harmony*, vol. 3 of 4, trans. Charles William Bingham (Edinburgh: Calvin Translation Society, 1853), 79, 83, 91-92.

[51]John Chrysostom, *Against the Games and Theaters*, *Homilies on Colossians* 12, etc.

[52]Marie Dentière, *Epistle to Marguerite de Navarre*, in *Marie Dentière: Epistle to Marguerite de Navarre and Preface to a Sermon by John Calvin*, trans. and ed. Mary B. McKinley, The Other Voice in Early Modern Europe (Chicago: University of Chicago Press, 2004), 53-54, 70-71, 76, 79.

[53]Clara Lucas Balfour, *Women of Scripture* (London: Houlston and Stoneman, 1847), 303-5, 311; Dwight Lyman Moody, "Salvation for Sinners," in *"The Gospel Awakening." Comprising the Sermons and Addresses, Prayer-Meeting Talks and Bible Readings of the Great Revival Meetings Conducted by Moody and Sankey*, 20th ed., ed. L. T. Remlap (Chicago: Fairbanks and Palmer, 1885), 531-32.

[54]Quoted in Dwight Lyman Moody, *Moody: His Words, Work, and Workers*, ed. W. H. Daniels (New York: Nelson & Phillips, 1877), 433-34.

used and abandoned by men represents the outworking of Victorian ideals of womanhood. When a woman's identity is so bound to sexuality, the loss of sexual "purity" ungenders her and pushes her outside social norms.[55]

The reports of assault, abuse, and rape in the twentieth and twenty-first century church are nothing new. But the #ChurchToo movement in particular has given victims and survivors a platform for exposing their assaults outside the reporting structures of churches (which have all too often silenced accusations).[56] There are two additional major differences between historical stories of assault in the church, and today: the sanctification of sex and purity culture.

Sanctified sex.

> *After many years, I finally told Grace that I needed more sex.*
> *I asked if we could have sex more days of the week and try a*
> *variety of positions. . . . I (Grace) loved Mark but also needed to*
> *obey God and be sensitive to my husband's physical needs.*

Mark Driscoll and Grace Driscoll, *Real Marriage*

From Tertullian to Moody, the church primarily regarded sex as sin, or so suspiciously like sin as to be indistinguishable. Following the sexual revolution of the 1960s, however, some parts of the church began identifying intercourse in marriage as a means of experiencing God. Heterosexual, marital intercourse became a divine blessing for the faithful.[57]

The sanctification of sex in marriage did not redeem sex outside of marriage. While the Driscolls celebrated marital sex in *Real Marriage*, they also condemned premarital sex and sexual sin in general.[58] Notably, Mark Driscoll also excoriated the Samaritan woman for her sexual sin.[59]

---

[55]See further Moslener, *Virgin Nation*, 33-34.
[56]See also DeMuth, *We Too*, 20-23; Anne Marie Miller, *Healing Together: A Guide to Supporting Sexual Abuse Survivors* (Grand Rapids, MI: Zondervan Reflective, 2019), 34; Everhart, *#MeToo*, 53, 75.
[57]See DeRogatis, *Saving Sex*, 42-92.
[58]Mark Driscoll and Grace Driscoll, *Real Marriage: The Truth About Sex, Friendship, and Life Together* (Nashville: Thomas Nelson, 2012), 9-13.
[59]Mark Driscoll, "The Woman at the Well," sermon preached at Mars Hill Church, Seattle, December 4, 2000. Available as "John's Gospel – The Woman at the Well – Mark Driscoll 8/34," May 18, 2017, video, https://youtu.be/0JkFWs5RxZw.

Humans have bodies, and bodies experience pleasure. The Bible itself recognizes the pleasures of sex (e.g., Deut 24:5; Prov 5:18-19; Song; 1 Cor 7:3-5). In many ways, this shift corrected a longstanding blind spot in Christian teaching. However, the Christian sexual revolution has also had more problematic effects.

First, the identification of marital sex as a divine blessing too often becomes the identification of a beautiful, sexy woman as a blessing for a man to enjoy (the "smokin' hot wife" phenomenon).[60] This blatant, reductive sexualization turns women into prizes for the faithful Christian man to win. But women are not prizes, nor is their purpose to "bless" a man by satisfying his sexual urges. This kind of sexual objectification dehumanizes women.

Second, according to a hierarchical view of gender, men should be the sexual aggressors, and women should submit to the man's desires. As Grace Driscoll wrote in *Real Marriage*, having sex with her husband was a way to obey God.[61] In this framework, refusing to have sex with a spouse becomes a sin. Wives may feel forced to agree to sex despite their own lack of desire.[62]

In *Real Marriage*, the Driscolls were careful to encourage mutuality and warn against abuse.[63] At the same time, as the quotation above suggests, they prioritized husbands' sexual desires over their wives' desires. Grace Driscoll experienced sexual abuse in her past, and it affected her experience of sex in her marriage. Nonetheless, when her husband wanted more sex, she had to find a way to comply.[64] The intersection of male authority and female subordination with sex complicates mutuality and consent.

---

[60]See, for instance, Jeremy Smith, "Godly Men and Smokin Hot Wives," *Hacking Christianity* (blog), August 5, 2013, https://hackingchristianity.net/2013/08/godly-men-and-smokin-hot-wives.html; Du Mez, *John Wayne*, 199.

[61]Driscoll and Driscoll, *Real Marriage*, 54-56, 66, 122.

[62]See DeRogatis, *Saving Sex*, 55-56, 61, 112-13; Linda Kay Klein, *Pure: Inside the Evangelical Movement That Shamed a Generation of Young Women and How I Broke Free* (New York: Touchstone, 2018), 139; Du Mez, *John Wayne*, 170, 178-79.

[63]Driscoll and Driscoll, *Real Marriage*, 164-66, 201-3.

[64]Driscoll and Driscoll, *Real Marriage*, 9-10, 16, 122-25. See further Klein, *Pure*, 140-43; Miller, *Healing Together*, 117-25.

Purity culture.

> *I was raised hearing horror stories about harlots (a nice, Christian*
> *term for a manipulative whore) who destroy good, God-fearing men.*
> *And then one day, my body began to change and I felt sexual stirrings*
> *within me and I thought, "Oh no. Is that me?*
> *Am I a manipulative whore?"*
>
> LINDA KLEIN, *PURE*

In contemporary Christianity, sanctified sex within marriage rewards sexual purity before marriage. Purity movements connect sexual purity (which primarily means abstinence from sex apart from heterosexual marriage) with spirituality. The value placed on virginity identifies sex outside of marriage as the worst sin, particularly for women. Purity culture teaches girls that their virginity, visible in their "modest" clothing and self-effacing behavior, is their salvation.[65]

> The association of superior sexual morality with White European identity I noted in the last chapter persists in the purity movements of the contemporary American evangelical church, which are primarily directed to White girls and women. This association reinforces the historic, racist sexualization of girls and women of color, which itself contributes to significantly higher rates of assault against women of color.[66]
>
> Of course, the message of sexual purity is present across various racial, ethnic, and denominational communities. Tamura Lomax addresses the consequences of the racist hypersexualization of Black women for concepts of sexual purity in the Black church; and Berta Esperanza Hernández-Truyol discusses the Latina experience of the messaging of sexual purity.[67]

---

[65]E.g., Moslener, *Virgin Nation*, 124-25; Klein, *Pure*, 11-13.

[66]See further Jessica Valenti, *The Purity Myth: How America's Obsession with Virginity Is Hurting Young Women* (Berkeley: Seal, 2010), 62-63, 76-78, 157-58; Moslener, *Virgin Nation*, 38-41; Emily Joy Allison, *#ChurchToo: How Purity Culture Upholds Abuse and How to Find Healing* (Minneapolis: Broadleaf, 2021), 45-46, 142.

[67]Berta Esperanza Hernández-Truyol, "Latinas—Everywhere Alien: Culture, Gender, and Sex," in *Critical Race Feminism: A Reader*, ed. Adrien Katherine Wing (New York: New York University Press, 2003), 57-69; Lomax, *Jezebel*, x-xiv, 30-38, and throughout.

Purity movements target young women and men. But as Linda Klein suggests in the quote above, girls and women bear a particular responsibility for maintaining purity. This responsibility reflects the intersection of masculinity with sexual desire and aggression. Since boys and men are (apparently) unable to control themselves, women—who are not (perceived to be) overcome with lust in the same ways—have to police their relationships.[68]

Women also must police their own bodies and behavior to protect men against temptation. Purity culture both desexualizes women by denying their sexual desires, and at the same time hypersexualizes them by defining them as the objects of male desire. Women's bodies become, as Klein says, stumbling blocks to trip men into sexual sin.[69] Girls and women may internalize this message in a sense of shame concerning their own bodies (reflected in Klein's worry that she was becoming a "manipulative whore") and a fear of exhibiting any assertiveness or authority.[70]

As Sara Moslener explains, contemporary evangelical purity movements are rooted in nineteenth-century social reform. Early purity movements centered on changing men's behavior to protect women.[71] Today, though, from adolescence onwards men hear that they are driven by physical desire and pleasure. The minimal expectation for their self-control is outweighed by the sexual objectification of women, who are simultaneously identified as inferior, weaker, and subordinate. As such, women are not taught how to say no. Instead of protecting women, purity movements endanger women.

Gender, sex, and violence.

> *The concept of consent is intrinsic to sexual activity, yet it is totally absent from purity culture. The emphasis on the submission of a wife to a husband downplays a woman's ability—or need—to exercise agency. If she* must *submit, how can she consent? Paradoxically, a woman is often seen as responsible for her own victimization.*
>
> RUTH EVERHART, *THE #MeToo Reckoning*

---

[68]See DeRogatis, *Saving Sex*, 28-31; Moslener, *Virgin Nation*, 162-63.
[69]Klein, *Pure*, 3, 137-39. See also Valenti, *Purity Myth*, 65, 79; Lomax, *Jezebel Unhinged*, x-xii.
[70]Klein, *Pure*, 8-9 (and throughout), explores the trauma of purity culture.
[71]Moslener, *Virgin Nation*, 16-20, 28-33, 162-63.

Eugene Hung defines rape culture simply as "the ways our society tells men that they're entitled to sex with women."[72] Rape culture considers women as less important or less deserving than men. It makes women into passive objects of male desire and action. By denying women the ability or right to consent, these perspectives normalize assault. According to Ruth Everhart, the messages (and culture) surrounding hierarchical definitions of gender, the sanctification of sex in Christian marriage, and purity movements overlap with rape culture in problematic ways.[73]

> Because of the significant number of cases of assault in conservative churches in recent years, I have been focusing on more conservative traditions of gender and sexuality. However, whether or not a particular community teaches the subordination of women, broader cultural contexts continue to be marked by patriarchal perspectives. Most churches expect congregants to respect and obey pastors, priests, or other leaders. In addition, women are generally socialized to be polite, nonconfrontational, and supportive to authority figures. These factors contribute to abuse across society, including in less conservative churches.[74]

As much as contemporary Christianity rejects the blatant sexualization of women apparent in the secular media, it has also accepted sexuality as a fundamental element of women's identity. Women are valued for their virginity, prized for their ability to satisfy their husbands' virility, or condemned for their nonmarital sexual experience. These categories turn women into seductive stumbling blocks, tripping men into harassment, assault, and rape.

As so many #ChurchToo stories indicate, when the responsibility for men's lust is born by women, sexual assault also becomes the woman's responsibility.[75] She dressed or behaved provocatively. She put herself in a

---

[72]Eugene Hung, "Defending My Daughters Against Rape Culture," *Mutuality* 24 (2017): 14-15.
[73]See further Klein, *Pure*, 92-94; Everhart, *#MeToo*, 123-29.
[74]Pamela Cooper-White, *Cry of Tamar: Violence Against Women and the Church's Response*, 2nd ed. (Minneapolis: Fortress, 2012), 157; Lomax, *Jezebel*, 54-57; Ross, "Feminist Theology," 639-43; Everhart, *#MeToo*, 8, 12; Allison, *#ChurchToo*, 155-57.
[75]E.g., Hannah Paasch, "Sexual Abuse Happens in #ChurchToo," *HuffPost*, December 4, 2017, https://www.huffpost.com/entry/sexual-abuse-churchtoo_n_5a205b30e4b03350e0b53131; Allison, *#ChurchToo*, 42-48.

position to be acted upon by a man. She had a body. In conjunction with the objectification and minimization of women, victim-blaming makes rape into (forgivable) "sin" that the perpetrator could not resist. The perpetrator becomes the woman's victim.[76]

These responses to assault hide the real reason for any and every rape: the presence of a rapist. By placing responsibility on women to police their own bodies and behavior, men's sexual aggression is left unchecked. By punishing the victim of assault rather than the assailant, assailants are free to continue their predatory behavior. These responses retraumatize victims by condemning their own personal, spiritual impurity and their sin of tempting a faithful Christian man into sex.[77]

The sexualization, objectification, and minimization of women in Christian tradition has had dangerous consequences for women from the second century on. When women are dehumanized as objects for men to see and use for their own pleasure, abuse does not just become possible. It becomes probable.

READING THE SAMARITAN WOMAN'S STORY AFTER #CHURCHTOO

The twentieth century was peppered with reports of abuse in Protestant churches and ministries. The scandals of abuse in the Catholic church have reverberated through the world since the 1980s. With the #MeToo and #ChurchToo movements, the extent of the problem has become clear.[78] The church in America faces a crisis of abuse.

As I noted in chapter one, alongside the abuse runs a history of poor responses: victim-blaming; demanding that victims forgive perpetrators; protecting institutions and their leaders against allegations. This pattern is changing as churches and parachurch organizations have begun to recognize the crisis, repent, and develop policies and procedures to protect vulnerable people against abuse.[79]

---

[76]See also Valenti, *Purity Myth*, 107-9; Klein, *Pure*, 90; Everhart, *#MeToo*, 140; Du Mez, *John Wayne*, 278.

[77]Valenti, *Purity Myth*, 151; Miller, *Healing Together*, 36.

[78]See Wietse de Boer, "The Catholic Church and Sexual Abuse, Then and Now," *Origins* 12, no. 6 (2019), http://origins.osu.edu/article/catholic-church-sexual-abuse-pope-confession-priests-nuns; Du Mez, *John Wayne*, 273-88. Survivors tell their own stories under #ChurchToo on social media. Miller, *Healing Together*, DeMuth, *We Too*, Everhart, *#MeToo*, and Allison, *#ChurchToo*, also include many stories of abuse in the church.

[79]For instance, J. D. Greear, president of the Southern Baptist Convention, has made responses to abuse a priority (he wrote the foreword to DeMuth's *We Too*). *Caring Well: A Report from the SBC*

And yet, in a sermon preached in December 2017, a White pastor in North Carolina condemned the Samaritan woman for adultery, suggesting she should be subject to the punitive consequences of Numbers 5. A post by a Black pastor at Piper's *Desiring God* in 2019 used the Samaritan woman to exemplify Jesus' power to save us from our sexual sins. From 2019 to 2020, alongside acknowledgment of the crisis of abuse, several sermons and posts at *The Gospel Coalition* repeated the identification of the Samaritan woman as a sexual sinner.[80]

This pattern of interpretation develops from and reinforces the reductive sexualization of women. It is, therefore, part of the problem. While this interpretation is the most common historically and today, though, it is not the only option. Abuse survivor Mary DeMuth characterizes the Samaritan woman as victim rather than victimizer.

The Samaritan woman as victim.

> We can imagine her carrying the shame of her past and the guilt of her present heavy on her shoulders. Here trudged a woman who loved others, but rarely felt love in return. . . . Her life became a collage of slammed doors, serial rejections, multiple failures, heartache, and probably abuse.
>
> FRANK VIOLA AND MARY DEMUTH, *THE DAY I MET JESUS*

Mary DeMuth writes for and ministers to the victims and survivors of abuse. As a survivor herself, she advocates for honesty, transparency, and the reformation of church practices with respect to abuse. She argues, "the church acts most like Jesus when it protects the victimized."[81] In DeMuth's

---

Sexual Abuse Advisory Group was released in June 2019. See https://caringwell.com/wp-content/uploads/2019/06/SBC-Caring-Well-Report-June-2019.pdf.
[80]Tyson Coughlin, "The Story of the Samaritan Woman at the Well Explained," sermon preached at Vizion Church, Charlotte, North Carolina, December 19, 2017, video, https://youtu.be/W3jE42chG2w; H. B. Charles, "The Woman at the Well," sermon preached at The Gospel Coalition National Conference, Indianapolis, Indiana, April 3, 2019, video, https://youtu.be/Xkw8RfgQ3qM; Bobby Scott, "Do You Wish to Be Pure?," *Desiring God*, October 12, 2019, www.desiringgod.org/articles/do-you-wish-to-be-pure; Brad Larson, "How to Have That Hard Conversation," *The Gospel Coalition*, January 27, 2020, www.thegospelcoalition.org/article/hard-conversation/; and Brett McCracken, "Exit the Echo Chamber," *The Gospel Coalition*, June 11, 2020, www.thegospelcoalition.org/article/exit-echo-chamber-persuade/.
[81]DeMuth, *We Too*, 198.

interpretation of John 4:4-42, Jesus' conversation with a victim of sexual marginalization provides a model for the church.[82]

DeMuth's fictional retelling of the story provides the Samaritan woman with a life history of abuse, divorce, and sexual slavery. While poverty led to the woman's immoral life, DeMuth also suggests that past abuse may have affected her ability to connect emotionally with her husbands. As is the case for many survivors, DeMuth's Samaritan woman internalized the abuse in a deep sense of shame.[83]

When the woman went to the well at noon (thus avoiding the gossip of her neighbors), she was afraid of the stranger, a man who might continue her story of abuse. Instead, he became her true husband, "a man who would never use or abuse her, but who would cherish her with the purest love in the universe."[84] For DeMuth, the woman's interaction with Jesus freed her (and all survivors of abuse) from the burden of shame.[85]

To interpret John 4:4-42 from the perspective of a survivor of abuse challenges the church to identify with the victim rather than the perpetrator. But while there is a vast difference between Piper's harlot and DeMuth's marginalized, abused woman, they both sexualize the Samaritan woman. She is a seductive sinner or a victim of abuse—very few interpreters imagine another possibility. This is the legacy of millennia of biblical interpretation.

REWEAVING THE THREADS

From Tertullian to the church today, the Samaritan woman has been narrowly viewed through her gender and marital history. This characterization intersects with the interpreters' views on women, gender, and sexuality. According to the majority interpretation, the Samaritan woman was the classic daughter of Eve: a sexually promiscuous sinner who tempted men to join her sin. Her words are either vilified or become reason for surprise (how could a woman like this hold her own in the conversation?).

---

[82]DeMuth, *We Too*, 46-48.
[83]Frank Viola and Mary DeMuth, *The Day I Met Jesus: The Revealing Diaries of Five Women from the Gospels* (Grand Rapids, MI: Baker, 2015), 80-86.
[84]Viola and DeMuth, *I Met Jesus*, 88, 107.
[85]DeMuth, *We Too*, 48.

Table 4.1. John 4 according to Liz Curtis Higgs, Barbara Essex, John Piper, and Mary DeMuth

Interpreter	Explanation of the Woman's Character and Participation in the Story	Significance of the Story for the Church
Liz Curtis Higgs, *Bad Girls of the Bible* (1999)	The woman's marriages ended with the deaths of her husbands, but she is guilty of sexual sin (living with her boyfriend). She is ostracized for her immorality. She attempts to deflect Jesus' attention from her sin with her question about worship. Her testimony to her neighbors comes from her changed life (rather than her words). Higgs classifies the Samaritan woman with Rahab and the "prostitute" of Luke 7:36-50.	The story shows that women who sin sexually can be saved.
Barbara J. Essex, *More Bad Girls of the Bible* (2009)	The woman has a "shady past," but the focus of the story remains on her long, theological conversation with Jesus about the place of worship. The woman is the first missionary in the New Testament story.	The story prompts readers to reconsider the sexual objectification of women. The woman gives Christians a model to follow in inviting others into the community of faith.
John Piper, sermons on John 4 at *Desiring God* (1984 and 2009)	The woman is guilty of sexual sin (adultery and prostitution). She is a social outcast. Her sin limits her spiritual understanding. She is manipulative and deflects attention from her sin with her question about the location of worship. Her testimony to her neighbors represents effective evangelism.	The story shows the inability of humans to fill their desires with anything other than God. The story also indicates the need for a gender hierarchy to protect women.
Mary DeMuth, *The Day I Met Jesus* (2015)	The woman experiences abuse, divorce, sexual slavery, and poverty. She internalizes her situation with a sense of deep shame. She is socially isolated. Jesus frees her from the abuse and her shame by becoming her true husband.	The story offers hope to victims and survivors of abuse.

The sexual objectification of the Samaritan woman and the corresponding minimization of her contribution to the narrative has consequences for women in the church. It authorizes the reductive sexualization of women and encourages the identification of women as dangers to men's salvation. It limits their active participation in Christian communities. This pattern of interpretation endangers women by placing them at the intersection of objectification and constraint.

Is another interpretation possible? In the second part of the book, I will return to the minority perspective: John Chrysostom's savvy apostle; Marie Dentière's woman preacher; Virginia Broughton's successful evangelist;

Barbara Essex's model missionary. These interpreters' emphasis on the Samaritan woman's words points toward a very different understanding of John 4:4-42. This version of the woman's story has the potential to challenge the reductive sexualization of women in Christian understanding.

Part Two

THE SAMARITAN WOMAN
IN HER DAY

*When [Jesus] was upon the Earth, he manifested his love,
and his will, and his mind, both to the Woman of Samaria,
and Martha, and Mary her Sister, and several others.*

MARGARET FELL, *WOMEN'S SPEAKING JUSTIFIED*

MARGARET FELL, ONE OF the founders of the Quaker movement in seventeenth-century England, incorporated the Samaritan woman into her defense of women's right to teach, preach, and lead Christian communities. She argued that in the Gospels, women like the Samaritan woman demonstrated a better understanding of Jesus than anyone else, including the twelve disciples. For Fell, the Samaritan woman's story demonstrated that women can receive and teach divine truth.[1]

We have reviewed similar interpretations from Marie Dentière and Virginia Broughton. This perspective is common among women writers: Christine de Pizan (writing in 1405), Argula von Grumbach (1523), Harriet Livermore (1824), Phoebe Palmer (1859), Elizabeth Baxter (1897).[2] These women identified the Samaritan woman as a model for their own ministry. Her story provided biblical justification for women's leadership in the church (and beyond).

> Marie Dentière wrote less than twenty years after Argula von Grumbach, but it is unlikely that she knew of Argula's interpretation of the Samaritan woman, and neither woman would have known Christine de Pizan's work. Margaret Fell would not have had access to these earlier interpreters. The women writing in the nineteenth century likely knew of each other, but not previous female interpreters. That these women independently found the same message in John 4:4-42 strengthens their challenge to the majority interpretation.[3]

---

[1]Margaret Fell, *Women's Speaking Justified, Proved, and Allowed of by the Scriptures* (London, 1666), 5.

[2]Christine de Pizan, *Book of the City of Ladies* 1.10.5 (France, 1405), trans. by Jeffrey Richards (New York: Persea, 1982); Argula von Grumbach, *To the University of Ingelstadt* (Germany, 1523) in *Argula von Grumbach: A Woman's Voice in the Reformation*, ed. Peter Matheson (Edinburgh: T&T Clark, 1995), 88; Harriet Livermore, *Scriptural Evidence in Favour of Female Testimony in Meetings for Christian Worship* (Portsmouth, NH: R. Foster, 1824), 81-82; Phoebe Palmer, *The Promise of the Father* (1859; repr. Eugene: Wipf & Stock, 2015), 11-13; Elizabeth Baxter, *The Women of the Word* (London: Christian Herald, 1897), excerpt in *Women in the Story of Jesus: The Gospels Through the Eyes of Nineteenth-Century Female Bible Interpreters*, ed. Marion Ann Taylor and Heather E. Weir (Grand Rapids, MI: Eerdmans, 2016), 144-47, here 146-47.

[3]See also Carol A. Newsom, "Women as Biblical Interpreters Before the Twentieth Century," in *Women's Bible Commentary*, 3rd ed., ed. Carol A. Newsom, Sharon H. Ringe, and Jacqueline E. Lapsley (Louisville: Westminster John Knox, 2012), 11-24, here 11; and Amanda W. Benckhuysen, *The Gospel According to Eve: A History of Women's Interpretation* (Downers Grove, IL: IVP Academic, 2019), 1-5, 9-12.

However, Livermore warned, a woman who imitated the Samaritan woman's public preaching in her day would be institutionalized.[4] (She nonetheless encouraged women readers to follow the Samaritan woman's example!) As we saw in part one of this book, interpreters who found support for women's leadership in John 4:4-42 were drowned out by the overwhelming representation of the Samaritan woman as the worst kind of sinner.

Like Dentière, Fell, and Broughton, many women interpreters did not address the Samaritan woman's marital history. Christine de Pizan, Balfour, and Baxter held the woman's supposed sinful sexuality in tension with her ministry. For other women (as for most men), the Samaritan woman's sin remained central to the story.[5]

These women (and the other interpreters reviewed in part one of this book) wrote for the church. Their conclusions are mirrored in contemporary academic analysis of John 4:4-42. A growing number of scholars echo Dentière, Fell, and Broughton in rejecting the identification of the Samaritan woman's marital history with sin.[6] The majority, however, identify sexual sin as a key theme of the story.[7] And, like Tertullian, Calvin, and Piper, some scholars utterly malign the Samaritan woman as an uneducated, rude, shameful, hypersexualized sinner.[8]

The majority interpretation of John 4:4-42 from Tertullian to today gives the Samaritan woman archetypal significance. Her story reflects the human

---

[4]Livermore, *Scriptural Evidence*, 81-82.

[5]For instance, Mrs. Frederick (Hannah) Locker, *Bible Readings from the Gospels for Mothers' Meetings, Etc.* (London: Religious Tract Society, 1877), 37-40; Elizabeth Cady Stanton, *The Women's Bible: A Classic Feminist Perspective* (1895–1898; repr. Mineola, NY: Dover, 2002), 140.

[6]For instance, Janeth Norfleete Day, *The Woman at the Well: Interpretation of John 4:1-42 in Retrospect and Prospect*, Biblical Interpretation Series 61 (Leiden: Brill, 2002), 167-72; J. Ramsey Michaels, *The Gospel of John*, New International Commentary on the New Testament (Grand Rapids, MI: Eerdmans, 2010), 246-48; Marianne Meye Thompson, *John: A Commentary*, New Testament Library (Louisville: Westminster John Knox, 2015), 102-3.

[7]See Ernst Haenchen, *John 1: A Commentary on the Gospel of John Chapters 1-6*, Hermeneia (Philadelphia: Fortress, 1984), 221; Leon Morris, *The Gospel According to John*, New International Commentary on the New Testament, rev. ed. (Grand Rapids, MI: Eerdmans, 1995), 225, 234; Bruce J. Malina and Richard L. Rohrbaugh, *Social-Science Commentary on the Gospel of John* (Minneapolis: Fortress, 1998), 98-101.

[8]So Raymond E. Brown, *The Gospel According to John (I–XII)*, Anchor Bible 29 (New York: Doubleday, 1966), 171, 175-77; D. A. Carson, *The Gospel According to John*, Pillar New Testament Commentary (Grand Rapids, MI: Eerdmans, 1991), 217-21; Craig Keener, *The Gospel of John: A Commentary*, 2 vols. (Grand Rapids, MI: Baker Academic, 2003), 1:593-95, 605-8.

condition (sin) and God's salvation. Although all humanity shares this story, the woman's gender remains central. The vilification of the woman on account of her marital history colors the interpretation of her conversation with Jesus, the reconstruction of her daily life, and the meaning of the story for the lives of women in the church. Instead of exemplifying women's leadership, her story offers a warning against the seductive dangers of women.

But what if the majority interpretation of John 4:4-42 has gotten the story wrong? Consider this:

- After exchanging only a few sentences with Jesus, the woman understands his identity as a prophet. She's not ignorant.

- The woman asks Jesus the serious theological questions of her time. She is not uneducated or unaware.

- The woman's neighbors listen to her and accept her testimony. They would not do this for a social outcast.

- Jesus warns other people about their sin in John 5:14, 8:21, 9:41, 15:22-24, and 19:11. If the woman's story centers on sin, repentance, and conversion, why is sin never mentioned in John 4?

These factors suggest that John 4:4-42 is not about sin or sex at all. If so, then the majority interpretation has misrepresented the Samaritan woman's story and character, reducing a story that emphasizes women's active participation in the life and ministry of Jesus to a warning against women's sexuality.

In chapter seven, I will work through a reinterpretation of the woman's story. But first, it is necessary to deal with the question of her marital history, the primary reason so many interpreters have accused her of sexual sin. In the next two chapters, I will explore women's lives in Jesus' world. I will question the possible explanations of the Samaritan woman's story in this context: how she ended up with five husbands, why she would cohabit with a man without a marriage contract, and what her neighbors might have thought of her in their social, historical, and cultural context.

> As we have seen with, for instance, Balfour and Piper, many interpreters refer to particular historical and cultural backgrounds to explain elements of the Samaritan woman's story: Jewish and Samaritan relations, marital customs,

> rabbinic views on women. They emphasize the restrictions on women's lives in the first century, often in order to highlight how different Jesus was (and sometimes to express Western superiority over Middle Eastern cultures).
>
> Women did face serious legal, social, political, and religious marginalization in the ancient Mediterranean world. Despite these limitations, though, women could also exercise power in their households and societies. The evidence for women's lives in the first century indicates more complex realities than their textual marginalization suggests.

There is another question to consider: Was the Samaritan woman a historical figure? Some scholars today identify John 4:4-42 as a literary fiction created to insert the Samaritan mission of the early Christians into the life of Jesus himself.[9] There are no other indications that Jesus preached his gospel to the Samaritans. Instead, in Matthew 10:5-6 Jesus forbids the disciples to preach to the Samaritans, and in Acts 8:4-25 the Samaritans do not seem to have heard of Jesus before Philip's arrival.

While the origins of the story told in John 4:4-42 are unclear, its characterization of the Samaritan woman reflects historical possibilities for women in the first century. Moreover, for the church the Samaritan woman has long represented an actual woman whose story provides a message for women in the church. In this part of the book, I will approach John 4:4-42 as a historically contextualized story to understand its representation of a first century woman's life.

---

[9]See R. Brown, *John*, 175-76; Muse W. Dube, "Reading for Decolonization (John 4:1-42)," *Semeia* 75 (1996): 37-59; Sandra M. Schneiders, *Written That You May Believe: Encountering Jesus in the Fourth Gospel* (New York: Crossroad, 1999), 134-35; John F. McHugh, *A Critical and Exegetical Commentary on John 1–4*, International Critical Commentary (London: T&T Clark, 2009), 264.

5

A WOMAN'S LIFE IN JESUS' WORLD

At that moment, his disciples arrived. They wondered why Jesus
was speaking with a woman, but no one said, "What do you want?"
or "Why are you talking with her?" So the woman abandoned
her water jar, returned to the city, and told everyone,
"Come, see this person who told me everything I've ever done.
He's not the messiah, is he?" They left the city and went to him.

JOHN 4:27-30

IN JOHN 4, WE MEET A SAMARITAN WOMAN, a resident of Sychar, at the village well. Throughout her conversation with Jesus, her questions and responses displayed her theological understanding. We learn that she had been married five times, and she currently had a man who was not her legal husband. She was initially surprised that a Jewish man would speak with her, just as Jesus' disciples were surprised to find him speaking with a Samaritan woman. But the woman was able and, apparently, willing to carry on a conversation with a stranger.

We know some things about the woman, and we can guess others based on the evidence of her encounter with Jesus at the well. But the story leaves a lot out, including the woman's name. We don't know why she was drawing water herself. The story does not indicate why she had so many marriages, or how they each ended. We don't know the circumstances of her current living situation. Even the reason for the disciples' surprise is unclear. Were they shocked that their teacher, an unmarried man, was speaking with a woman he didn't know? Were they surprised to hear a woman speak with intelligence? Or were they concerned by the woman's Samaritan identity?

In John 4:4-42, we see only a glimpse of this woman's life. Interpreters tend to fill in the blanks based on their assessment of the woman's character. The result represented in a majority of commentaries, sermons, and other interpretations is a depiction of the Samaritan woman as an ignorant, uneducated, foolish, adulterous prostitute. Clara Balfour warned that to judge the woman's marital history by contemporary Christian standards of sexual morality is not entirely fair (though she herself condemned the woman's degrading homelife).[1] Is another reconstruction possible?

In this chapter, I will survey the common experiences of life for women in Jesus' world from birth to death. I will distinguish social ideals from more complex realities and explore the range of experiences women might have had depending on their social status, age, wealth, family situation, and geographic location. I will set the Samaritan woman in this context to understand the possibilities of her life before turning in chapter six to the particularities of her marital history.

SEEKING THE WOMEN OF JESUS' WORLD

In Mark 5:21-43, Jesus interacts with three Jewish women: a twelve-year-old girl, the girl's mother, and a woman independent of familial connections. These three women represent different stages of life. They open a window into women's experience of the world in the first century. In this chapter, I will use the three women of Mark 5 as a framework for exploring women's lives in the Samaritan woman's world.

Before beginning this work, though, it is important to notice how the women in Mark 5:21-43 are represented. The only named characters in the story are men: Jesus, Jairus, Peter, James, John. The independent woman acts for herself, but secretly, without drawing attention to herself (a sharp contrast to Jairus's behavior). The unnamed women of Jairus's household are acted upon rather than doing things themselves. The

---

[1]Clara Lucas Balfour, *Women of Scripture* (London: Houlston and Stoneman, 1847), 311.

absence of any sustained attention to their experience in this story reflects the tendency of authors in the ancient world to prioritize men's words, actions, and perspectives.

Across the Roman Empire, including among Jews and Samaritans, women of all legal, social, and economic classes were marginalized in various ways. Laws restricted their rights with respect to property ownership, marriage, and divorce. Social customs limited "respectable" women from a public presence, or even from going outside the home without adequate chaperonage. In literary sources, legal codes, and inscriptions, we see women portrayed from the perspective of men (often, wealthy, powerful, elite men).

These factors limit our knowledge of the lives and perspectives of women in the first century.[2] Exploring women's own experiences of their world therefore requires creativity. What are the spaces women inhabited, and how might they have navigated those spaces? We need to read elite male perspectives carefully and critically, questioning how the authors' own goals may have influenced their presentation of women's stories. The women themselves may have narrated their own lives quite differently.

I will proceed with caution through this chapter's reconstruction of women's lives in the first century, aware of all that we simply cannot know—and aware of the ways the sources we do have may mask the complexities of women's experiences. We have to remember the contrast between the representation of women in men's words, and the lived experiences of the women themselves glimpsed in personal letters, inscriptions, legal documents, and archaeological remains.

These concerns are particularly important for the Jewish and Samaritan women. Interpreters have often relied heavily on Jewish rabbinic traditions in their analysis of John 4. Some of this material reflected first-century understandings and practices. However, the majority of rabbinic material recorded the debates and perspectives of a small group of highly educated men in the third century (and beyond). It is not always the most useful source for reconstructing life in the Samaritan woman's world.[3]

---

[2]On these points, see Lynn H. Cohick, *Women in the World of the Earliest Christians* (Grand Rapids, MI: Baker Academic, 2009), 19-26 (and throughout).

[3]See further Seth Schwartz, "The Political Geography of Rabbinic Texts," in *The Cambridge Companion to the Talmud and Rabbinic Literature*, ed. Charlotte Elisheva Fonrobert and Martin S. Jaffee (Cambridge: Cambridge University Press, 2007), 75-96; Laura S. Lieber, "Jewish Women:

There are, in fact, few sources for understanding Jewish women's experience in the first century: the stories of the New Testament; Philo of Alexandria, a Jewish theologian in the early first century, and Josephus, a Jewish historian in the late first century; scattered comments in Greek and Roman sources; and a handful of letters, legal contracts, and inscriptions. The resources for studying and understanding life among the Samaritans in the first century are even more limited. We primarily meet the Samaritans in the writings of others (especially of Jews, whose comments reflect their own prejudices).

Scholars today recognize the Samaritans as a sectarian community with deep roots in ancient Israel. Reading between the lines of the Jewish sources on the Samaritans and the Samaritans' own accounts, they were culturally and religiously similar to the Jews in the first century.[4] They worshiped God, kept the Sabbath, and lived by the Torah. Moreover, in the first century in Judea, Samaria, and Galilee, Jews and Samaritans alike lived under Roman rule, with Roman laws, soldiers, and officials in their cities and villages.

In this chapter, then, I will use material from Jewish, Greek, and Roman sources to explore what life might have been like for a Samaritan woman. The peoples of the ancient Mediterranean shared a broadly similar cultural context. Stories, laws, and personal documents recording the lives of Jewish and Roman women can help us understand what the Samaritan woman's own experience may have been as a daughter, as a wife and mother, and as a woman independent of familial connections.

> The next two chapters refer to various sources from the ancient Mediterranean world. Many of these are available in Jane Rowlandson, *Women and Society in Greek and Roman Egypt: A Sourcebook* (Cambridge: Cambridge University Press, 1998); Jo-Ann Shelton, *As the Romans Did: A Sourcebook in Roman Social History*, 2nd ed. (Oxford: Oxford University Press, 1998); Mary R. Lefkowitz and Maureen B. Fant, *Women's Life in Greece and Rome: A Source Book in Translation*, 3rd ed.

Texts and Contexts," in *A Companion to Women in the Ancient World*, ed. Sharon L. James and Sheila Dillon, Blackwell Companions to the Ancient World (Oxford: Wiley-Blackwell, 2012), 329-42, esp. 330, 341-42.

[4]See Lidija Novakovic, "Jews and Samaritans," in *The World of the New Testament: Cultural, Social, and Historical Contexts*, ed. Joel B. Green and Lee Martin McDonald (Grand Rapids, MI: Baker Academic, 2013), 207-16.

[Baltimore: Johns Hopkins University Press, 2005]; and Emily A. Hemelrijk, *Women and Society in the Roman World: A Sourcebook of Inscriptions from the Roman West* [Cambridge: Cambridge University Press, 2021]. Many sources are also accessible online [try www.perseus.tufts.edu/hopper/].

BEING A DAUGHTER

> *Jairus, one of the leaders of the synagogue, came,*
> *and when he saw Jesus, he fell at his feet. He was begging*
> *Jesus: "My little daughter is about to die! Come and put*
> *your hands on her so that she will be saved, and live."*
>
> MARK 5:22-23

A twelve-year-old daughter is the first woman mentioned in Mark 5:21-43, though the girl herself does not appear until the very end of the story. For most of the story, she is sick in bed, at the point of death. This was not an unusual occurrence in the Roman Empire. In the first century, at least 50 percent of children died by the age of ten from injury, illness, or the consequences of poverty.[5] The threat of childhood mortality helps explain why the parents in Mark 10:13-16 wanted to bring their children to Jesus for a blessing. They hoped that the blessing would protect their children.

The value of a daughter. We first meet the girl in Mark 5 in the words of her father, Jairus, one of the synagogue leaders in the village. Although Jairus is an important man, he does not approach Jesus with expressions of his authority. Rather, he falls to the ground before Jesus, begging him to come and heal his daughter. Actually, Jairus calls the girl his "little daughter," a diminutive that suggests his love for her.

This is an important point. Visible displays of affection are rarely evident in ancient stories, letters, or documents. In part, the lack of expressions of affection reflected the constraints of poverty and subsistence living. In

---

[5]Maureen Carroll, *Infancy and Earliest Childhood in the Roman World: 'A Fragment of Time'* (Oxford: Oxford University Press, 2018), 147-48, notes that excavations of several cemeteries have found mortality rates of 60 percent by age six, and between 30 and 40 percent within the first year of life.

addition, cultural expectations of emotional restraint hid intense private
emotions from public view, especially for people of high social status.[6]

> Scholars sometimes cite the high rates of infant and childhood mortality as rea-
> son for Roman parents to have limited their emotional attachment to their chil-
> dren. However, there are many representations of parental love in burial and
> memorial practices. There is no reason to think that parents in the first century
> were less invested in their children than parents today.[7]

Common definitions of childhood and expectations for children also
contributed to unemotional or unsentimental representations of children in
ancient texts. For Jews, Romans, and so probably the Samaritans too,
children were defective humans who lacked basic skills, understanding, and
self-control. This perspective explains why the disciples tried to turn away
the parents who brought their children to Jesus. Like many in the first
century, they did not consider children valuable enough to bother an important teacher (Mk 10:13-16).[8]

This devaluing was particularly marked with respect to daughters.[9]
Parents, nurses, teachers, and other adults had the responsibility of molding
and shaping children into reasonable, educated, disciplined adults. But after
raising, feeding, clothing, and investing in a daughter, parents sent her out
of the house in marriage, taking a dowry with her. Daughters were an expense not every family could afford, as this letter from a migrant laborer to
his wife indicates: "I beg and beseech of you to take care of the little child,
and as soon as we receive wages I will send them to you. If—good luck to
you!—you bear offspring, if it is a male, let it live; if it is a female, expose it."[10]

To expose a newborn meant to leave the child in a public space such as a
garbage dump or a town square. Infant abandonment was legally permitted

---

[6]See further Carroll, *Infancy*, 6-7, 238-43.

[7]Carroll, *Infancy*, 4-9, 212-15.

[8]Caryn A. Reeder, "Child, Children," in *Dictionary of Jesus and the Gospels*, 2nd ed., ed. Joel B.
Green, Jeannine K. Brown, Nicholas Perrin (Downers Grove, IL: InterVarsity Press, 2013),
109-13, here 111-12.

[9]See also Lieber, "Jewish Women," 332.

[10]Personal letter, Egypt, Oxyrhynchus Papyrus 744, translation in Mary R. Lefkowitz and Maureen
B. Fant, *Women's Life in Greece and Rome: A Source Book in Translation*, 3rd ed. (Baltimore: Johns
Hopkins University Press, 2005), 187.

across the Roman Empire, though it probably was not practiced by Jews (nor, presumably, by Samaritans). While some abandoned babies were taken to be raised as slaves, most would have died.[11]

> Several authors, including the Jews Philo (*On the Special Laws* 3.117) and Josephus (*Against Apion* 2.202) and the Roman Tacitus (*Histories* 5.5), claimed that Jews did not expose their infants. However, there may be evidence of the practice among Jews in Palestine.[12]
>
> Note that the rabbis accused the Samaritans of infanticide (Mishnah Niddah 7.4), but this reference probably tells us more about rabbinic perspectives than Samaritan practice.

It is not clear how common the custom of infant exposure was. According to the reports and stories of infant exposure, the choice was difficult for families to make. But for some families, practical concerns demanded difficult decisions. For a wealthy family, an additional child might result in financial loss through inheritance. For a poor family, raising a daughter might mean the inability to care adequately for the rest of the household.[13]

A girl's education.

Now is the time to order her character,
now is the time to shape it; instruction that is stamped
upon the plastic years leaves a deeper mark.

SENECA, CONSOLATION TO HELVIA 18.8[14]

In the United States today, we tend to idealize childhood as a period of innocence, freedom, and play. The first-century definition of children as defective humans, as this quotation from Seneca indicates, made childhood a

---

[11]Judith Evans Grubbs, "The Dynamics of Infant Abandonment: Motives, Attitudes and (Unintended) Consequences," in *The Dark Side of Childhood in Late Antiquity and the Middle Ages: Unwanted, Disabled, and Lost*, ed. Katariina Mustakallio and Christian Laes, Childhood in the Past 2 (Oxford: Oxbow, 2011), 21-36, here 21-27.

[12]So Catherine Hezser, *Jewish Slavery in Antiquity* (Oxford: Oxford University Press, 2005), 136-38.

[13]See further Cohick, *Women*, 38-41.

[14]Seneca, *Moral Essays, Volume 2*, translated by John W. Basore, Loeb Classical Library (Cambridge: Harvard University Press, 1932), 481.

time of disciplined training for adulthood.[15] What this training looked like for a young girl depended on her family's social status and wealth.

For freeborn girls, learning how to navigate society was paramount. They were taught the behavioral expectations that would allow them to bring honor to the household as daughters, wives, and mothers. Education in social values, cultural customs, and religious traditions primarily happened informally, as part of daily life in a household. In Jewish families, instruction in Torah and the stories of Israel were important.[16] Among the Roman elite, girls learned imperial identity, culture, and values.[17]

Formal education in schools or with private tutors in the home was the privilege of elite families.[18] There were well-educated women authors, philosophers, and public speakers in the Roman Empire. But some Roman and Jewish authors questioned the value of education for girls, wondering if too much learning would distract a girl from her future as an honorable wife and mother.[19]

In most families in the Roman Empire, including among Jews and Samaritans, children began working at simple household tasks as soon as they were able. This inscription, for instance, commemorates a girl who, at the age of nine, was already trained and at work in a specialized trade: "Vicentia, sweetest daughter, spinner of gold thread, who lived nine years and nine months."[20] Children also worked in family-run businesses, kitchen gardens, and farms (though women did not normally participate in fieldwork). Girls like Jairus's daughter learned to manage a household from their mothers.[21]

---

[15]Reeder, "Child," 109-11.

[16]See Deut 6:20-25; Josephus, *Apion* 2.204.

[17]Lieber, "Jewish Women," 333; Janette McWilliam, "The Socialization of Roman Children," in *The Oxford Handbook of Childhood and Education in the Classical World*, ed. Judith Evans Grubbs and Tim Parkin (Oxford: Oxford University Press, 2013), 264-85; Lauren Caldwell, *Roman Girlhood and the Fashioning of Femininity* (Cambridge: Cambridge University Press, 2015), 35-38.

[18]Beryl Rawson, *Children and Childhood in Roman Italy* (Oxford: Oxford University Press, 2003), 155-56, 162-65; Caldwell, *Roman Girlhood*, 18-26.

[19]Lieber, "Jewish Women," 333-34; Caldwell, *Roman Girlhood*, 27-33.

[20]Funerary inscription, Rome, CIL 6.9213, translated by Emily A. Hemelrijk, *Women and Society in the Roman World: A Sourcebook of Inscriptions from the Roman West* (Cambridge: Cambridge University Press, 2021), 144.

[21]Richard Saller, "The Roman Family as Productive Unit," in *A Companion to Families in the Greek and Roman Worlds*, ed. Beryl Rawson (Chichester: Wiley-Blackwell, 2011), 116-28, here 124-27; McWilliam, "Socialization," 272-73.

Enslaved children.

> Hilara, slave of Hermia. 14 years old.
>
> FUNERARY INSCRIPTION, ROME[22]

The Roman Empire was a slave society in which enslaved people, including children, were defined as property. We know from sales contracts, Jesus' parables, and later rabbinic material that slavery existed in Galilee, Judea, and Samaria. In addition, Jews and Samaritans captured in Rome's wars were enslaved across the Empire.[23]

Enslaved people were dehumanized by slave owners. They lacked legal rights, including property ownership, marriage, and parental rights over their own children. Enslaved people could not protect their own bodies against violence. Slave owners regularly beat and raped their slaves (note 1 Pet 2:20).[24]

Enslaved girls were, like their poorer freeborn peers, trained to labor from an early age. They might be educated if their particular work required literacy. Unlike freeborn daughters, enslaved girls were apprenticed to learn skills like weaving.[25] Overall, they had significantly less experience with play, education, or affection. While all children faced violence in their daily lives (since physical discipline was considered to be an essential part of raising children), enslaved children were especially vulnerable to physical, emotional, and even sexual violence.[26]

Leaving childhood.

> [Minicia Marcella's] death is all the more bitter for its timing. She
> was engaged to marry an excellent young man. The date was set
> and we were all invited. But our joy was changed to sorrow. I
> cannot find the words to describe my grief when I heard Fundanus

---

[22]CIL 6.6395, translation in Lefkowitz and Fant, *Women's Life*, 224.

[23]See Hezser, *Jewish Slavery*, 116-19, 271-73, and throughout. Hezser argues that enslavement among Jews (and likely Samaritans) generally resembled Roman practices (e.g., 380-87).

[24]Caryn A. Reeder, *Slavery in the New Testament*, Grove Biblical (Cambridge: Grove Books, 2019), 4-6.

[25]Cf. Saller, "Roman Family," 125-27.

[26]Hanne Sigismund-Nielson, "Slave and Lower-Class Roman Children," in *Handbook of Childhood*, ed. Grubbs and Parkin, 286-301; Reeder, "Child," 110.

himself (so grief multiplies itself) ordering that the money that
had been delegated to clothes, pearls, and gems for the wedding
be spent on incense, ointments, and spices for the funeral.

PLINY THE YOUNGER, *LETTER* 5.16

When Minicia Marcella died at age twelve, her father had already arranged a marriage for her. While men tended to be in their twenties or even thirties at the time of their first marriage, the young age of new brides in elite and non-elite households is attested across the Roman Empire.[27]

We will explore the practices of marriage more thoroughly in the next chapter. For now, note that parents arranged daughters' marriages for the economic and social benefits offered by alliances with a wealthy household or a family with higher status. Daughters' marriages represented an investment in the family's future. Marriages connected communities together, giving daughters an important social role.[28]

Marriage marked a girl's transition into adulthood. Girls therefore became adults at what we would today consider a relatively young age. Since girls moved into their husbands' households (which were often multigenerational), an older woman—the husband's mother or other female relation—could help the new bride adjust to married life.

Jairus's actions and words in Mark 5:22-23 express his love for his daughter. But her death at age twelve, at the cusp of marriageability, also meant a loss of financial and social capital for the family. Like Minicia Marcella, Jairus's daughter died just as her own adult life should have begun.

BEING A WIFE AND MOTHER

Jesus took the girl's father and mother and the disciples who were
with him, and he went into the room where the girl was.

MARK 5:40

---

[27]Lieber, "Jewish Women," 339; Caldwell, *Roman Girlhood*, 106-16.
[28]See also Suzanne Dixon, *The Roman Family* (Baltimore: Johns Hopkins University Press, 1992), 62-63.

This verse contains the only direct reference to Jairus's wife in Mark 5:21-43. Unlike Jairus, she is not described in any way, and she does not speak. She is only acted upon. Jairus's wife is marginalized in this story.

We can imagine some of what the mother's experience was. She was likely a primary caregiver for her daughter during her illness. In her husband's absence, she may have taken on the responsibility of organizing the mourning that was in process by the time of his return. She surely grieved the loss of her child. Her emotions and actions are hidden behind her limited representation in the story.

Similarly, the marginalization of women in historical records and narratives hides their valuable, necessary contributions to first-century life. These contributions gave wives a certain amount of power in the household and broader society. Moreover, women had the important responsibility of bearing and raising children. Mothers' influence could extend into their children's adult lives, giving women a potentially powerful voice in politics and society.

The value of a wife.

> Here I lie, a married woman, Veturia is my name and descent, wife
> of Fortunatus, daughter of Veturius. I lived for three times nine
> years, wretched me, and I was married for twice eight. I slept with
> one man, I was married to one man. After having given birth to
> six children, with one surviving, I died. Titus Iulius Fortunatus,
> centurion of the second legion Adiutrix Pia Fidelis, erected this for his
> wife, who showed unequalled and extraordinary devotion to him.
>
> FUNERARY INSCRIPTION, AQUINCUM (BUDAPEST)[29]

This epitaph from the second century gives us insight into both a woman's life and what a husband might value in his wife. Although the inscription was written in the first person as if from Veturia's perspective, it reflected her husband's perspective. The inscription allowed Fortunatus to participate in the economy of social status. By highlighting particular aspects of his wife's life and character, he praised himself.

---

[29]CIL 3.3572, translated in Caldwell, *Roman Girlhood*, 111.

The inscription outlines Veturia's life. She married at age eleven and died at age twenty-seven. By the time of her death, she had given birth six times. She may have had other pregnancies end in miscarriage, a common occurrence in the ancient world. Veturia's repeated pregnancies offer a sober reminder of the primary duty of wives to bear children for their husbands.

As the physician Soranus said, men did not marry for pleasure. "Pleasures" of all sorts were easily available without the trouble of marriage. Rather, men married in order to have legitimate children.[30] Roman laws in the first century reinforced this message by rewarding husbands and wives who had three or more children. As Veturia's story indicates, the high rates of childhood mortality made it necessary for families to have multiple children so that one or two might survive to adulthood.[31]

Beyond the outline of Veturia's life, Fortunatus's inscription celebrated her faithfulness to him. First, Fortunatus was Veturia's sole husband. Roman society honored women who were married only once for their fidelity to their husbands.[32] Anna in Luke 2:36-37 exemplified this feminine virtue. But to be married only once was more of an ideal than a reality. For women who were widowed or divorced, remarriage was often a necessity, as I will discuss in the next chapter.

Second, Fortunatus emphasized his wife's fidelity by claiming that he was her only sexual partner. A wife's sexual fidelity was an important asset to her husband. It provided evidence of her familial loyalty and devotion (which the Romans called *pietas*). These descriptions in Veturia's epitaph identified her as an honorable Roman matron, a woman worthy of praise. Her good character would raise Fortunatus's own status.[33]

Notice, however, that Fortunatus did not proclaim his own sexual fidelity. As we saw in chapter two, men in the Roman Empire were not expected to be virgins at marriage, nor were they expected to have sex only with their own wives. Roman sources indicate that freeborn men took advantage of broad sexual rights:

---

[30]Soranus, *Gynecology* 1.34.

[31]See Rawson, *Children and Childhood*, 5-7; Saller, "Roman Family," 119.

[32]Cohick, *Women*, 104-5.

[33]See also Cohick, *Women*, 69-71. Judith P. Hallett, "Women in Augustan Rome," in *A Companion to Women in the Ancient World*, ed. Sharon L. James and Sheila Dillon (Oxford: Wiley-Blackwell, 2012), 372-84, here 377-84, discusses the complicated realities beyond the rhetoric of fidelity and devotion.

If therefore a man in private life, who is incontinent and dissolute in regard to his pleasures, transgresses with a lover or a slave, his wedded wife ought not to be indignant or angry, but she should reason that it is respect for her which leads him to share his debauchery, licentiousness, and wantonness with another woman (Plutarch, *Advice to a Bride and Groom* 16).[34]

The only bodies off-limits were the bodies that belonged to other men—wives, children, and slaves. Roman sexual freedom was critiqued by Jews and Christians, though it is difficult to say what, exactly, counted as off-limits in these communities.[35]

We learn more about Veturia in her epitaph than about Jairus's wife in Mark 5. But the inscription is still quite short. It does not tell us about Veturia's personal wealth. She may have inherited money or property from her father, as many women in the Roman Empire did. She may have run a business in addition to managing her husband's household. We don't know from this inscription whether she had any special skills or interests, or even what her personality or character were like. The inscription gives only a brief glimpse into this woman's life.

Ideals and realities.

> Likewise, teach older women to behave reverently. They shouldn't
> be slanderers or addicted to wine. Instead, they should teach what
> is good: they should advise young women to love their husbands
> and children, and to be self-controlled, chaste, contributors
> to the household, good, submissive to their husbands.

Titus 2:3-5

Roman moralists of the first and second centuries detailed the behavior and character of an ideal wife. She did not drink wine, leave the house without her husband's permission, have friends of her own, or worship any

---

[34]The translation is modified from Plutarch, *Moralia, Volume 2*, translated by Frank Cole Babbitt, Loeb Classical Library (Cambridge: Harvard University Press, 1928), 309.

[35]Note, for instance, Mt 5:27-32; Acts 15:28-29; Josephus, *Apion* 2.201. The questions of the sexual use of slaves among Jews and Christians is explored by Carolyn Osiek, "Female Slaves, *Porneia*, and the Limits of Obedience," in *Early Christian Families in Context: An Interdisciplinary Dialogue*, ed. David L. Balch and Carolyn Osiek, Religion, Marriage, and Family (Grand Rapids, MI: Eerdmans, 2003), 255-74, here 264-74; and Hezser, *Jewish Slavery*, 189, 193.

gods her husband did not worship.[36] The Jewish writer Josephus pro
claimed similar standards for Jewish women, and several New Testament
texts echoed this message.[37]

Many of the women we meet in the Gospels are located inside their
homes: Peter's mother-in-law in Mark 1:29-31, Mary and Elizabeth in Luke 1,
Martha and Mary in Luke 10:38-42. Their physical location inside houses
reflected the larger cultural context of the ancient Mediterranean world.
Jairus's wife did not go with him to beg Jesus for help for their daughter. She
stayed in the house, in restricted space. By placing her in the relatively protected space of the home, the narrative marks her honorable status.

> As noted in chapter two, households in the Roman world were not private
> space in the way we think of privacy today. The home was restricted space,
> however. Women in households were protected from the harassment and ac-
> cusations of immorality that women experienced outside the home in the
> streets and markets.[38]

In analyzing this evidence, it is important to remember that the home
was the site of social engagement and household productivity. Wives participated in society and the economy as they carried out the essential daily
tasks of the household: food preparation, cleaning, weaving cloth and sewing
clothing, and managing slaves (if the family owned slaves). Wives also contributed to the household by working in family-run shops and businesses.[39]

> Claudia Severa greets her Lepidina. On the third day before the Ides of
> September, sister, for the day of the celebration of my birthday, I gladly invite
> you to make sure that you come to us, to make the day more enjoyable for me
> by your presence, if you come. . . . I shall expect you, sister. Farewell, sister,
> my dearest soul, and be well, just as I hope to prosper (Vindolanda Letter 291).[40]

---

[36]See, for instance, Valerius Maximus 6.3; Pliny the Elder, *Natural History* 4.27; Plutarch, *Advice*
9, 19, 26.

[37]Josephus, *Apion* 2.201; Eph 5:22-24; 1 Tim 5:3-16; 1 Pet 3:1-6. See also Lieber, "Jewish Women,"
330-32, 338.

[38]See further Susan E. Hylen, *A Modest Apostle: Thecla and the History of Women in the Early Church*
(Oxford: Oxford University Press, 2015), 15.

[39]See Saller, "Roman Family," 116; Lieber, "Jewish Women," 338; Hylen, *Modest Apostle*, 21-24.

[40]Translated by Hemelrijk, *Women*, 185.

The ideals expressed by elite male authors do not fully reflect women's lives. This letter from Claudia Severa to Lepidina, both married to military commanders stationed along the northern border of the Roman Empire in Britain, offers an example of a close friendship between women. Women went out in public without their husbands to shop, worship, and watch gladiator fights. Wives and mothers advised emperors, governors, and senators. Elite women also spoke publicly to protect household honor, argue for or against political decisions, and participate in the planning for war.[41]

> To Italia, dressmaker of Cocceia Phyllis. She lived twenty years. Acastus, her fellow slave, paid for this tombstone because she was poor.
>
> Aurelia Nais, freedwoman of Gaius, fish vendor in the Warehouse of Galba. Gaius Aurelius Phileros, freedman of Gaius, her patron, and Lucius Valerius Secundus, a freedman of Lucius, set this up.
>
> Sweet Amemone is buried in this tomb, dear to her husband, a well-known innkeeper, whose fame has spread beyond the boundaries of her sweet home town. Because of her, many people used to frequent Tibur. . . . I, Philotechnus, have made this inscription for my venerable wife, since her name should last forever.[42]

Elite women had the privilege of avoiding public assemblies or appearances if they so desired. These funerary inscriptions from Rome indicate that for non-elite women, both enslaved and free, working outside the home was a normal part of life. They ran taverns and shops. They worked as servers in restaurants and bars. They managed businesses, either alongside other family members or independently.[43] Despite elite male disapproval (and disproving the stereotypical dismissal of women's intelligence and capabilities), women were visible actors in politics, culture, and the economy.

Motherhood. Jairus's wife had at least one child and possibly more. Perhaps, like Veturia and many other first-century women, she had multiple pregnancies in the hope that one or two children would survive to adulthood. Repeated pregnancies had serious physical consequences for women's health.

[41]See Hylen, *Modest Apostle*, 26-28, 77; Caryn A. Reeder, *Gendering War and Peace in the Gospel of Luke* (Cambridge: Cambridge University Press, 2019), 92.
[42]CIL 6.9980, 6.9801, 14.3709, translations in Lefkowitz and Fant, *Women's Life*, 223; Hemelrijk, *Women*, 153, 169.
[43]See further Saller, "Roman Family," 121-23.

Childbirth is hard today. In antiquity, giving birth was much more dangerous. Many funerary inscriptions and personal letters record the deaths of women in childbirth.[44]

In some households, enslaved people nursed, raised, and educated the children of their owners and other slaves. This system allowed elite women to participate in society and politics on behalf of their household, and it allowed less wealthy or powerful women (and other enslaved mothers) to contribute to household productivity.[45]

In other households, mothers were the primary caregivers for their children. These women were agents of social reproduction, teaching cultural values and traditions to their children. Some Roman and Jewish sources emphasized mothers' influence on their children's political, moral, and spiritual formation.[46]

In Mark 5:21-43, the mother is bereaved. Despite the high probability of children's deaths, parents' reflections on their children in letters and funerary inscriptions show the grief and pain of loss. To lose five children must have been quite painful and devastating for Veturia and her husband. To watch a daughter die must have left Jairus's wife as grief-stricken as her husband.

Enslaved mothers.

> *On the following conditions Sophrona, acting with the consent of*
> *her son Sosandros, sets free the female house-born slave named*
> *Onasiphoron. . . . Onasiphoron is to remain with Sophrona for the*
> *whole period of Sophrona's life, doing whatever she is ordered to*
> *do without giving cause for complaint. If she does not do so, then*
> *Sophrona is to have the power to punish her in whatever way*
> *she wishes to. And Onasiphoron is to give Sosandros a child.*
>
> MANUMISSION DECLARATION, DELPHI[47]

---

[44]Carroll, *Infancy*, 55-62.

[45]See also Cohick, *Women*, 147-48.

[46]Tacitus, *Dialogue* 28; Plutarch, *Life of Tiberius Gracchus* 1.5; Tobit 1:8; 2 Tim 1:5, 3:15; and also Cohick, *Women*, 143-46; Alicia D. Myers, *Blessed Among Women? Mothers and Motherhood in the New Testament* (Oxford: Oxford University Press, 2017), 114-18.

[47]Translation in Thomas Wiedemann, *Greek and Roman Slavery* (1981; repr., London: Routledge, 2005), 46-47.

As we've already noted, the Roman Empire was a slave society. Male owners could use enslaved people for their own benefit, including to satisfy their sexual desires. Slaves did not have the right to give or withhold consent to sexual advances. They also had no rights over any children born to them. Enslaved mothers could not treasure their children, educate them, or protect them from the horrors of enslavement.[48]

The document quoted above recorded the freedom of an enslaved woman named Onasiphoron in the early first century. "House-born" meant that Onasiphoron was born into slavery in the home of Sophrona. Her owners, Sophrona and Sophrona's son Sosandros, chose to free Onasiphoron. This was the dream for enslaved people across the Roman Empire.

Notice, though, what Onasiphoron's life of freedom looked like. She had to continue to live with her former owner Sophrona, through Sophrona's entire life. She had to do whatever Sophrona asked of her. Sophrona could punish her for wrongdoing. Finally, as a condition of freedom, Onasiphoron owed Sosandros a child.

This requirement suggests Onasiphoron had been freed so that her child (born after her manumission) would be freeborn. In this way, Sophrona and Sosandros would gain an heir from Onasiphoron's body (whether she was willing or not). Onasiphoron's rights over her own child in this situation are uncertain. The language of "giving" Sosandros a child at least suggests Onasiphoron would not have significant influence over her child's life.

In all, Onasiphoron's freedom does not seem to be very different from her enslavement. Her "freedom" came by the decision and power of her owners, and they retained control over her and her (freeborn) child. The story of an enslaved woman like Onasiphoron reminds us that not all mothers in the Roman Empire were honorable wives, or dishonorable wives, for that matter. Not all mothers could care for, raise, or grieve for their children. Not all mothers had the privilege of remaining within the safe, private space of the home. The range of women's experiences in the Samaritan woman's world was broad.

---

[48]Osiek, "Female Slaves," 259-60, 263-64.

A WOMAN ALONE

> *Now, there was a woman who had been menstruating continually for*
> *twelve years. She suffered many things under many doctors. She spent*
> *all that she had, but it didn't do any good. She just kept getting worse.*

MARK 5:25-26

The third woman in Mark 5:21-43 appears on her own. Unlike Jairus's daughter, no father spoke for her or sought healing on her behalf. Unlike Jairus's wife, she did not remain within the household. She apparently had control over her own resources, though she spent everything on her search for healing from her physical ailment. That physical ailment—continual vaginal bleeding for twelve years—would have prevented her from carrying out women's responsibility of reproduction. These elements of the narrative locate the woman outside the structures of the household.

> The woman's ailment meant she was constantly in a state of ritual impurity. Since strict ritual purity was primarily for the purpose of worship in the temple in Jerusalem, normal menstrual cycles would not be a problem. However, twelve years is a very long time to live in a state of impurity. In addition, in the first century many people associated illness and disability with punishment for sin (e.g., Jn 5:14, 9:2), which may have added to the woman's suffering.[49]

In the absence of any father or husband to speak for her, the woman went out in public and acted for herself. She touched Jesus' clothes without even asking permission, effectively stealing Jesus' power to heal herself (note Mk 5:27-30). This third woman in Mark 5 does not represent the ideals of women's behavior in the first century. But notably, no one reprimanded her. Instead, Jesus publicly acknowledged the saving power of her faith (Mk 5:34). He also made her part of his family, calling her "daughter."

This woman's presence in Mark 5 is instructive. Not all women fit into the neatly defined categories of daughter, wife, and mother, and not all women

---

[49]See further Cohick, *Women*, 219-22; and Algirdas Akelaitis, "The Practice and Experience of the Menstrual Rituals in the Ancient Israel," *Soter* 73 (2020): 5-19.

were defined with respect to their connection to a man. Despite the marginalization of women in a male-centric, hierarchical social structure, women in the first century owned their own property, supported themselves, and functioned independently of male authority.

A captive slave.

> *Claudia Aster, a captive from Jerusalem. The imperial freedman*
> *Tiberius Claudius Proculus has taken care (that this was set up).*
> *I ask you, ensure by law that you take care that nobody*
> *knocks down my inscription. She lived twenty-five years.*
>
> FUNERARY INSCRIPTION, NAPLES[50]

This inscription recorded the life of a Jewish woman who survived the five-month-long siege of Jerusalem during the First Jewish Revolt, only to be taken from her home and sold in a Roman slave market. The enslavement of the survivors of a captured city was a common practice of war in antiquity. The Roman Empire grew rich from the sale of human lives (see Lk 21:23-24; Rev 18:13).

We don't know how old this woman was when she was captured, though she was apparently mature enough to remember her origins in Jerusalem.[51] She was purchased by Tiberius Claudius Proculus, a freed slave who had belonged to and worked for the emperor. The "Claudia" in her name marked her as part of his household ("Aster" may be a Latinized version of "Esther").

> Usually enslaved people were given only one name. When a slave owner freed a slave, formerly enslaved persons were required to add the owner's family name to their own. It's possible, then, that Claudia Aster had been set free, possibly to marry her former owner. However, the inscription clearly identifies Claudia Aster as a captive. It lacks the vocabulary commonly found in inscriptions for freed slaves or spouses. Her status is somewhat ambiguous.

---

[50]CIL 10.1971, translation from Hemelrijk, *Women*, 216.

[51]Captives who were enslaved as young children, taken far from home, and integrated into a new household may not have had this capacity.

Even though the inscription commemorates Claudia Aster's origins in Jerusalem, it is unlikely that she could have maintained her Jewish identity with any integrity. An enslaved person could not keep the Sabbath or the dietary laws. Claudia Aster would have come into contact with pagan idols inside her new owner's household, and she might have been expected to participate in non-Jewish ceremonies and festivals.[52]

Along with her freedom, Claudia Aster lost the privilege of chastity. She could not protect her body against sexual advances. As an enslaved woman, Claudia Aster could not be a mother like Jairus's wife. Her pre-captivity identity as a daughter and, possibly, a wife and mother was taken from her. The trauma she would have experienced during the revolt and siege would be compounded by the dehumanization of her enslavement.[53]

The inheritance.

> *Judah son of Eleazar Khthousion, an En-gedian living in Maoza, willed*
> *to Shelamzious, his daughter, all his possessions in En-gedi as follows: half*
> *of the courtyard across from (?) the synagogue (?). . . . Shelamzious shall*
> *have the half of the previously mentioned courtyard and rooms from today,*
> *and the other half after the death of the said Judah, validly and securely*
> *for all time, to build, raise up, raise higher, excavate, deepen, possess, use,*
> *sell and manage in whatever manner she may choose, all valid and secure.*
>
> PROPERTY DEED, ROMAN PALESTINE[54]

This deed detailed property given by Judah to his daughter in the early second century. Shelamzious was not a woman alone, outside the standard relationships of patriarchal society. She had a father, and she was married (as another document in the same collection records). However, she owned property independently of male authority or oversight. The deed gives us a sense of what was possible for women, including Jewish women, in the first and second centuries.

---

[52]See Hezser, *Jewish Slavery*, 19-22, 117.
[53]See further Reeder, *War and Peace*, 139-42.
[54]Papyrus Yadin 19, modified translation from Naphtali Lewis, *The Documents from the Bar Kokhba Period in the Cave of Letters: Greek Papyri*, Judean Desert Studies 2 (Jerusalem: Israel Exploration Society, 1989), 85.

Judah gave Shelamzious authority over half the property during his life, with full rights of ownership over the entire property after his death.[55] While the language of the deed reflected the practices of legal documentation of the time, the authority given to this woman to hold on her own, apart from male guidance or control, is remarkable. Perhaps family inheritance provided the woman in Mark 5:25-33 with the resources to finance her search for healing.

Women inherited, purchased, managed, and sold property across the Roman Empire in the first century (and beyond). In fact, scholars estimate between a fifth and a third of land in the Empire was owned by women.[56] Like Shelamzious, many of them had independent control over their property. Wealthy women used their resources for the good of their communities by funding public building projects, programs to feed the hungry, and temples and synagogues.[57]

They supported individuals too. As Lynn Cohick describes, patrons provided housing for dependents, loaned money for businesses or dowries, and helped dependents make valuable social and economic connections.[58] Several women mentioned in the New Testament supported Jesus and the earliest churches in these ways (Lk 8:1-3; Acts 16:15; Rom 16:1-2). In return for their patronage, women were honored with inscriptions, statues, and the respect of their dependents.

A farmer.

> *Valeria Maxima, mother, owner of a farm, dearest daughter of Valeria, who lived 36 years, 2 months, 12 days, on her farm in the district of Mandela in the precinct of Hercules, rest in peace.*
>
> FUNERARY INSCRIPTION, TIVOLI[59]

This funerary epitaph commemorated a matriarchal family. The younger Valeria owned a farm near Rome. She may have worked the farm herself or (more likely) managed enslaved and free farmworkers. The younger Valeria

---

[55]The deed described a dwelling built around an open courtyard, a common building design in Roman-era Judea and Galilee.

[56]See Saller, "Roman Family," 120; Hylen, *Modest Apostle*, 21-22.

[57]See the inscriptions in Lefkowitz and Fant, *Women's Life*, 158-61; Lieber, "Jewish Women," 335-36.

[58]Cohick, *Women*, 285-301.

[59]CIL 4.3482, translation in Lefkowitz and Fant, *Women's Life*, 209.

was a mother, though we are not given details about her children. The elder Valeria may have lived with her daughter and grandchildren. Remarkably, no father, husband, or any other man appeared in this inscription.

Similar households are represented in the New Testament. Martha owned a home in which she lived with her sister Mary (Lk 10:38-42). In John 11, this same household included their brother Lazarus. Martha took responsibility for welcoming Jesus and his followers into her home, indicating her authority over the household. Likewise, Lydia ran a business in Philippi. As the authority in her household, she hosted Paul and his associates and converted her entire household to Christianity (Acts 16:14-15).

Mary in Jerusalem, Chloe in Corinth, Nympha in Colossae, the women Paul greeted in Romans, the unnamed woman of 2 John: these women are recognized in the New Testament on their own merits, without any obligatory reference to male family members (Acts 12:12-17; Rom 16:1-15; 1 Cor 1:11; Col 4:15; 2 Jn 1). Their presence challenges us to recognize the different circumstances of women's lives and the considerable wealth, power, and authority women could hold independently of men.

Men wrote, recorded, and preserved most of the stories, histories, legal documents, and private letters of the Roman Empire. Consequently, we primarily see women's lives, experiences, and identities through a male perspective. The glimpses into the lives of Claudia Aster, Shelamzious, Valeria the mother and Valeria the daughter, Martha, and the nameless woman in Mark 5:25-34 add complexity to our understanding of women's existence in the Roman Empire.

WONDERING ABOUT THE SAMARITAN WOMAN'S LIFE

We learn very little about the Samaritan woman in John 4:4-42. The stories, letters, and inscriptions about other women in the Roman Empire provide a framework for cautiously reconstructing the possibilities of her life.

First, the woman's interaction with Jesus shows her intelligence and education. She knew Samaritan traditions and the history of the divide between the Samaritans and the Jews. While we don't know her family's social status or wealth, her ability to speak knowledgeably with Jesus suggests she was educated or was able to educate herself by listening to and participating in household conversations.

She may have been trained to specialized skills like weaving as a young girl. She certainly learned household management within her family. The woman's father (or other male family member) would have arranged her first marriage, probably when she was between twelve and fifteen years old. We don't know how her marriages ended (we'll explore some of the options in the next chapter), but her father's household would have continued to be involved in her subsequent marriages.

To have five husbands may mean the woman brought significant resources to her marriages. Her father's household may have been wealthy or well-connected, or perhaps the woman herself owned property like Shelamzious and Martha.

As a wife, the woman participated in household productivity. If her household was wealthy, she may have managed enslaved people. In a poorer household, she may have worked in or run a business in addition to completing the daily work of the household. Her trip to the well to draw water was one of her contributions to household life.

The possibility of wealth suggested by the woman's ability to converse and her multiple marriages contrasts with the fact that she went to the well herself to draw water rather than sending someone else. There are unfortunately few references to anyone collecting water in first-century sources, so it is difficult to know how to interpret this contrast.

The story does not mention the woman's children. It is unlikely that the woman was unable to conceive or bear children, since childlessness would have limited her ability to remarry. She probably did raise and educate children.[60] She may have transitioned her daughters into adulthood and marriage and seen sons take their places in society. Given the high rates of childhood mortality, she probably had endured the deaths of some of her own children.

We don't know how old the woman was when she met Jesus. Allowing time for six different marital relationships, she may have been in her thirties (or even older). Her maturity is borne out by the respect her neighbors showed her. Like Claudia Severa and Lepidina, the Samaritan woman would

---

[60]The legends of the Samaritan woman's life in the early church included several children. See Eva Catafyglotu Topping, *Saints and Sisterhood: The Lives of Forty-Eight Holy Women* (Minneapolis: Light and Life, 1990), 138-41.

have had friends in her community. It did not shock her neighbors to hear her speak publicly, or that she met a stranger, a man, in public on her own. The ideal of women's seclusion in the household and silence in public space was just that—an ideal, not a reality.

Against the context of women's lives in Jesus' world, the representation of the Samaritan woman is relatively normal. The woman did, however, have an unusual marital history. In the next chapter, I will dig deeply into the laws and practices of marriage, divorce, widowhood, remarriage, and cohabitation in the first-century world. The woman was certainly unlucky in the sheer number of marital households she had been part of. But, as we'll see, unlucky is not the same as sinful.

6

MARRIAGE FROM BEGINNING TO END

Jesus said to the woman, "Go, call your husband,
and come back here." The woman answered,
"I don't have a husband." Jesus said to her, "You're correct when you say,
'I don't have a husband.' You've had five husbands, and now the
one you have is not your husband. You speak the truth."

JOHN 4:16-18

THE MAJORITY INTERPRETATION OF the Samaritan woman as an adulterer, prostitute, and social outcast develops from this exchange between the woman and Jesus. As we've seen in the history of interpretation, the standard characterization of the woman rests on several overlapping assumptions regarding sex, marriage, and women.

Until very recently in Christian tradition, sexual intercourse was correlated with sin. The only sanctioned option for a sexual relationship was marriage, but even sex with one's own spouse was (often) morally suspect. Contemporary interpreters are more likely to celebrate marital sex, but nonmarital sex remains apparently the worst sin a person—especially a woman—can commit.

By these standards, a woman who had at least six sexual relationships, one of which was not marital, can be condemned as a sinner. Interpreters assume some or all of the woman's husbands divorced her because she had sex with other men. Since they also claim that divorce was uncommon in the first century, her multiple divorces are seriously problematic.

Interpreters also assume the woman chose to remarry either as an expression of her own sexual sinfulness or, for contemporary interpreters, because of her longing for an intimate relationship. Whether the woman is working as a prostitute or living with a boyfriend (as some interpreters today say), her nonmarital cohabitation confirms her sinful sexuality.

According to the majority interpretation of John 4:4-42, then, the Samaritan woman's marital history is the result of her own choices, decisions, and actions. Very few interpreters pay attention to the men in the woman's story. Those who do often imply that the woman's husbands are the victims of her immorality. All women tempt men into sexual sin, whether they intend to or not. But a woman like this, who—interpreters claim—acted out of her own desire to initiate sexual relationships with men, perverts pious, chaste womanhood.

In this chapter, I will question the accuracy and viability of these assumptions within the first-century context. I will explore what marriage was in the first century: its purposes, how marriages were arranged, and its social significance. I will consider alternatives to formal marriage for those without the right to marry. I will examine the end of marriages in death and in divorce and the options for life after marriage.

The limitations addressed in the beginning of chapter five still apply. The clearest evidence of marital values and practices in the first century comes from elite Roman families. The practices of non-elite Romans and non-Romans in general, preserved primarily in legal documents and inscriptions, are not always as clear. The sources are also limited by their male-centric perspective. The realities of marriage, divorce, and cohabitation were doubtless more complex and variable than the ideals, laws, and narratives might suggest.

ESTABLISHING A MARRIAGE

What are our marriage laws? The Law recognizes no sexual connections, except the natural union of man and wife, and that only for the procreation of children. . . . The law commands us, in taking a wife, not to be influenced by dowry, not to carry off a woman by force, nor yet to win her by guile and deceit, but to betroth her from the man who is authorized to give her away.

JOSEPHUS, *AGAINST APION* 2.199-200

In *Against Apion*, Josephus explained Jewish customs to non-Jews. Writing after the Jewish revolt against the Roman Empire in the first century, he was particularly concerned to show that Judaism was an honorable, respectable way of life. His discussion of the purpose and practice of marriage shows the differences between marriage in the first century and today.

According to Josephus, the primary and most significant reason for two people to marry was not love, or relationship, or the human desire for intimacy. Rather, the purpose of marriage was conceiving, bearing, and raising children. Similar expectations appear in Roman marriage contracts, personal letters, census records, and more. The physician Soranus even encouraged men to consider a prospective bride's reproductive potential before contracting a marriage.[1]

This purpose of marriage was reinforced by first-century laws demanding that elite Romans marry, procreate, and raise children. Emperor Augustus celebrated men who fathered many children with their wives, and imperial artwork portrayed parents surrounded by children as a symbol of imperial success. By Roman law, women of various social classes who had multiple children were rewarded with legal independence from male guardianship.[2]

Love, friendship, and intimacy were not excluded from marriage, of course. Jews and Romans valued close familial bonds. Funerary inscriptions celebrated marital love, companionship, and harmony: "we were bound by mutual love as soon as we met . . . we should have continued to live in happiness."[3] But, in contrast to the understanding of marriage in America

---

[1]Soranus, *Gynecology* 1.34.1. See also Pliny the Younger, *Letters* 1.14.2; Papyrus Michigan 7.434; Aulus Gellius, *Attic Nights* 17.21.44-45; Suzanne Dixon, *The Roman Family* (Baltimore: Johns Hopkins University Press, 1992), 67-69.

[2]Suetonius, *Life of Augustus* 34; Dio Cassius, *History of Rome* 54.16.1-2; Ulpian, *Fragments* 11.28a; Dixon, *Roman Family*, 120-21; Susan E. Hylen, *A Modest Apostle: Thecla and the History of Women in the Early Church* (Oxford: Oxford University Press, 2015), 20-21.

[3]CIL 6.18817, translation from Jo-Ann Shelton, *As the Romans Did: A Sourcebook in Roman Social History*, 2nd ed. (Oxford: Oxford University Press, 1998), 48. See also CIL 6.15346, 6.29580, 13.1983; Pliny the Younger, *Letters* 4.19, 8.5; Dixon, *Roman Family*, 69-70, 83-89.

today, in antiquity emotional connections developed after marriage, as a consequence of sharing a common life. They were not prerequisites for marriage nor the purpose of marriage.

In *Against Apion*, Josephus defined marriage as a legal contract arranged by the prospective groom and the bride's father or legal guardian. Both families were involved from the beginning. Parents, guardians, and family friends identified potential spouses for their children and made the financial and legal arrangements for a marriage. This process reinforces the fundamental distinction between marriage in the first century and today. For Jews, Romans, and Samaritans in antiquity, a daughter represented a powerful means of forming political, social, and economic alliances between two families.

A girl's first marriage.

Marry a virgin, so you can teach her good habits.

HESIOD, WORKS AND DAYS 699[4]

Hesiod lived in Greece in the seventh century BCE, but his books were still being read and cited in the first century. His perspective on the advantages of marrying a young woman is borne out by the age of girls at their first marriage in the first century. We saw this reflected in the previous chapter in the examples of Minicia Marcella, the twelve-year-old who died just as she should have been getting married, and Veturia, who married at age eleven (before the legal minimum of twelve years).

Marriage between the ages of twelve and fifteen was normal among elite families. For non-elite women, marriage might be slightly delayed, but most freeborn girls were married by their late teens. Their husbands tended to be at least ten years older.[5] For example, the philosopher Cicero married his first wife when he was twenty-seven and she was eighteen. He divorced this wife when he was nearly sixty, subsequently marrying a girl who was

[4]Translated in Mary R. Lefkowitz and Maureen B. Fant, *Women's Life in Greece and Rome: A Source Book in Translation*, 3rd ed. (Baltimore: Johns Hopkins University Press, 2005), 24-25.
[5]Laura S. Lieber, "Jewish Women: Texts and Contexts," in *A Companion to Women in the Ancient World*, ed. Sharon L. James and Sheila Dillon, Blackwell Companions to the Ancient World (Oxford: Wiley-Blackwell, 2012), 339; Lauren Caldwell, *Roman Girlhood and the Fashioning of Femininity* (Cambridge: Cambridge University Press, 2015), 3-4, 106-16.

fourteen or fifteen. He married his own fifteen-year-old daughter to a thirty-year-old man.[6]

The relative youth of girls at marriage reflects the intersecting concerns of virginity, trainability, and reproduction. First, virginity was a valuable commodity for Jews, Romans, and presumably also Samaritans. A lack of sexual experience ensured that any children born to the woman belonged to her husband—a factor particularly important among Jews and Samaritans, who understood a man's name and property as an inheritance to protect.[7]

> The concept of virginity was not primarily about a woman's purity, or an internal state of being (though it could incorporate such ideas). Instead, virginity was an externally defined status with social and economic value to a family.[8]

Across the Roman Empire, virginity also provided an indication of a girl's character. A girl who maintained her virginity until marriage honored her father's authority over her body. Therefore, she would presumably also honor her husband by preserving her sexual availability for him alone. A girl's virginity was a public concern. A woman's sexual fidelity contributed to her household's status.[9]

The second concern behind a young age at marriage for girls was malleability. The status of virginity overlapped with youthfulness. It's not always easy to tell if "virgin" refers to a woman who has not yet had sexual intercourse, or if it simply means a young, unmarried girl (who may or may not have had sexual intercourse). A very young bride could be trained to the traditions and customs of their new household. This is Hesiod's reasoning in encouraging men to marry young girls.

The age difference between husbands and wives increased the husband's authority over his wife. An adolescent bride was still growing, developing, and learning about the world. Her adult husband essentially took over the

---

[6]Tim Parkin, "The Roman Life Course and the Family," in *A Companion to Families in the Greek and Roman Worlds*, ed. Beryl Rawson (Chichester: Wiley-Blackwell, 2011), 276-90, here 283.

[7]Caryn A. Reeder, *The Enemy in the Household: Family Violence in Deuteronomy and Beyond* (Grand Rapids, MI: Baker Academic, 2012), 45-52, 125-26, 163.

[8]See further Caldwell, *Roman Girlhood*, 45-52.

[9]The consistent references to women's virginity in marriage contracts and funerary inscriptions represent its cultural value. See also Hylen, *Modest Apostle*, 28.

woman's education from her own parents. As one funerary inscription says, a woman's husband was a second father for her.[10]

Third, childbirth was an important responsibility for wives, especially considering the high rates of childhood mortality in the ancient world. The extension of a woman's reproductive years into her teens meant more opportunities for successful childbirth and a higher probability that one or two children might survive childhood.[11]

> You will be very sad to hear that your granddaughter [Pliny's wife] has had a miscarriage. She's a young girl and didn't even realize that she was pregnant. . . . She has paid for her ignorance, and her lesson has been costly; she was herself gravely ill. . . . Although this pregnancy was not successful, it gives us confidence that we are capable of having children (Pliny the Younger, *Letters* 8.10).[12]

Some physicians in the Roman Empire recognized that younger girls were less likely to conceive and that pregnancy and childbirth were dangerous for younger girls. As Pliny's letter concerning his (much younger) wife's miscarriage indicates, though, these concerns did not restrain early marriage and reproduction.[13]

Contracting a marriage.

> *Judah son of Eleazar also known as Khthusion gave over Shelamzion,*
> *his very own daughter, a virgin, to Judah surnamed Cimber son of*
> *Ananias son of Somalas . . . for Shelamzion to be a wedded wife to*
> *Judah Cimber for the partnership of marriage according to the laws.*
>
> MARRIAGE CONTRACT, ROMAN PALESTINE[14]

---

[10]CIL 1.2.1221, translated in Shelton, *As the Romans*, 37. (This inscription says the relationship began when the woman was only seven years old.) See also Quintilian, *The Orator's Education* 6, preface 4-5; Peter Garnsey and Richard Saller, with Jaś Elsner et al., *The Roman Empire: Economy, Society, and Culture*, 2nd ed. (Oakland: University of California Press, 2015), 155-56.

[11]See further Garnsey and Saller, *Roman Empire*, 165-66.

[12]Translation in Shelton, *As the Romans*, 25.

[13]In fact, some doctors prescribed early marriage for girls to avoid physical ailments. Extended virginity was thought to be dangerous for women's bodies. See Caldwell, *Roman Girlhood*, 80-97.

[14]Papyrus Yadin 18, translation in Naphtali Lewis, *The Documents from the Bar Kokhba Period in the Cave of Letters: Greek Papyri*, Judean Desert Studies 2 (Jerusalem: Israel Exploration Society, 1989), 80.

Marriages were established through legal contracts like this one belonging to Shelamzious (also known as Shelamzion), whom we met in chapter five. The two parties to the contract are the bride's father (or other male guardian) and the groom. Sometimes the bride also signed the contract. The contracts detailed the financial arrangements, expectations for behavior on each side, and protective measures for both families' investments.

> There were two types of marriage in the Roman world. In one [known as *cum manu* marriage], husbands assumed legal authority over their wives. In the first century, it was more common for fathers to retain authority over their daughters by establishing *sine manu* marriages for them. In a *sine manu* marriage, the husband had no rights over his wife's personal, familial property.[15]

In this marriage contract, Judah promised to feed and clothe Shelamzious and any children she may bear to him. Other marriage contracts were significantly more detailed. One brother in Alexandria ensured his sister's husband could not abuse his new wife or have sex with anyone else in their home. Brides promised to live with their husbands (marking the husband's authority over the household), and in one case, a new wife promised not to poison her husband with love potions.[16] The rabbis included requirements for a wife's modest behavior, the household work she would perform, and the frequency of sexual intercourse.[17]

Shelamzious's marriage contract specified the amount she brought with her: five hundred silver denarii (one denarius was about one day's wage). The bride's dowry represented a major concern in marriage contracts. The husband held the dowry in trust for the wife, both to support her and any children during the marriage and to provide for her following his death or their divorce. In this way, the dowry protected the bride in her new household and gave her resources to survive after the marriage ended.

---

[15]See Lynn H. Cohick, *Women in the World of the Earliest Christians* (Grand Rapids, MI: Baker Academic, 2009), 42-43, 100-101.

[16]See PSI 1.64; Tebtunis Papyrus 1.104.

[17]Mishnah Ketubbot 4-5. See also Jacobine G. Oudshoorn, *The Relationship Between Roman and Local Law in the Babatha and Salome Komaise Archives: General Analysis and Three Case Studies on Laws of Succession, Guardianship, and Marriage*, Studies on the Texts of the Desert of Judah 69 (Leiden: Brill, 2007), 380-87.

The dowry belonged to the bride herself. Judah had to return Shelamzious's money immediately, with no objection, if she or her legal representative asked for it (if, that is, she wanted to divorce her husband). The legal and financial arrangements of marriage contracts protected the bride's family's investment by ensuring the money or property they provided would stay within the family (with the bride and her children).[18]

I now pronounce you . . .

> *Herais requests your company at dinner in celebration*
> *of the marriage of her children at her house*
> *tomorrow, the fifth, at nine o'clock.*
>
> A WEDDING INVITATION[19]

Many families celebrated a marriage with ceremonial elements to mark the bride's shift from childhood to adulthood, a procession through town to take the bride to her new home, a dinner party, and entertainment. Religious elements were included, but the celebrations were not primarily religious for Romans or Jews. Moreover, none of these celebrations were necessary. A bride could simply move into her new husband's home—he did not even have to be present for the marriage to be official.[20]

Depending on local customs, the bride and groom may have occasionally stayed together or even lived together after the contract was signed but before the marriage was finalized. Roman couples sometimes cohabited while waiting for the bride to be old enough to legally marry. According to the rabbis of the third century, the Jews of Judea traditionally permitted couples to have sex during their engagement.[21]

These practices helpfully contextualize Matthew 1:18-19. Mary's pregnancy during her engagement may not have been too shocking to her community. They would have assumed that she and Joseph had anticipated the finalization of their marriage. Joseph, however, knew Mary's child was not

---

[18]Cohick, *Women*, 112-15.
[19]Papyrus Oxyrhynchus 111, translation in Lefkowitz and Fant, *Women's Life*, 205.
[20]See further Dixon, *Roman Family*, 64-65; Cohick, *Women*, 57-61; Caldwell, *Roman Girlhood*, 119-20, 138-39.
[21]Mishnah Ketubbot 1.5. See also Caldwell, *Roman Girlhood*, 107-14.

his own. The natural conclusion was that his contracted wife had committed adultery against him. He therefore wanted a divorce.

Joseph's desire to divorce Mary suggests that their marriage began with the contract rather than at cohabitation (a practice known as inchoate marriage). This particular practice was unusual in the first century. However, Jews and Romans both debated if a woman who had sex during her betrothal, whether with her fiancé or another person, was guilty of adultery.[22] Without standardized ceremonies, the beginning of a marriage could be ambiguous.

A bride's consent.

> *Thermion daughter of Apion and Apollonius son of*
> *Ptolemaeus agree that they have come together for the*
> *purposes of sharing their lives with one another.*
> MARRIAGE CONTRACT, EGYPT[23]

Marriages were arranged and contracted by families. The contracts were signed by the bride's father (or male guardian) and by the groom. However, as this marriage contract shows, the bride herself also had the right to consent to or reject a marriage. A bride's consent was expected, in fact, in Roman and Jewish custom.

How seriously a young girl's opinion would be taken is unclear, especially since young girls were socialized to obey their parents. According to Roman legal debates, a woman's right to object was limited, and the lack of an objection counted as consent. However, there is evidence that at least some parents discussed potential marriages with their daughters.[24]

"A rich young man committed rape. Before the girl made her option, he sent his relatives to her to ask her to marry him. After hearing their pleas, she wept in silence" ([Quintilian], *Lesser Declamations* 247).[25] In Roman rhetorical schools, boys debated theoretical legal cases. This particular exercise proposed a

[22]Philo, *On the Special Laws* 3.72; *Digest* 48.5.14.3, 8; Cohick, *Women*, 62-63.
[23]BGU 4.1052, translation in Shelton, *As the Romans*, 43.
[24]*Digest* 23.1.11-12; Caldwell, *Roman Girlhood*, 118-19.
[25]The quotation is from [Quintilian], *The Lesser Declamations*, translated by D. R. Shackleton Bailey, 2 vols., Loeb Classical Library (Cambridge: Harvard University Press, 2006), 1:27.

> fictional law in which the victim of rape could choose either to marry her rapist
> or have him executed. Similar cases repeat in several other exercises. I wonder
> what the boys who argued these cases in school learned from them about sex-
> ual assault, male power, and female consent. The assumption that there would
> be pressure on the victim to marry the rapist regardless of her own trauma
> certainly reinforces the ambiguity of a girl's ability to consent.[26]

A woman who waited until her late teens to marry may have had a stronger voice in the proceedings. Women who remarried after the death of a spouse or divorce had the best opportunity to participate in choosing a new husband, though the woman's male guardians would still arrange the marriage contract on her behalf.[27] However, remarriage still centered on the advantages of a connection for families and communities, not romantic attachment.

MARRIAGE IN ALL BUT NAME

A wife is acquired by money, or by contract,
or by sexual intercourse.

MISHNAH QIDDUSHIN 1.1

As I've already noted, to use rabbinic evidence for life in the first century is problematic. This particular tradition, however, is also represented by a marriage contract dating to the early second century. The contract de-clared that Jesus (not that Jesus) and Salome would continue to live to-gether as before. This language indicates that their formal, contracted marriage began with cohabitation.[28]

> One marriage contract identifying a situation of cohabitation may not seem
> like significant evidence. However, given how few Jewish marriage contracts

---

[26]See further Caldwell, *Roman Girlhood*, 74-76.
[27]For instance, Cicero's wife and daughter arranged the daughter's third marriage during Cicero's absence, under the cover of his general permission to act (see Cicero, *Letters to Friends* 75).
[28]Papyrus Hever 65; Oudshoorn, *Relationship*, 424-28; Lieber, "Jewish Women," 341. A third example of this pattern of marriage is found in a contract from the fifth century BCE Jewish community of Elephantine in Egypt (TAD B3.3).

> (or other written documentation of the lives of ordinary people) exist for the time period, this single reference represents a significant proportion of the available evidence.

Similar practices were known across the Roman Empire. Suppose a family wanted to make an alliance with another household, but the daughter whose marriage could cement the alliance was too young for legal marriage. They could begin the marriage informally through cohabitation. Roman lawyers identified cohabitation as a form of marriage, and in Egypt cohabitation was an alternative to contracted marriage.[29]

This type of uncontracted marriage was just as legitimate as contracted marriage. Spouses referred to each other as husband and wife. Instead of the formal marriage contract to protect wives' wealth, women made contracts for financial loans to their husbands. Cohabitation essentially replaced the marriage contract as the marker of intent to marry.

The right to marry.

> *Lucia Macrina through her advocate Fannius demanded her deposit*
> *from the property of the deceased soldier Antonius Germanus. Lupus*
> *[the judge] said, "We recognize that deposits are dowries. For such*
> *reasons as these I cannot give a trial. For a soldier cannot marry."*
>
> LEGAL CASE, EGYPT[30]

Lucia Macrina lived with a Roman soldier, Antonius Germanus, in Egypt. She had apparently brought money with her into their common household. After the soldier's death, she sued for the return of this money. The judge, however, identified the money as a dowry. Since soldiers could not legally marry, Lucia Macrina had no right to the return of her property.

Formal, contracted marriage was a privilege reserved for those with wealth, social status, or particular identity markers. Roman citizens could

---

[29]See *Digest* 23.2.24, 48.5.14.8; Papyrus Oxyrhynchus 2.267; Papyrus Kronion 52; and Papyrus Family Tebtunis 20.

[30]Papyrus Cattaoui 1.5-13, modified translation from Sara Elise Phang, *The Marriage of Roman Soldiers (13 BC–AD 235): Law and Family in the Imperial Army*, Columbia Studies in the Classical Tradition 24 (Brill: Leiden, 2001), 399.

not legally marry noncitizens. Elite Romans could not marry slaves, freed slaves, or entertainers. Roman soldiers and enslaved people lacked the right to contract a legal marriage at all.[31] The rabbis also prohibited marriage with slaves. Jews who were illegitimate by birth could not marry legitimately born Jews, and priests were restricted in their options for marriage.[32]

So, in a relationship in which one person fell into these restricted categories, the couple could establish an informal marriage by cohabitation instead of a legally contracted marriage. People in an informal marriage shared a common household and finances. As in the case of Lucia Macrina, the wife might bring a dowry into the marriage. The family raised children together. These relationships were marriages in all but name.[33]

These informal marriages were not illegal. The cohabitors could not be prosecuted for an offense.[34] But the relationships were also not legally recognized. Therefore, as in the case of Lucia Macrina, spouses did not have the rights of a formal, legal marriage with respect to inheritance, the legitimacy of children, or protection for a woman's economic investment.

The lack of legal protection had potentially devastating consequences for enslaved people. Both spouses and their children belonged to their owner, who had the right to sell any one of them, or to free one person without the others. Enslaved men and women did not have the ability to be sexually faithful to their spouses, since slave owners could use their slaves for sex without the slaves' consent. Any relationships between slaves happened at the owner's discretion. Owners could forbid certain alliances or demand sexual relationships between particular slaves.[35]

The absence of legal rights and protections in an informal marriage were serious drawbacks, especially for women and their children. People who could legally marry generally did. However, informal marriage by cohabitation was an acceptable, normal, moral alternative to legally recognized

---

[31]Livy 43.3.1-2; Seneca, *On Benefits* 4.35.1; *Digest* 23.2.44; Ulpian 5.3-5.

[32]Mishnah Gittin 4.5; Ketubbot 1.10; Yevamot 2.4; Qiddushin 3.2, 4.1.

[33]See further Dixon, *Roman Family*, 90-95.

[34]The only ambiguity came when the status of the spouses was unequal. A freeborn woman who entered an informal marriage with a slave, for instance, risked the loss of her own free status (Paul, *Opinions* 2.21A.1-3).

[35]Mt 18:24-25; Seneca the Elder, *Controversies* 4, preface 10; Martial, *Epigrams* 2.48; Plutarch, *Advice* 16; Jennifer Glancy, *Slavery in Early Christianity* (2002; repr. Minneapolis: Fortress, 2006), 21-24, 28-29, 50-53.

marriage. For poor women, soldiers, enslaved people, or others who could not enter a formal, contracted marriage, cohabitation provided a way to live in family life with mutual support.

Concubines.

> *After the death of his wife Vespasian resumed his relations with Caenis,*
> *freedwoman and amanuensis of Antonia, and formerly his mistress; and*
> *even after he became emperor he treated her almost as a lawful wife.*
>
> Suetonius, *Vespasian* 3

For elite men like the emperor Vespasian, concubines provided another alternative to a formal, contractual marriage. Before Vespasian married, he had a committed relationship with a freed slave named Caenis. After his wife died, he resumed his relationship with Caenis. The two were never formally married, but in all other respects, the biographer Suetonius said, their relationship was marital.

The marital aspect of a man's relationship with a concubine included monogamy. A man could have either a wife or a concubine, but not both at the same time. A concubine had to be a legitimate partner for the man (she could not, for instance, be a prostitute, a close relative, or underage). The relationship was marked by the attributes of marriage: companionship, respect, and affection. The concubine, moreover, received the same social respect as a woman in a formal, contracted marriage.[36]

There were distinctions between a formal marriage and concubinage. Cohabitation with a concubine required consent but no contract. Women who were concubines often held a lower social status than their companions. Like Caenis, many were freed slaves. Men were not expected to have children with concubines. Any children were illegitimate and unable to inherit the father's property.[37] This was a significant advantage of concubinage for elite men who already had heirs.

Romans, Jews, and likely therefore also Samaritans recognized a variety of noncontractual, permanent (or semi-permanent) relationships as

---

[36]See Plautus, *Braggard Soldier* 508-509, 1094-1096; Chariton, *Callirhoe* 2.1.5; *Digest* 25.7.1.1-2, 32.49.4, 45.1.121.1; Dixon, *Roman Family*, 94.

[37]See Dixon, *Roman Family*, 93; Cohick, *Women*, 105-106.

acceptable alternatives to a formal, contracted marriage. The range of household situations reminds us that "marriage" is flexible. It is defined and practiced differently in different times, cultures, and spaces. In the first century, the lack of a contract did not make the marital relationship any less legitimate.

THE DEATH OF A SPOUSE

> *To the Spirits of the Deceased Aeturnia Zotica. Annius Flavianus, one of*
> *the ten lictors of Fufidius Pollio, governor of Galatia, to his well-deserving*
> *wife. She lived for fifteen years, five months, and eighteen days; she died*
> *sixteen days after giving birth to her first child, leaving a son alive.*
>
> FUNERARY INSCRIPTION, GALATIA[38]

Scholars estimate that, given the probability of death from childbirth, illness, or injury, marriages in the Roman Empire lasted fifteen years on average.[39] The inscription quoted here was put up by a husband, Annius Flavianus, for his wife Aeturnia Zotica. Their marriage lasted significantly less than fifteen years.

If this was Annius Flavianus's first marriage (and his first child), he might choose to remarry to increase the chance of having an heir survive to adulthood. Remarriage also offered social, political, or economic advantages. On the other hand, Aeturnia Zotica could have been Annius Flavianus's second or third wife. An older widower who had surviving children might choose to protect their inheritance by remaining unmarried or establishing a relationship with a concubine. A poor man might rely on his own (adult) children for sustenance and companionship, as numerous sources indicate.[40]

Given the general lack of good medical care for illness or injury in the ancient world, many wives survived their husbands. The Roman ideal of the *univira*, a woman who had only one spouse in her lifetime, discouraged

---

[38]ILS 1914, translated by Jane F. Gardner and Thomas Wiedemann, *The Roman Household: A Sourcebook* (London: Routledge, 1991), 100.
[39]Richard Saller, "The Roman Family as Productive Unit," in Rawson, *Companion to Families*, 119.
[40]Parkin, "Life Course," 285-89.

remarriage. The fidelity of a wife to her husband's memory brought her honor and praise. However, the ideal did not translate into reality for many women (and, in fact, a law instituted by Augustus required remarriage for childless widows). The demands of poverty, a family's social advancement, and the need for young women to bear children all encouraged women to remarry after a spouse's death (or divorce).[41]

A widow's story.

> It shall be the established right of Babatha, our daughter, that if she
> is widowed and will have no husband, that she may reside in the
> storage room which is a part of the sites of this gift, and may have
> access and egress together with you in that courtyard of the storage
> room, for as long as she is a widow without a husband. But she shall
> not have the rightful authority to bring a husband into that house.
>
> A PROPERTY DEED, ROMAN PALESTINE[42]

In the early second century, a Jewish man in Roman Palestine deeded a portion of his property to his wife. In Jewish practice, a man's property was inherited by his male heirs and unmarried daughters. This property deed circumvented this expectation. The deed includes the provision quoted above: the wife must offer living space to their daughter, Babatha, if her husband died and she needed a home. The daughter's rights were limited, however. If she remarried, she would lose this living space.[43]

> The "Babatha Archive," found in a cave in the Judean desert, preserves a collection of early second-century CE legal documents belonging to Babatha and her family. Babatha's second husband was the father of Shelamzious, whom we have met already. Shelamzious's documents were part of the collection.[44]

---

[41]Plutarch, *Life of Tiberius Gracchus* 1.4; Suetonius, *Galba* 5.1; CIL 5.7453, 6.10230; Cohick, *Women*, 104-5.

[42]Papyrus Yadin 7, modified translation from Yigael Yadin, *The Documents from the Bar Kokhba Period in the Cave of Letters: Hebrew, Aramaic, and Nabatean-Aramaic Papyri*, 2 vols. (Jerusalem: Israel Exploration Society, 2002), 1:81-87.

[43]Oudshoorn, *Relationship*, 241-44.

[44]See Ross S. Kraemer, "Typical and Atypical Jewish Family Dynamics: The Cases of Babatha and Berenice," in *Early Christian Families in Context: An Interdisciplinary Dialogue*, ed. David L. Balch

Babatha was probably married to her first husband when this deed was written. Other documents in the collection indicate that her first husband did die, leaving her a widow with a young son. We don't know whether she moved back into her father's house at that point or made other arrangements.

Babatha's son continued to live with her, though her husband had appointed legal guardians for him in his will. Under the terms of the will, Babatha's brother-in-law was supposed to provide financial support for her son. Various documents relating to legal cases brought by Babatha against her son's guardians suggest the support they provided was not sufficient.[45]

Eventually, like many widows, Babatha remarried. Her second husband, Shelamzious's father, had been married before. In fact, he was possibly still married to his first wife when he married Babatha (it is not clear if he divorced his first wife, or if they had a polygamous marriage). The situation was certainly complicated, and the two wives had several legal disputes over the husband's property.[46]

A widow's vulnerability.

> *This is worship which is pure and faultless before God the*
> *Father: To take care of orphans and widows in their troubles,*
> *and to keep yourself away from the world's pollution.*
>
> JAMES 1:27

In Roman law, women inherited part of their fathers' property. However, relatively few women would have been wealthy enough to support themselves independent of familial connections. The many legal cases in Babatha's archive and the attention to widows in the New Testament represent the potentially precarious social position of women following a husband's death.[47]

---

and Carolyn Osiek, Religion, Marriage, and Family (Grand Rapids, MI: Eerdmans, 2003), 130-56; Cohick, *Women*, 117-18.

[45]Oudshoorn, *Relationship*, 218-20.

[46]Kraemer, "Typical and Atypical Jewish Family Dynamics: The Cases of Babatha and Berenice," in *Early Christian Families in Context*, ed. Balch and Osiek, 139, 149; Oudshoorn, *Relationship*, 221-25.

[47]See also Hylen, *Modest Apostle*, 36-37.

The vulnerability of widows provides an intriguing context for the situation mentioned in 1 Corinthians 5:1: a man had sex with his father's wife (his stepmother). Assuming this woman had remained in her husband's home after his death, she was probably dependent on her stepson for support. Her dependency would complicate her ability to consent.

Paul condemned the man for his actions, but he did not say anything about the woman. This absence may indicate that she was not a member of the church. But it is at least possible that part of the problem with the man's behavior was his abuse of a dependent. The message of not taking advantage of others in 1 Corinthians 6 supports this interpretation.[48]

Since wives did not inherit from their husbands, a widow often had to leave her home. She could take only what she brought to the marriage: her dowry and personal possessions. Under a strict interpretation of the law, the clothing, jewelry, or other items her husband gave her during the marriage all belonged to his estate, and therefore to his heirs. Even regaining the dowry could require legal wrangling.[49]

Babatha had the option of returning to her father's home after her first husband's death. An adult son or married daughter could also provide a living space and support for a widowed mother. If her children were young, though, the widow's legal and financial position was more tenuous. The children belonged to her husband's family, not to the widow herself. Young children often remained with their mothers (as in Babatha's case), but the legal guardians appointed for the children could make other arrangements.[50]

Wealthier widows and older widows with familial connections might choose to remain unmarried. For many women, however, remarriage provided the necessary security of a home, familial relationships, and a social support network.

---

[48]See also Cohick, *Women*, 281.
[49]BGU 4.1104.
[50]See Dixon, *Roman Family*, 42-44, 74-77; Parkin, "Life Course," 281-82.

Unnatural death.

> *Restutus Picenesis and Prima Restuta made this [inscription] for*
> *Prima Florentia, their dearest daughter, who was deprived of her*
> *life by Orfeus, her husband, and thrown into the Tiber. December,*
> *her relative, set this up. She lived sixteen and a half years.*
>
> FUNERARY INSCRIPTION, ROME[51]

Not all wives died of natural causes. This inscription, written by parents in memory of their daughter, recorded her murder at age sixteen. Comparable inscriptions and stories indicate that Prima Florentia was not the only wife to die at her husband's hands.[52]

We do not know anything more about the circumstances of this marriage, or how or why Prima Florentia's murder occurred. But the commonality of violence in Roman society, from a man's power to discipline members of his household to gladiator shows to public crucifixions, makes such occurrences nearly unsurprising. Prima Florentia's story reminds us of the harsh realities of life in the first century.[53]

DIVORCE

> *Zois and Antipatros agree that they have separated from one*
> *another, severing the union which they had formed. . . . It shall*
> *be lawful both for Zois to marry another man and for Antipatros*
> *to marry another woman without either of them being liable.*
>
> DIVORCE AGREEMENT, ALEXANDRIA[54]

With this agreement, Zois and Antipatros announced they had decided to divorce. They stopped living together, and with the return of Zois's dowry,

---

[51]ISIS 321, translated by Emily A. Hemelrijk, *Women and Society in the Roman World: A Sourcebook of Inscriptions from the Roman West* (Cambridge: Cambridge University Press, 2021), 38.

[52]CIL 13.2182; Tacitus, *Annals* 4.22, 16.6; Philostratus, *Lives of the Sophists* 555-556.

[53]See further Caryn A. Reeder, "1 Peter 3:1-6: Biblical Authority and Battered Wives," *Bulletin for Biblical Research* 25 (2015): 527-29.

[54]BGU 4.1103, modified translation from Jane Rowlandson, *Women and Society in Greek and Roman Egypt: A Sourcebook* (Cambridge: Cambridge University Press, 1998), 170.

their marriage was officially over. The documentation of a divorce was not necessary, but (as the last sentence in the agreement indicates) it prevented any accusations of adultery if either spouse established another marriage with someone else.

The procedure for divorce was relatively simple. Under Roman law, husbands and wives both had the right to initiate a divorce. A divorce could be completed by the couple themselves, without the involvement of legal courts. There was no shame associated with divorce, and people who had been divorced could remarry.[55]

Of course, individual circumstances complicated the simplicity of divorce. Zois and Antipatros both agreed to divorce, but sometimes only one spouse wanted the divorce. Since children remained with their father, some mothers might be reluctant to pursue divorce. The return of a woman's dowry sometimes had to be negotiated through legal courts. The involvement of each spouse's family in both arranging and ending a marriage also added difficulties. Nonetheless, Suzanne Dixon says, divorce was "quite common and casual."[56]

Jewish customs of divorce varied slightly from Roman practices. According to Josephus and to rabbinic tradition, only husbands had the right of divorce, not wives. However, Jewish women could (and did) divorce under Roman law instead. The provision in Shelamzious's marriage contract that her husband must return her dowry if she or her representatives asked for it implied the potential for divorce.[57]

The rabbis also detailed specific regulations for the divorce papers mentioned in Deuteronomy 24:1. Their concern with ensuring the legitimacy of the woman's future children indicated that divorced people were expected to remarry.[58] As in Roman society, there was apparently no shame in divorce.

> According to Mark 10:1-12, Jesus rejected divorce. A parallel text in Matthew 19:3-9 allows divorce only in the case of adultery. Both texts assume that divorce was

---

[55]See Dixon, *Roman Family*, 81.
[56]Dixon, *Roman Family*, 77.
[57]Josephus, *Jewish Antiquities* 15.259-260, 18.136; Cohick, *Women*, 116; Lieber, "Jewish Women," 340.
[58]Mishnah Gittin 3.1, 9.4.

enacted by husbands against wives. Prohibiting this kind of unilateral divorce could protect women against unjust situations.

Paul also discouraged divorce, though he admitted the possibility of divorce when the husband and wife were not both Christians (1 Cor 7:15).

Deciding on divorce.

> *Augustus gave his daughter Julia in marriage first to Marcellus,*
> *son of his sister Octavia and hardly more than a boy; and then after*
> *his death to Marcus Agrippa, prevailing upon his sister to yield*
> *her son-in-law to him. For at that time Agrippa was married to one*
> *of Octavia's daughters and had children from her. When Agrippa also died,*
> *Augustus, after considering various alliances for a long time,*
> *even in the equestrian order, finally chose his stepson Tiberius,*
> *obliging him to divorce his wife, who was with child*
> *and by whom he was already a father.*
>
> Suetonius, Augustus 63.1-2

The marital history of Julia, daughter of emperor Augustus, demonstrates familial involvement in marriage and divorce. In order to advance his own political goals, Augustus forced first his nephew and then his stepson to divorce their wives in order to marry his daughter.

Elsewhere, Suetonius described Tiberius's distress at divorcing his first wife to marry Julia. Despite Augustus's machinations, Julia and Tiberius did not have a successful marriage. She was accused of adultery and exiled from Rome. When Tiberius became emperor after Augustus's death, he ended the support her father had provided for her, and she died as a result.[59]

Adultery was defined by the marital status of the woman (a married man was only guilty of adultery if his partner was a married woman). Laws instituted under Augustus made adultery a criminal offense. Husbands had to divorce wives who were convicted of adultery. The wives and their lovers were further

---

[59]Suetonius, *Tiberius* 7.2-3; Tacitus, *Annals* 1.53.

> punished by the loss of personal property (including part of the dowry) and exile to separate islands.[60]

Augustus had his own complex marital history. He ended one betrothal so that he could marry the stepdaughter of a political rival to mark their reconciliation. However, he divorced this woman before they lived together because of a disagreement with her mother. He also divorced his next wife (who had herself been married twice before), this time because she irritated him. Augustus then forced another woman to divorce her husband, even though she was pregnant at the time, in order to marry him.[61]

Augustus's family history covers a range of reasons for beginning and ending a marriage: political, social, and economic advantages for families; fundamental incompatibility; a wife's infidelity. Infertility was also sometimes cited as reason for a divorce (though its acceptability was debated).[62] Rabbinic tradition added a bad reputation, burned meals, and the opportunity to pursue a more attractive woman as reasons for a man to divorce his wife.[63] While the Romans and the Jews valued long-lasting marriages that ended only with a spouse's death, they also recognized many reasons for ending a marriage that was no longer satisfactory to the various people involved.

A woman's rights.

> *To Protarchos. From Tryphaine, daughter of Dioskourides.*
>
> *Asklepiades, to whom I am married, persuaded my parents, though*
> *I was unwilling, to give me to him as my caretaker. . . . My accuser,*
> *Asklepiades, since he kept going off throughout the marriage for no*
> *reason, squandered my dowry, abused me and insulted me, and*
> *laying his hands on me, he used me as if I were his bought slave.*
>
> LEGAL DOCUMENT, ALEXANDRIA[64]

---

[60]See *Acta Divi Augustus*, quoted in Jo-Ann Shelton, *As the Romans Did: A Sourcebook in Roman Social History*, 2nd ed. (Oxford: Oxford University Press, 1998), 55; Dixon, *Roman Family*, 78-81.
[61]Suetonius, *Augustus* 62.1-2.
[62]See Laudatio Turiae 2.31-47; Valerius Maximus 2.1.4; Dixon, *Roman Family*, 68-69.
[63]Mishnah Gittin 4.7-8, 9.10. See also Josephus, *Jewish Antiquities* 4.253, *Life* 426.
[64]BGU 4.1105, translation from Rowlandson, *Women*, 324-25.

Women had the right to divorce under Roman law, but it was not always easy for a woman to pursue her rights. Tryphaine's parents married her to her husband against her own expressed desire in the first place. In this document, she sought the assistance of the legal system to end her marriage and regain her property.

Tryphaine made two complaints against her husband Asklepiades. First, he wasted her dowry, the money that he should have preserved for her. Second, he also abused her, treating her like a slave rather than a freeborn woman. Excessive physical abuse, misuse of dowry, and abandonment are common reasons cited in the (admittedly sparse) examples of women's choice to divorce a husband.[65]

Women's legal right to divorce husbands was constrained by various factors. Could she get her full dowry back? Did she have children? Lacking an arrangement between the parents, they would stay with the father, adding to the wife's emotional and social loss. Where (and how) would she live? These questions made the exercise of the right to divorce more problematic for a woman.

THE SAMARITAN WOMAN'S MARITAL HISTORY

According to the majority interpretation of John 4:4-42, Jesus' review of the Samaritan woman's marital history represented his condemnation of her sin. She forced her husbands to divorce her on account of her disobedience, adultery, or infertility. She chose to remarry out of her own sinful sexual desires or, alternatively, to satisfy her longing for relationship. The woman's five marriages and current cohabitation were the result of her own actions. The men were the victims of her sin.

The expectations, practices, and laws of marriage among Jews and Romans provide a context for reconsidering the Samaritan woman's marital history. First, marriage in the first century had two primary purposes. It functioned to ally two households for their mutual economic, social, and political advantage, and it provided a means for the birth of legitimate children. Marriage was not fundamentally emotional or romantic. Marital respect and love were the consequence of a shared life rather than the reason for sharing life.

---

[65]See also BGU 8.1848; Quintilian, *Orator's Education* 7.8.2; Seneca, *On Benefits* 4.27.

This point is worth emphasizing. In the first century, marriage was not about relationship. It was not even about the two people who were married. Marriage was instead about family, community, and economy. To be married was to participate in and contribute to communal life.

Second, women did have legal rights in the first century. Their consent was necessary for a valid marriage, and they could divorce their husbands. But these rights were limited by social and cultural expectations of a father's authority over even adult daughters and of daughters' obedience to their fathers. Finances, housing, and children also constricted women's ability to refuse a marriage, to divorce, or to remain unmarried following the end of a marriage.

This context undermines the characterization of the Samaritan woman as sexual sinner. Instead of a woman looking for love in all the wrong places, we have a woman who was socialized into the expectation that she would marry for the good of her family and community. She would have prepared for marriage by learning how to manage a household and by gaining skills that would allow her to contribute to the household economy. Her spouse (and his family) was selected by her family. Her consent was essentially inevitable.

For one woman to have six marital relationships is certainly unusual (though see Mk 12:18-23!). Among other records, the Roman general Pompey comes closest with five marriages (two ending in divorce, and three in death), followed by Augustus and his four wives (plus one fiancée). Three seems to be the most marriages recorded for a woman. We can't know the exact circumstances of the Samaritan woman's multiple marriages or her current situation. But the practices of marriage, mortality, divorce, and remarriage in the first century suggest some possibilities.

First, she may not have cohabited with each husband. In Matthew 1:18-19, Joseph wants to divorce his fiancée before their marriage was completed, and the rabbis recognized that betrothals could end with divorce or death before the marriage began.[66] Augustus also divorced his first wife before they lived together. These parallels offer a possible explanation for one or more of the Samaritan woman's marriages.

Second, the woman probably married for the first time between ages twelve and fifteen, to a man at least ten years older than herself. Her husband

---

[66]Mishnah Ketubbot 4.2.

could have died due to age, injury, or disease. The woman may, in fact, have survived the deaths of several husbands, as Augustus's daughter Julia did. Some of the woman's marriages may have ended in divorce for a variety of reasons: abuse; incompatibility; a more advantageous match for either the woman's family or her husband's.

Adultery was one reason for divorce among Romans or Jews, but there is no reason to assume the Samaritan woman was divorced by her husbands for adultery. Rather, the fact of her remarriages suggests she was not suspected or convicted of adultery. Likewise, the evidence for divorce on account of infertility is slim (and again, the woman's remarriages would argue against a reputation for infertility).[67] The Samaritan woman may have had several children, or she may have had several childless marriages end for a variety of causes.

Third, remarriage following the death of a spouse or divorce was very common across the Roman Empire. Depending on the woman's family circumstances, she may have needed to remarry for her own thriving, to advance her family's financial, social, or political standing, or for the social value of shared life. Despite Tertullian's assertions, remarriage did not make the woman into a prostitute.

Finally, cohabitation was an acceptable alternative to formal, contractual marriage in the Roman Empire. Perhaps the woman could not formally marry her sixth man due to differences in their status or identity. Perhaps the man was a Roman citizen or soldier stationed in Sychar as part of the imperial administration. Perhaps he was a freed slave or from a priestly family. An alliance with a man like this could have benefited her family and community with access to economic and political resources.

> Other suggestions for the Samaritan woman's sixth man include a situation of levirate marriage and polygamy.[68] In addition, David Lose raises the possibility that the woman's sixth relationship was nonsexual. Maybe she was simply a dependent on the man.[69] However, John 4:16-18 parallels her current situation with

---

[67]See also Cohick, *Women*, 123-24.

[68]See Gail R. O'Day and Susan E. Hylen, *John*, Westminster Bible Companion (Louisville: Westminster John Knox, 2006), 53; Cohick, *Women*, 126.

[69]David Lose, "Misogyny, Moralism and the Woman at the Well," *HuffPost*, March 21, 2011, www .huffpost.com/entry/misogyny-moralism-and-the_b_836753.

> her five previous marriages. "Having" and "man" (or "woman") together refer to marital relationships and sexual encounters throughout the Bible (for instance, Deut 28:30; Mt 22:28; 1 Cor 5:1, 7:2).

Perhaps the woman's current man already had heirs, and he did not want to split his property with additional children from their relationship. Considering the time needed to establish and end five marriages, the woman herself was probably older by the time she met Jesus at the well. As an elder in the community, she may have sought her current relationship for security and companionship rather than procreation.[70]

If we understand marriage as a business arrangement rather than a romantic endeavor, then the woman's five marriages become significantly less scandalous. If we remember that cohabitation was a culturally acceptable alternative to contracted marriage, then her current situation becomes a practical solution rather than an indication of sexual sin. In all of this—marriage, death, divorce, remarriage, informal marriage—the woman was not (necessarily) at fault in any way.[71] Her marital history was simply the consequence of her time and place.

Jesus did not accuse the Samaritan woman of sin, as he did with others in the Gospel of John. Neither sin nor forgiveness is mentioned in John 4:4-42. To interpret the reference to the woman's marital history as a condemnation of sin is problematic.[72] This story is about something else altogether.

---

[70]See also Cohick, *Women*, 125-27.

[71]So also Janeth Norfleete Day, *The Woman at the Well: Interpretation of John 4:1-42 in Retrospect and Prospect*, Biblical Interpretation Series 61 (Leiden: Brill, 2002), 169-72; John F. McHugh, *A Critical and Exegetical Commentary on John 1–4*, International Critical Commentary (London: T&T Clark, 2009), 281; Marianne Meye Thompson, *John: A Commentary*, New Testament Library (Louisville: Westminster John Knox, 2015), 102-3.

[72]See Lynn Cohick, "The 'Woman at the Well': Was the Samaritan Woman Really an Adulteress?" in *Vindicating the Vixens: Revisiting Sexualized, Vilified, and Marginalized Women of the Bible*, ed. Sandra Glahn (Grand Rapids, MI: Kregel Academic, 2017), 249-53, esp. 252-53.

7

THE SAMARITAN WOMAN'S STORY REIMAGINED

The woman said to him, "Sir, I see that you are a prophet.
Our ancestors worshiped on this mountain. But you and your
people say that the place for worshiping God is in Jerusalem."

JOHN 4:19-20

ONCE SIN AND SEX are removed from the interpretation of John 4:4-42, we're left with a knowledgeable, thoughtful woman who met Jesus beside a well. As they talked, she realized the person she was speaking with was a prophet. Her question about worship opened the space for Jesus to explain his own identity and the new reality that he brought.

The woman did not keep her knowledge about Jesus to herself. She returned to the village to tell all her neighbors. Their immediate response indicated their regard for this woman. They trusted her. Moreover, they believed Jesus because of the woman's witness. Her words had power.

In this chapter, I will explore the Samaritan woman's story again, listening carefully to her words and to Jesus' words. I will consider the structure of the narrative, the echoes of biblical themes and historical contexts, and the ways this story fits into John's Gospel as a whole. This reimagining of John 4:4-42 disrupts the reductive sexualization of the Samaritan woman that has been so common in Christian interpretation. How might the Samaritan woman's story empower women and men in the church today?

THE CONVERSATION

In John's Gospel, Jesus' conversations often turn into monologues about his own identity. In John 3:1-21, for example, the conversation between Jesus and Nicodemus consists of three exchanges. Nicodemus speaks about five sentences, and Jesus replies with approximately twenty sentences. There is little give-and-take represented in this interaction. Rather, Nicodemus's brief, basic questions provide the opportunity for Jesus to preach his own message. This pattern repeats in a number of stories in John (see, for instance, Jn 4:31-38, 6:25-58, and 7:14-29).

By contrast, the conversation between Jesus and the Samaritan woman is lengthy, progressing through seven exchanges. The woman speaks eleven sentences, and Jesus speaks about twenty sentences.[1] Only one of Jesus' responses is long enough to count as a mini-sermon (Jn 4:21-24). Moreover, the woman's questions and comments are integral to the conversation.[2]

Jesus begins the conversation with the Samaritan woman. Initially, she only responds to him. However, between verses 19 and 20, the pattern shifts. After acknowledging Jesus as a prophet, the woman introduces the question of the two places of worship. This opening prompts Jesus' declaration of an entirely new way to worship. In their last exchange, the woman's astute introduction of messianic expectations leads to Jesus' self-revelation.

The attention, space, and initiative given to the Samaritan woman in her conversation with Jesus are remarkable. Her active participation contrasts with the first-century ideal of women's seclusion and silence.[3] However, despite the restrictions on women's lives, women did engage in their

---

[1] Because the earliest Greek manuscripts do not include punctuation marks, counting the number of sentences depends on the interpreter's choice. Jesus speaks between seventeen and twenty sentences.

[2] See also Christine de Pizan, *The Book of the City of Ladies* 1.10.5; Sandra M. Schneiders, *Written That You May Believe: Encountering Jesus in the Fourth Gospel* (New York: Crossroad, 1999), 141; Margaret M. Beirne, *Women and Men in the Fourth Gospel: A Genuine Discipleship of Equals*, Journal for the Study of the New Testament Supplement Series 242 (London: Sheffield Academic, 2003), 73, 81; Frances Gench, *Back to the Well: Women's Encounters with Jesus in the Gospels* (Louisville: Westminster John Knox, 2004), 112.

[3] Livy 34.2.8-13; Plutarch, *Advice to the Bride and Groom* 32; etc. See especially Bruce J. Malina and Richard L. Rohrbaugh, *Social-Science Commentary on the Gospel of John* (Minneapolis: Fortress, 1998), 98-101; Jerome H. Neyrey, "What's Wrong with This Picture? John 4, Cultural Stereotypes of Women, and Public and Private Space," in *A Feminist Companion to John,* ed. Amy-Jill Levine, Feminist Companion to the New Testament and Early Christian Writings 4, 2 vols. (London: Sheffield Academic, 2003), 1:109-11.

communities and contribute to public discourse in the first century. Against this context, the representation of the Samaritan woman in John 4:4-42 is unusual, but it fits into the acceptable, expectable ways women participated in social life.[4]

THE MARRIAGE PLOT

An unmarried man sits down by a well. When a woman comes to draw water, the man asks her for a drink. She offers him water, and they get married. This basic marriage plot repeats (with some variation) through Genesis and Exodus: Isaac's matchmaker finds Rebekah by a well (Gen 24:10-51); Jacob meets Rachel at a well (Gen 29:1-20); Moses meets Zipporah by a well (Ex 2:15-21).

> Zipporah and her sisters are harassed by men at the well, and the rabbis mention a spring as a place a woman might be raped (Mishnah Kettubot 1.10). Jacob's daughter Dinah was assaulted in Shechem, near the well where Jesus met the Samaritan woman (Gen 34:2). The potential for abuse in public spaces is also present in Roman sources. The marriage plot sanitizes the danger by legitimating the relationship.

Weddings are part of the Gospel of John. Jesus, his mother, and his followers attend a wedding dinner in John 2:1-11. This party became the venue for Jesus' first "sign." In John, Jesus' miracles are identified as signs that reveal Jesus' identity (see Jn 2:11, 20:30-31). The location of this first sign at a wedding connects Jesus with the wedding imagery used by the prophets to symbolize Israel's restoration (Is 54:4-8, 62:4-5; Hos 2:19-20).[5]

This message reappears in John 3:28-30. When questioned about Jesus, John the Baptist explains that he is only the friend of the bridegroom. He rejoices to hear the bridegroom's voice—but it is the groom, Jesus, who has the bride. The imagery primes the reader to hear wedding bells when Jesus

---

[4]Compare especially Susan E. Hylen, *A Modest Apostle: Thecla and the History of Women in the Early Church* (Oxford: Oxford University Press, 2015), 10-15, 24-30.
[5]Compare also Mt 22:1-14, 25:1-13; Rev 21:9-10; Raymond E. Brown, *The Gospel According to John (I–XII)*, Anchor Bible 29 (New York: Doubleday, 1966), 105; John F. McHugh, *A Critical and Exegetical Commentary on John 1-4*, International Critical Commentary (London: T&T Clark, 2009), 267.

sits down by a well and asks a woman for a drink.[6] The bridegroom is looking for his bride. If this woman offers Jesus water, readers know what will happen next.

But, in the first of several twists in the expectations provoked by the narrative, the woman doesn't offer Jesus water. Instead, she challenges him: "How do you, a Jew, from me—a Samaritan woman!—ask for a drink?" (Jn 4:9). The awkward word order here emphasizes the ethnic distinction between Jesus and the woman. The marriage plot is disrupted by questions of identity.

DIVIDED IDENTITY

Questions of identity run through the story of the woman's conversation with Jesus. The problem is clarified in the explanation of her response to Jesus' request for water: "For Jews don't associate with Samaritans" (Jn 4:9). The woman's references to Jacob and the place of worship draw attention to the divide between the two peoples. This story is about contested identity and the tensions that result.

The history of the divide between the Jews and Samaritans is complex. Each group tells their own versions of their respective origins, and scholars today offer different interpretations of these traditions and their historical realities. Before exploring the tensions represented in John 4:4-42, then, I will review the development of the divide and the effects of the divide for Jews and Samaritans in the first century.

Origin stories. Samaritan traditions dating to the Middle Ages claim that the Samaritans are the true Israelites. The people who later became the Jews broke away from them in the time of the priest Eli, who set up his own worship site at Shiloh (though the rest of the people already worshiped at Mt. Gerizim).[7] These traditions reflect the identification of Mt. Gerizim as the place chosen by God for worship in the Samaritans' version of the Pentateuch (the first five books of the Bible).

---

[6]See especially Adeline Fehribach, *The Women in the Life of the Bridegroom: A Feminist Historical-Literary Analysis of the Female Characters in the Fourth Gospel* (Collegeville, MN: Liturgical, 1998), 29-30, 47-50; Schneiders, *Written That*, 135; Gench, *Back to the Well*, 112-13.

[7]Abu'l-Fath, *Kitab al-Tarikh*, quoted in Robert T. Anderson and Terry Giles, *The Keepers: An Introduction to the History and Culture of the Samaritans* (Peabody, MA: Hendrickson, 2002), 11-12. See also Lidija Novakovic, "Jews and Samaritans," in *The World of the New Testament: Cultural, Social, and Historical Contexts*, ed. Joel B. Green and Lee Martin McDonald (Grand Rapids, MI: Baker Academic, 2013), 211.

The Samaritans only identify the five books of the Pentateuch as Scripture. Their version of the Pentateuch is mostly the same as the text preserved in the Jewish and Christian Bibles. However, Mt. Gerizim is identified as the place God chose for worship. Moses' singular importance is emphasized, and so is the expectation for a new prophet like Moses to teach the people (Deut 18:15-18).[8]

The Jews tell a different version of this story. Josephus (a historian in the late first century) identified the Samaritans with the foreigners who were forced to move into Samaria, the central hill country of ancient Israel, following the Assyrian conquest (2 Kings 17:24-41). These people learned to worship Israel's God. Then, in the fourth century BCE, some Jewish priests who had married non-Jewish women, along with other Jews accused of breaking the Torah, joined the Samaritans and built a temple on Mt. Gerizim. Josephus's Samaritans are sort of Jewish, and sort of not—a perspective shared by later rabbinic tradition.[9]

Scholars today suggest both versions of the Samaritans' origins are partially accurate. As Lidija Novakovic explains, the Samaritans were probably Israelites from the northern kingdom. Like other Israelites, they were monotheistic and lived according to the Torah. Though they worshiped at Mt. Gerizim rather than in Jerusalem, there was significant interaction between the Samaritans and other Israelites.

The division between "the Jews" and "the Samaritans" occurred slowly from the construction of the temple on Mt. Gerizim in the fifth century until its destruction in the second century BCE by John Hyrcanus (king of the Jewish Hasmonean kingdom).[10] Following this act of war, each group claimed to be the true people of God, to the exclusion of the other.[11] The contested identity that runs through John 4:4-42 reflects this division.

[8]See Robert T. Anderson and Terry Giles, *The Samaritan Pentateuch: An Introduction to Its Origin, History, and Significance for Biblical Studies*, SBL Resources for Biblical Study 72 (Atlanta: Society of Biblical Literature, 2012), 74-102.
[9]Josephus, *Jewish Antiquities* 9.288-290, 11.306-312, 11.346-347; Mishnah Demai 3.4; Nedarim 3.10; Sheqalim 1.5. See also 2 Macc 5:22-23; Anderson and Giles, *Keepers*, 42-47; Novakovic, "Jews and Samaritans," 209-11.
[10]Josephus, *Jewish War* 1.62-65.
[11]See Novakovic, "Jews and Samaritans," 212-13; and also Anderson and Giles, *Samaritan Pentateuch*, 16-22.

Jews and Samaritans in the first century. In the first century, some Jews and Samaritans got along with each other, did business together, and shared meals together. One of Herod the Great's wives was Samaritan. Jews and Samaritans allied against Herod's son Archelaus. Samaritans celebrated holy days in the temple in Jerusalem.[12] Jews from Galilee traveled through Samaria on their way to and from Jerusalem, as Jesus and the disciples did in John 4:4-42. It was not a problem for the disciples to purchase food from the Samaritans.

There were also incidents of violence between Jews and Samaritans. Josephus recorded the murder of a Jew as he traveled through Samaria to Jerusalem, followed by violent reprisals by Jews against the Samaritans.[13] Jesus' disciples' desire to call down fire from heaven to destroy a Samaritan village in Luke 9:52-56 represents similar hostility. Josephus and the rabbis both accused the Samaritans of deliberately disrupting Jewish worship.[14] Rabbinic traditions also identified the Samaritans as unclean: "Someone who eats the bread of the Samaritans is like to one who eats the flesh of swine," in one strong statement![15]

Despite their common origins and instances of neighborliness, the Jews and the Samaritans in the first century had a troubled relationship.[16] Acts of violence and accusations of impurity reflect what we might today identify as racism. This context helps explain the association of being a Samaritan with being possessed by a demon in John 8:48. The people who accuse Jesus of both clearly intend to insult him. This context also frames the Samaritan woman's conversation with Jesus.

Contested identity in John 4:4-42. The tension between the Jews and Samaritans is overt in John 4:4-42. The woman questions Jesus' request for water precisely because of their ethnic identities (v. 9). She then mentions "our ancestor Jacob" who dug the well. The explanation of the significance of the site in verses 5-6 and 12 offers a reminder of the historical

---

[12]Josephus, *Jewish War* 1.562, 2.111; *Jewish Antiquities* 18.30. See also Lk 17:11-19; Mishnah Berakot 7.1, 8.8.

[13]Josephus, *Jewish War* 2.232-235.

[14]Josephus, *Antiquities* 18.30; Mishnah Rosh Hashanah 2.2.

[15]Mishnah Shevi'it 8.10, modified translation from Herbert Danby, *The Mishnah: Translated from the Hebrew with Introduction and Brief Explanatory Notes* (Oxford: Oxford University Press, 1933), 49. See also Mishnah Niddah 4.1.

[16]Anderson and Giles, *Samaritan Pentateuch*, 106-17.

tensions between the two communities, both of whom claimed ownership of the land on account of their ancestry.

> In Genesis 33:18-20, Jacob purchases land near Shechem for his family. The Samaritans were historically associated with Shechem (many Samaritans still live nearby in the modern Palestinian city of Nablus).

The "our" in the woman's statement in John 4:12 is ambiguous. She may mean that Jacob is the common ancestor of the Jews and the Samaritans. However, given the emphasis on ethnic identity, she may mean Jacob is the ancestor of the Samaritans alone, not the Jews. The woman's question implies Jesus the Jew is nothing like "our" Jacob (later, in Jn 4:20, the woman clearly distinguishes between the Samaritans' ancestors and the Jews).[17]

Tensions over identity remain central through the story. But before we turn to the divisive issue of worship, notice what has happened in John 4:10-15. This story began with a marriage plot, but the woman's questions disrupted the expected conclusion. Now, Jesus has upended the marriage plot entirely by offering the woman water—and she accepts! The bridegroom has become the bride.

THE WATER

John's Gospel is full of symbolism, metaphor, and imagery. Jesus is the Word, the vine, a lamb, the good shepherd. The temple is a building in Jerusalem and Jesus' own body. Entering the kingdom of God requires rebirth (Jn 1:1, 1:29, 2:14-21, 3:3-7, 10:11, 15:1). And in John 4:7-15, water is both actual water that a person can draw from a well to drink and something more: living water that becomes an internal spring, leaping up into eternal life.

> "Living water" in the Bible refers to spring water or running water in a river, in contrast to standing water (in a cistern, for instance). Wells can be fed by

---

[17]See further J. Ramsey Michaels, *The Gospel of John*, New International Commentary on the New Testament (Grand Rapids, MI: Eerdmans, 2010), 242; Anderson and Giles, *Samaritan Pentateuch*, 128-29.

> underground springs or filled with (living) rainwater. In John 4:6, Jacob's well is described as a spring, suggesting it had a living water source.[18]

In the early fourth century, a Christian pilgrim visited the Samaritan woman's well. At that time, the well was used to fill a baptismal pool at the site (another pilgrimage account also mentions a church). This liturgical use of the well represents one interpretation of the imagery of water in John 4:7-15.[19] The references to the work of baptism by Jesus and John the Baptist in John 3:22-23 and 4:1-3 encourage this connection.

Later in the narrative, Jesus repeats his offer of water to the thirsty. In John 7:37-39, the living water flowing out of a believer is identified with the Holy Spirit. The similar descriptions layer this meaning into John 4:13-14.[20] The connection circles back to the baptism with the Spirit in John 1:32-33 (note also Jn 3:5-8).

These associations are deepened by the water imagery that flows through the Bible. Wisdom, righteousness, and the fear of the Lord are represented as living springs in Proverbs (Prov 10:11, 13:14, 14:27, 16:22). In Jeremiah 2:13, God is a spring of living water. Wells of salvation, springs of water, and rivers flooding the land symbolize the salvation of Israel's restoration from exile in Isaiah (Is 12:3, 41:17-18, 44:3, 49:10, 55:1, 58:11).[21]

This background enriches the imagery of springs of water, the gift of water, and thirstiness in John 4:7-15.[22] Of course, the Samaritan Bible included only the first five books of the Jewish Bible, so if the Samaritan woman recognized the symbolism of Jesus' references, she may not have made all these connections.[23] She might, however, have remembered Hagar, to whom God

---

[18]Ernst Haenchen, *John 1: A Commentary on the Gospel of John Chapters 1-6*, Hermeneia (Philadelphia: Fortress, 1984), 219, describes how a well like this would work, and Michaels, *John*, 236-37, 241-43, discusses the differences between springs, wells, and the kinds of water they give.

[19]"Pilgrim from Bordeaux" 588; Jerome, *Letter* 108.13. The same connection is made by Cyprian, *Epistle* 62.8; and in early Christian art, which is discussed by Janeth Norfleete Day, *The Woman at the Well: Interpretation of John 4:1-42 in Retrospect and Prospect*, Biblical Interpretation Series 61 (Leiden: Brill, 2002), 56-63. See further R. Brown, *John*, 179-80.

[20]See also Marianne Meye Thompson, *John: A Commentary*, New Testament Library (Louisville: Westminster John Knox, 2015), 99.

[21]See also Joel 3:18, Zech 14:8.

[22]See further R. Brown, *John*, 178-79; Craig Keener, *The Gospel of John: A Commentary*, 2 vols. (Grand Rapids, MI: Baker Academic, 2003), 1:603-5; McHugh, *John*, 273-75.

[23]See, however, Gail R. O'Day and Susan E. Hylen, *John*, Westminster Bible Companion (Louisville: Westminster John Knox, 2006), 53.

showed a well of living water when she and her son were dying of thirst (Gen 21:19), or God's provision of water during Israel's exodus from Egypt (Deut 8:14-16). In John 4:10 (and even more clearly in Jn 7:37-38), Jesus assumes this divine function for himself.

THE FINAL TWIST: THE WOMAN'S MARITAL STATUS

The marriage plot hovering behind John 4:7 is disrupted first by the ethnic divide between Jews and Samaritans and second by the woman's failure to offer Jesus water. A third disruption comes in John 4:16-18: the woman is not available. She has been married five times, and she currently has a man.

> For Origen, the woman's marriages were an allegory of seeker's spiritual growth. Augustine, Aquinas, and others adapted similar interpretations with the husbands representing the senses and reason, or the Pentateuch and heterodox teachers. These interpretations draw attention to the woman's gradual growth in understanding in John 4:4-42.
>
> A number of scholars and pastors today propose another possibility: the five husbands represent the gods of the five peoples resettled in Samaria by the Assyrians, with the sixth man being Israel's God (see 2 Kings 17:29-33). In this reading, the woman's marital history symbolizes Samaritan history. The consistent use of marriage as an image for God's relationship with Israel through the prophets strengthens this interpretation. It fits well with the identification of Jesus as bridegroom in John too.[24]
>
> John's Gospel relies heavily on symbolism throughout. It is certainly possible that the woman's marital history is itself symbolic. Despite Josephus's interpretation of Samaritan origins, though, it's not clear that many Jews or Samaritans in the first century would have made a particular connection with the five nations (who worshiped seven gods, according to 2 Kings). J. Ramsey Michaels also suggests that the woman's reference to "all she had done" in John 4:29 argues against an allegorical interpretation.[25]

---

[24]See especially Fehribach, *Bridegroom*, 65-69; Schneiders, *Written That*, 139-41; McHugh, *John*, 281-82.
[25]Michaels, *John*, 247.

As we have seen, interpreters from the third century onwards have understood the woman's marital history as her own sin. The review of the evidence of women's lives in the first century in the previous two chapters suggests this approach is fundamentally flawed. Women had limited rights or choice with respect to marriage and divorce. Rather than being a sinful abnormality, remarriage was expected for widows and divorced women. Finally, cohabitation was a common, acceptable alternative to formal, contractual marriage.

In this context, the Samaritan woman's marital history may be unusual. However, unusual does not mean immoral or sinful. If John 4:4-42 was primarily about sin, we would expect sin to be mentioned. It is not. The woman's marital history and current cohabitation are not identified as sin. Jesus does not condemn her, nor does he offer her forgiveness.[26]

By contrast, Jesus warns a man against continuing to sin in John 5:14. He frequently addresses sin when speaking with "the Jews," and they accuse him of sin too (Jn 8:21-34, 8:46, 9:16-31, 9:41, 15:22-24, 16:8-11). The Gospel also highlights the forgiveness of sin made possible through Jesus (Jn 1:29, 8:24, 8:34-36, 20:23). The threads of sin and forgiveness running through the book make the absence of any reference to sin or forgiveness in John 4:4-42 really quite remarkable and important.

Sometimes interpreters bring Jesus' words in John 8:11 into John 4. The story of the woman accused of adultery in John 8:2-11 is not found in the earliest manuscripts of John's Gospel. It interrupts the narrative time of John (Jn 8:12 and following continue the story that begins in Jn 7:37). For these reasons, I think John 8:2-11 may be part of the oral tradition of Jesus' life that circulated in the early church, but it probably was not original to the Gospel of John.[27]

Since the story has long been incorporated into the Gospel of John, it is useful to contrast John 8:2-11 with John 4:4-42. Sin is explicitly present in the story of the woman accused of adultery, though notably the story equates adultery with other sins (that is, the woman's act is not somehow worse than her accusers' sins). The presence of sin in John 8:2-11 again underscores its absence from John 4:4-42.

---

[26]See also McHugh, *John*, 281; M. Thompson, *John*, 102-3.
[27]See further R. Brown, *John*, 332-38.

According to the majority interpretation, the timing of the story re-inforces the Samaritan woman's sin. Only a social outcast would fetch water alone at noon.[28] The evidence cited as support is very slim (Gen 24:11 and 1 Sam 9:11), though. An equal amount of evidence places women at wells in broad daylight (Gen 29:7 and Josephus, *Jewish Antiquities* 2.257-258). As Lynn Cohick says, it would be nice to share the work of drawing water with others at a cool time of day, but doing so alone at noon is not immoral.[29]

There is no suggestion of social ostracism in John 4:4-42, either. Rather, the woman's neighbors (who certainly know her marital history) listen to her and believe in Jesus on account of her testimony (Jn 4:39-42). Their lack of concern or judgment against the woman gives interpreters a model to follow.

The timing of the story is important, but it points to salvation rather than sin. In John's Gospel, Jesus is associated with light, while darkness symbolizes unbelief and wickedness.[30] In his last words prior to John 4:7, Jesus told Nicodemus (who came to Jesus in the dark of night) that evildoers hate the light. They refuse to enter it so that their deeds won't be exposed. Those who enact truth, however, come into the light so that everyone can see their deeds have been done in God (Jn 3:20-21).[31]

The bright light of noon reveals the Samaritan woman's deeds (note Jn 4:29!). She was human, and presumably as fallible as any other human. But, according to the contrast set out by Jesus in John 3:20-21, she was not an evildoer. For the reader of the Gospel, the timing of the story associates her with the truth, with God, and with Jesus himself.

In John 4:11, 15, and 19, the Samaritan woman calls Jesus "sir," a word that could also be translated as "lord." For the woman within the story, the title acts as a polite term of respect for a stranger. For the reader of the story, the title

---

[28]See Leon Morris, *The Gospel According to John*, New International Commentary on the New Testament, rev. ed. (Grand Rapids, MI: Eerdmans, 1995), 228; Neyrey, "What's Wrong," 109; etc.

[29]Lynn H. Cohick, *Women in the World of the Earliest Christians* (Grand Rapids, MI: Baker Academic, 2009), 123.

[30]See Jn 1:4-5, 8:12, 9:5, 11:9-10, 12:35-36, 12:46.

[31]For the extension of Jesus' words through Jn 3:21 (represented in many translations, including CEB and NRSV), see also M. Thompson, *John*, 77.

anticipates the honor given to Jesus (e.g., Jn 6:23, 6:68, 9:38, 11:2). The Samaritan woman is the first person in the Gospel to call Jesus "lord."

Rather than condemning her sin, Jesus' knowledge of the Samaritan woman's life leads to her recognition of his identity (as happens with Nathanael in Jn 1:47-49).[32] The story of the woman at the well is about the woman, and Jesus' reference to the woman's own history gives readers insight into one aspect of her life. The point of the reference is not to record one woman's life, however, but to reveal Jesus' own identity.

As the disrupted marriage plot concludes, a new narrative window opens. Because Jesus is a prophet, the woman can ask the burning question of her day. Where should God be worshiped, in Jerusalem or Mt. Gerizim? Who are the true people of God—the Samaritans, or the Jews?

TEMPLES, WORSHIP, AND THE PEOPLE OF GOD

The Samaritan woman's reference to the two places of worship reintroduces the divide between the Samaritans and Jews. Both peoples agreed that there should be only one place in which sacrifices could be offered to God. For the Jews, of course, this place was Jerusalem. For the Samaritans, the place for worship was Mt. Gerizim.

In Deuteronomy 11:29, 27:11-26, Moses instructs the Israelites to pronounce the blessings of the covenant from Mt. Gerizim, and the curses from its neighbor, Mt. Ebal. Mount Gerizim is only referenced a few other times in the Jewish Bible. In the Samaritan Bible, however, Mt. Gerizim is clearly identified as the one place God has chosen for worship.[33] Jacob's well is located in the valley at the foot of Mt. Gerizim. When the woman says her ancestors worshiped on "this mountain," she means the mountain right beside them.

Archaeological evidence suggests a temple was built on Mt. Gerizim in the mid-fifth century BCE. Samaritans offered sacrifices and celebrated festivals there. In the late third century, following the destruction of the major city of Samaria during Alexander the Great's invasion, the temple on Mt.

---

[32]See also Beirne, *Women and Men*, 82-83; Gench, *Back to the Well*, 117; O'Day and Hylen, *John*, 54; Michaels, *John*, 247.

[33]See Anderson and Giles, *Samaritan Pentateuch*, 90-96.

Gerizim became an even more important site of social, economic, and political power. As mentioned above, this temple was destroyed by the Jewish ruler John Hyrcanus in the late second century BCE.[34]

By the Samaritan woman's day, any temple buildings were long gone, though the Samaritans continued to offer sacrifices and celebrate festivals on Mt. Gerizim (as they do today). The lack of a temple did not change the identification of Mt. Gerizim as the one and only chosen place for worship in the Samaritan community.

> Mt. Gerizim was the only location for sacrificial worship, but the Samaritans did not only pray or praise God in that single space. In the first century, they also had synagogues for study of the Bible and prayer, and religious practices were incorporated into the daily life of households.[35]

When Jesus and the Samaritan woman met at Jacob's well, they were overshadowed by the mountain and by the debate over the place of worship. The woman's contrast between "our" ancestors and "you" Jews in John 4:20 connects the location of worship with identity. Her comment raises the key underlying question: Who is right? Are the Samaritans the people of God, or the Jews?

Jesus' response reinforced the differences between the two peoples. He said that the Samaritans worshiped what they did not know. Salvation came from the Jews, not the Samaritans. That is, the Jews have the entire scope of the Bible, while the Samaritans accepted only the Pentateuch as authoritative Scripture. The Jews, therefore, had the prophetic, Davidic expectations for a messianic restoration—the Samaritans did not.[36]

While Jesus affirmed the distinction between Jewish and Samaritan traditions, his affirmation is sandwiched within a challenge to both. Neither the temple in Jerusalem nor Mt. Gerizim were the one right place for worship. Both were replaced by "spirit and truth."

---

[34]See Anderson and Giles, *Samaritan Pentateuch*, 16-20; Novakovic, "Jews and Samaritans," 212-13.
[35]Anderson and Giles, *Keepers*, 131.
[36]See also D. A. Carson, *The Gospel According to John*, Pillar New Testament Commentary (Grand Rapids, MI: Eerdmans, 1991), 223; Keener, *John*, 1:610-11. Note the critique of the imperialistic superiority running through the story in Muse W. Dube, "Reading for Decolonization (John 4:1-42)," *Semeia* 75 (1996): 50-52.

This message reflects a theme developed through John 1–2. For first-century Jews, God's presence dwelt in the temple in Jerusalem. Access to this holy space was restricted. In Jesus, however, God "camps out" among the people (Jn 1:14). The word used here is the verbal form of "tabernacle," recalling the presence of God dwelling among the Israelites during the exodus from Egypt. In other words, in Jesus, God tabernacles among the people, making God's glory visible. Jesus replaces the function of the temple with his own person (Jn 2:13-21).[37]

The Samaritan woman missed the grand symbolism of Jesus' action performed in Jerusalem days earlier. But as a representative of the Samaritan people, she now heard the significant consequences of Jesus' identity. First, access to the holy spaces of worship was no longer restricted. Second, the historic divide between the Samaritans and Jews was over.[38] The shift from "place" to "spirit and truth" opens the opportunity for worship to all.

JESUS' IDENTITY, PART TWO

> *The woman said, "I know that when the messiah (that*
> *is, the christ) comes, he will tell us everything." Jesus said*
> *to her, "That's me, the one speaking with you."*
>
> JOHN 4:25-26

The Samaritan woman's immediate response to Jesus may indicate a certain amount of confusion. Jesus has, after all, just challenged a fundamental theological understanding held by both Jews and Samaritans, so perhaps she wants more explanation. On the other hand, O'Day and Hylen point out that the woman's introduction of messianic expectations recognizes the eschatological connotations of Jesus' words.[39] Read in this way, her comment advances the conversation.

---

[37]See George R. Beasley-Murray, *John*, Word Biblical Commentary 36 (Waco: Word, 1987), 59; Keener, *John*, 1:408-12; M. Thompson, *John*, 104-5.

[38]See further Keener, *John*, 1:611; F. Scott Spencer, "'You Just Don't Understand' (or Do You?): Jesus, Women, and Conversation in the Fourth Gospel," in *Feminist Companion*, ed. Levine, 15-47, esp. 37; Teresa Okure, "Jesus and the Samaritan Woman (Jn 4:1-42) in Africa," *Theological Studies* 70 (2009): 401-18, esp. 409-10; Michaels, *John*, 255.

[39]O'Day and Hylen, *John*, 54.

Many Jews in Jesus' day expected a messianic king who would restore Israel to political independence and faithfulness to the covenant. The Qumran community added two more: a priestly messiah who would restore worship in the temple in Jerusalem and a prophet like Moses promised in Deuteronomy 18:15-18 (1QS 9.10-11).

The Samaritans expected only the prophet like Moses (called the Taheb), who would teach God's Word and restore all things. The Samaritan woman's reference to a messiah who would explain all things reflects this hope (though it is probably unlikely that a Samaritan would use the language of "messiah").[40]

In English translations (including mine above), Jesus' words in John 4:26 are generally represented with some variant of "I am he"—that is, I am the Messiah you expect. Jesus has already said that the eschatological "hour" has begun (Jn 4:23). His response to the woman redirects her messianic expectation from the future to the present.

The identification of Jesus as the Messiah is only one level of meaning in John 4:26. A more exact translation would be "I am, the one speaking to you." "I am" is a significant phrase in John's Gospel. A series of "I am" statements explain Jesus' identity: the bread of life (Jn 6:35, 48, 51); the light of the world (Jn 8:12); the gate for the sheep (Jn 10:7, 9); the good shepherd (Jn 10:11, 14); the resurrection and the life (Jn 11:25); the way, the truth, and the life (Jn 14:6); the true vine (Jn 15:1, 5).

In addition, in several places Jesus says simply "I am." He said this to the disciples when they see him walking across the Sea of Galilee (Jn 6:20), and to the soldiers who came to arrest him in the Garden of Gethsemane (Jn 18:5, 8). He said it repeatedly to his audience in the temple in John 8. "If you do not believe that I am, you will die in your sins" (Jn 8:24). "When you lift up the Son of Man, then you will know that I am" (Jn 8:28). "Truly I say to you, before Abraham was, I am" (Jn 8:58).

In response to this last statement, the people in the audience picked up stones to execute Jesus. They recognized the biblical reverberations of his claim. When Moses asked God's name, God replied, "I am who I am" (Ex 3:14). The Greek translation of the Old Testament frequently uses "I am"

---

[40]See further Schneiders, *Written That*, 138; Anderson and Giles, *Samaritan Pentateuch*, 83-90.

within revelations of God's identity.[41] Jesus' "I am" statements in John connect to this background.

The Gospel identifies Jesus with God from its first verses, and the "I am" statements reinforce this identification. The Samaritan woman heard the first "I am" in John.[42] The clear declaration of Jesus' identity given to the woman contrasts with the questions throughout the rest of the Gospel. As Tertullian and Margaret Fell emphasized, Jesus' self-revelation to the woman sets her story apart from most others.[43]

RESPONDING TO JESUS

The reactions of the Samaritan woman, the disciples, and the people of Sychar weave together through the rest of the story. First, the disciples returned from their shopping. They were surprised to find Jesus speaking with a woman (Jn 4:27). Their surprise may relate to the woman's Samaritan identity or her gender, as the repetition in the verse (speaking with a woman, speaking with her) suggests.

For some interpreters, the disciples' surprise reflects first-century expectations for respectable women's seclusion and silence (or, as John Piper says, first-century misogyny). These interpreters often cite a rabbinic warning against speaking too often with women, including the rabbis' own wives.[44] But as we've seen, these expectations represented social ideals rather than realities. The ancient world was patriarchal, but women also participated in public life.

> Later rabbinic traditions praised a women scholar named Beruriah for her intelligence, her ability as an interpreter, and her active participation in the community. According to one story, she used the words of Mishnah Avot 1.5 to tease a male rabbi for saying four more words to her than he needed to (Babylonian

---

[41]For instance, Gen 17:1; Ex 20:2; Lev 11:44; Is 41:4, 43:25; Jer 9:24.

[42]See also D. Moody Smith, *John*, Abingdon New Testament Commentaries (Nashville: Abingdon, 1999), 118; Schneiders, *Written That*, 139; O'Day and Hylen, *John*, 54-55; McHugh, *John*, 288.

[43]Contrast with, e.g., Jn 1:19-28, 6:41-42, 7:11-13, 8:48, 10:24. See Tertullian, *Modesty* 11.1; Margaret Fell, *Women's Speaking Justified, Proved, and Allowed of by the Scriptures* (London, 1666), 4; and also Keener, *John*, 1:472.

[44]Mishnah Avot 1.5; R. Brown, *John*, 173; Malina and Rohrbaugh, *Social-Science Commentary*, 100; John Piper, "The Food of Christ Is to Give Eternal Life" (message given August 9, 2009), *Desiring God*, www.desiringgod.org/messages/the-food-of-christ-is-to-give-eternal-life.

Talmud Eruvin 53b]. Beruriah exemplifies women's ability to engage despite the limitations imposed by men.[45]

The disciples' surprise is more than misogyny. The two questions they didn't ask in John 4:27 connect their surprise to Jesus rather than the woman—what was he seeking? Why was he speaking with her? For the reader (though not for the disciples within the story), these questions have already been answered. God seeks worshipers (Jn 4:23), and Jesus was speaking with her in order to reveal his identity (Jn 4:26).[46]

From the reader's perspective, the disciples were surprised for the wrong reasons. Instead of the woman's gender, they should have been concerned with Jesus' challenge to long-held Jewish and Samaritan understandings of worship and with his redefinition of the identity of the people of God in "spirit and truth."

While the disciples were busy not asking their questions, the woman returned to her village. She invited her neighbors to meet the person who told her everything she had done. "Could this possibly be the messiah?" (Jn 4:29). The phrasing of her question in Greek suggests that she expected her neighbors to say no (the same construction is found in Jn 8:22 and Jn 18:35). Perhaps then, as some interpreters have argued, the woman wasn't sure about Jesus' identity.[47]

However, the climax of the conversation in Jesus' clear announcement of his own identity, the immediacy of the woman's reaction (she even left her water jar behind at the well), and her neighbors' prompt exodus from the village indicate rather more certainty.[48] So does Jesus' conversation with the disciples, placed in the narrative between the woman's witness in Sychar and the Samaritans' arrival at the well.

Jesus told the disciples to look around them at the fields, full of ripe crops ready for harvest. The sandwiching of the harvest analogy between the woman's announcement to her neighbors and the villagers' approach to the

---

[45]See Brenda Socachevsky Bacon, "Reader Response: How Shall We Tell the Story of Beruriah's End?" *Nashim* 5 (2002): 231-39, especially 232-34.

[46]See also Michaels, *John*, 257-58.

[47]Fehribach, *Bridegroom*, 76-77; Gench, *Back to the Well*, 118.

[48]Compare Mt 12:22-24, and see also D. Smith, *John*, 119; Beirne, *Women and Men*, 91; Okure, "Jesus," 408-9.

well to meet Jesus provides a framework for interpretation. Jesus and the woman are the sowers, and the Samaritans are their harvest.[49]

The woman's witness.

> *Many of the Samaritans from that city believed in Jesus because of*
> *the woman's word as she testified, "He told me everything I've done."*
>
> JOHN 4:39

Jesus' analogy draws attention to the connection between the Samaritans' belief and the woman's testimony (or witness). Witnessing to Jesus is a central theme in John's Gospel.[50] Jesus' own testimony; the testimony of the actions he performs; the testimony of John the Baptist, the Spirit, the Father, and the Scriptures—all offer evidence for the truth of Jesus' identity.[51] In John 15:27, Jesus gives the work of testimony to his followers. Along with John the Baptist, the Samaritan woman models this work in the narrative.[52]

Many Samaritans believed in Jesus because of the woman's word. Many more believed because of Jesus' own word (Jn 4:39, 41). The Samaritans tell the woman that it is "no longer" because of her testimony that they believe, because they have now heard for themselves (Jn 4:42). As we've seen, the contrast here has encouraged some interpreters to denigrate the woman's testimony. For Calvin, for instance, the woman's announcement only got the people interested. It took Jesus himself to create true faith.[53]

> The woman's witness in John 4:42 is described as "speech," which is sometimes used to identify gossip. For Calvin, *St. John 1–10*, 109-10, and Haenchen, *John*, 226, this term confirmed the worthlessness of the woman's testimony. However,

---

[49]So also D. Smith, *John*, 121; Beirne, *Women and Men*, 91; Gench, *Back to the Well*, 119. R. Brown, *John*, 183-84 (among others), however, identifies the sowers with Jesus, John the Baptist, and the biblical prophets.

[50]The verbal form, "I testify," appears thirty-three times in John and the noun, "testimony," fourteen times. The noun and verb are used only six times total in all the other Gospels.

[51]For instance, Jn 1:15, 3:11, 5:31-39, 8:14, 15:26.

[52]See also Harriet Livermore, *Scriptural Evidence in Favour of Female Testimony in Meetings for Christian Worship* (Portsmouth, NH: R. Foster, 1824), 81-82; Schneiders, *Written That*, 142, 144; O'Day and Hylen, *John*, 56-57.

[53]John Calvin, *The Gospel According to St. John 1–10*, trans. T. H. L. Parker, Calvin's Commentaries (1961; repr., Grand Rapids, MI: Eerdmans, 1978), 109-10. See also Fehribach, *Bridegroom*, 77.

> Jesus' own testimony is described with the same term in John 8:43 (the only
> other time the word is used in John), and the word comes from the same root as
> Jesus' self-identification in John 4:26 ("the one speaking with you"). For John,
> "speech" is not gossip, but witness.[54]

However, the development of faith through the witness of disciples con-
firmed by Jesus himself is characteristic of John's Gospel (Jn 1:35-51, 20:18-20).
The parallel between John 4:39 and John 4:41 equates the word of the woman
and the word of Jesus as reasons for the Samaritans' faith. The deliberate
echo gives the woman's words their due.[55] The connection with Jesus'
harvest analogy makes the effectiveness of her testimony even more clear.
She and Jesus sow together, and the harvest is the belief of the villagers.

THE SAVIOR OF THE WORLD

The Samaritan woman's conversation with Jesus began with the recognition
of the divide between Jews and Samaritans. The tensions between the two
peoples remain in focus through the story, emphasized through the woman's
references to "our" ancestor Jacob, her insinuation that Jesus could not be
greater than Jacob, and her question concerning the theologically correct
place of worship.

Jesus challenged this division by moving worship out of the two "places"
into the realm of spirit and truth. The last words of the story clarify these
implications with a bold declaration: Jesus is savior of the world (Jn 4:42). The
faith expressed by the Samaritans in John 4 begins to realize Jesus' mission in
John 3:16-17. Their acceptance of the testimony of the woman and Jesus means
that, even if salvation comes from the Jews, it is not limited to them.[56]

THE SAMARITAN WOMAN IN THE GOSPEL OF JOHN

John's Gospel is a literary work of art. The narrative is carefully constructed
with repetitive patterns, dramatic irony, and more. The Samaritan woman's

---

[54]See also McHugh, *John*, 288, 295.

[55]So also D. Smith, *John*, 121; Schneiders, *Written That*, 143-44; Gench, *Back to the Well*, 119;
Michaels, *John*, 269.

[56]See also Schneiders, *Written That*, 147; Spencer, "You Just Don't Understand," 37; Okure, "Jesus,"
409-10; Michaels, *John*, 255.

story echoes elements of Nicodemus's encounter with Jesus in John 3:1-21 and the story of a man born blind in John 9:1-41. In addition, the Samaritan woman is part of a good company of women in John's Gospel: Mary, Martha, Mary Magdalene. These connections add to our understanding of John 4:4-42.

The Samaritan woman and Nicodemus. The stories of Jesus' conversations with Nicodemus and the Samaritan woman are separated only by a brief scene with John the Baptist and his followers. Moreover, the two conversations have important similarities, which draw readers' attention to the equally important ways they differ.[57]

Nicodemus is named in John 3:1-21. As a Pharisee and a "leader of the Jews," he was an important, well-educated, powerful man. By contrast, the Samaritan woman goes unnamed. She was just a woman, and she had to draw water for her household herself. Unlike Nicodemus, she had no obvious social power or religious authority.

Nicodemus sought Jesus out in the middle of the night. Jesus rather pointedly told him that evildoers hate the light, choosing to remain in the darkness so that no one would see their actions (Jn 3:19-20). The woman did not seek Jesus out. Their chance conversation happened publicly, in broad daylight. She proclaimed to her neighbors that Jesus told her everything she ever did (Jn 4:29, 39). Her actions, in other words, were exposed by the light, and this exposure convinced the woman and her neighbors of Jesus' identity.

Nicodemus initiated his conversation with Jesus; Jesus initiated his conversation with the woman. But, as I noted above, Nicodemus said very little in comparison with Jesus. He essentially disappears from the story after John 3:9. The Samaritan woman remained an equal partner throughout her conversation with Jesus.

Neither Nicodemus nor the woman initially understood Jesus' imagery. They both tried to make the figurative symbolism into something more concrete. In John 3:1-21, there is no indication that Nicodemus gained understanding. Instead, Jesus critiqued his failure to understand (Jn 3:10). The woman, on the other hand, recognized Jesus' identity and testified about him to her community.[58]

---

[57]See especially Beirne, *Women and Men*, 67-104.
[58]This contrast in particular challenges interpreters' assertions of the woman's ignorance (e.g., R. Brown, *John*, 176; Morris, *John*, 231-33). See also Chrysostom, *Hom. Jo.* 32.1; D. Smith, *John*, 109.

The pairing of these stories challenges readers' expectations. The educated, powerful, Jewish man should understand who Jesus is and respond, yet Nicodemus's choice to seek Jesus out at night associates him with darkness and unbelief. The Samaritan woman should not understand Jesus. But she holds her own in the conversation, and by the end she clearly sees who Jesus is. In a surprising twist, the Samaritan woman becomes the model for readers to follow.

The Samaritan woman and a sighted man. In John 9:1-41, a man who was born blind is given the ability to see through Jesus' intervention. The majority of the story addresses the aftermath, particularly the concern of the Jewish leaders and the man himself with Jesus' identity. Jesus appears only at the beginning and end of this story. Despite the very different narrative structures, though, the story of the sighted man and the Samaritan woman have several important similarities (including their shared lack of names!).

First, the sighted man's journey to understanding Jesus resembles the Samaritan woman's own process. The Samaritan woman first identified Jesus as a Jew, then as a prophet, and finally as the Messiah. The sighted man first called Jesus a man, then a prophet, a man from God, and finally the Son of Man (Jn 9:11, 17, 33, 35-36). Together, the two stories narrate the development of faith.

The man's growing recognition of Jesus results, second, in his belief and worship (Jn 9:38). The location of the story outside the temple—the man met Jesus on the steps leading into the temple, and by the end of the story he had been cast out of the temple by the Jewish leaders—intersects with Jesus' message about worship in spirit and truth in John 4:23-24. Neither the Samaritan woman nor the sighted man needed to enter a temple building to worship.

Third, the disciples and the Pharisees accused the sighted man, his parents, and Jesus of sin in John 9:2, 16, 24-34. At the end of the story, Jesus turned these accusations onto those who claim to be sighted (an echo of the light and darkness motif of the Gospel; Jn 9:39-41). The emphasis on sin in John 9:1-41 calls attention to its absence from John 4:4-42. Neither the Samaritan woman nor the sighted man were defined as sinners by Jesus (note Jn 9:3). Instead, both represent the development of faith, witness, and worship.

The women of John's Gospel. A number of narratives in John's Gospel place women in the center of Jesus' ministry. His public ministry began at his mother's request at the wedding in Cana. She overrode his reluctance to begin his work by telling the household slaves to do what he said. Turning water into wine was Jesus' first sign, and Jesus' followers believed in him because of it (Jn 2:1-11).

In John 11:21-27, Martha—a woman whom Jesus loved—made a significant confession of faith: Jesus, the resurrection and the life, is the Messiah. She did not understand the immediacy of Jesus' power of resurrection (she expected, as other Jews did, for the resurrection to be an eschatological event). But, Marianne Meye Thompson argues, Martha's connection of Jesus' identity as Messiah with his "power of life" provides an interpretive center for the story of Lazarus.[59]

Finally, at the end of John, Mary Magdalene was the first disciple to meet the risen Jesus face to face, and "woman" was the first word the risen Jesus said. Jesus sent Mary Magdalene to tell the rest of the disciples about his resurrection (Jn 20:1-18). She accordingly became, as many interpreters have noted, the apostle to the apostles.

The Samaritan woman is in good company—a company of women who speak the truth as witnesses to Jesus.[60] Obviously, men also witness to Jesus in John's Gospel. But the presence of these women is deeply significant (and distinctive). As Margaret Fell commented centuries ago, Jesus' own recognition of these women, the respect he gave them, and their importance in John's Gospel provide a witness to the equality and leadership of women in Christian community.[61]

THE SAMARITAN WOMAN'S STORY IN CONTEXT

In John 4:4-42, Jesus and the Samaritan woman discussed questions of Jesus' identity, messianic expectations, and the historic division between the Jews and Samaritans. They delved into deep matters of theology. They worked together to preach to a village of Samaritans who, from the combined power of their words, recognized Jesus as the Savior of the world.

---

[59]M. Thompson, *John*, 246-47.
[60]See also Spencer, "You Just Don't Understand," 28-30; M. Thompson, *John*, 106.
[61]Fell, *Women's Speaking*, 10-11. See also Beirne, *Women and Men*, 219; Okure, "Jesus," 415-16.

I began this chapter with a question: How might the Samaritan woman's story empower women and men in the church today? John's Gospel gives us the answer. The Samaritan woman models Christian discipleship. Through her questions and challenges to Jesus, she grows in understanding. She brings her deeds into the light to be seen. She witnesses to Jesus among her neighbors.

Along with the formerly blind man, the Samaritan woman represents John's ideal disciple. Along with the other women of this Gospel, the Samaritan woman is instrumental in Jesus' ministry. Her work as an evangelist sets a precedent for all disciples to follow. Her story should empower women and men today to seek understanding and to witness to the identity of Jesus.

CONCLUSION

Reading the Bible After #ChurchToo

A woman was the first Samaritan
convert to the christian faith, and by a woman
the proclamation was given first in the city Sychar,
that Messiah was come; she was instrumental in a reformation.

HARRIET LIVERMORE, SCRIPTURAL EVIDENCE
IN FAVOUR OF FEMALE TESTIMONY
IN MEETINGS FOR CHRISTIAN WORSHIP

THE INTERPRETATION OF THE STORY of the Samaritan woman in John 4:4-42 offers a microcosm of the dehumanizing, reductive sexualization of women in Christian theology and practice, from Tertullian in the second century to the church today. As we have seen in the *Life of Maria the Harlot*, Marie Dentière's *Epistle to Marguerite de Navarre*, and the #ChurchToo movement, such messages have significant, dangerous consequences for girls and women.

The majority interpretation of John 4:4-42 is not the only option. In this book, we have listened to interpreters who challenge the reductive sexualization and minimization of women in the church. Harriet Livermore's focus on the Samaritan woman's act of proclamation is representative of this approach. For Livermore, Margaret Fell, Virginia Broughton, and many others, the Samaritan woman modeled women's vocal participation and leadership in the church.

In this final chapter, I will review the historical sexualization and minimization of women in Christian tradition, and the ways such messages connect with John 4:4-42. I will also consider how the reinterpretation of biblical stories of women can contribute to a new reformation—a reformation of the church's perspectives on women, a reformation that is necessary as the church addresses the abuse revealed by #ChurchToo victims and survivors.

GENDER, SEX, AND THE CHURCH

> *It is frighteningly easy for a woman in the church to absorb a*
> *message that she is lesser, inferior, and lacking in some way.*
> Lucy Peppiatt, *Rediscovering Scripture's Vision for Women*

As I argued in part one, Christian tradition has conditioned us to see biblical women through the lenses of sex and sin. Recognizing that the details vary, a basic narrative told about women in the church begins in Genesis 2–3 with a hierarchy of creation in which women are (created to be) inferior to men, and therefore must submit to male authority in the household and beyond. Women's inferiority and submission are only strengthened by the punishment of Eve's sin (sometimes defined as her challenge to the man's authority).

This narrative receives further reinforcement from the problem of sex. Theologians and pastors expressed discomfort with human sexuality from the second century to the twentieth. The desires, pleasures, and releases of sex undermine the self-control and discipline of Christian faith. The classification of sexual intercourse outside of a marital relationship as sin affected perceptions of sex inside marriage too.

The sanctification of marital sex in the contemporary church has challenged some of these assumptions with the recognition and celebration of embodied experience. However, the identification of marital sex as a blessing too often turns into the identification of women as prizes for faithful men. The incorporation of sexual desire and aggression into definitions of masculinity further reduces women to passive subjects of men's action.

In addition, sanctifying sex in marriage inversely emphasizes the sinfulness of sex outside marriage. The purity movements of the contemporary church teach girls that their salvation depends on maintaining their virginity until marriage. Since sexual desire is a masculine quality, girls must take responsibility for guarding this element of their identity. Confusingly, purity culture also warns that girls are seductive stumbling blocks, tempting boys and men into sin. The sexualization of young girls and women is pervasive in the church.

As Lucy Peppiatt reminds us, these messages have troubling consequences for women's self-understanding. Moreover, the perceived inferiority of women correlates with the limitation of women's participation in worship, teaching, and preaching. The association of all women with their mother Eve sometimes translates into authoritarian relationships that allow for abuse. With respect to sex, the passivity and submissiveness assigned to women makes them both the objects of male attention and the dangerous temptations that cause men's sexual sin.

The #ChurchToo movement bears witness to the bodily dangers such messages pose for girls and women in our churches. Harassment and assault certainly develop out of the evil of human sin. But the pervasiveness of these experiences through time, across denominations, and in different racial and ethnic communities suggests there are also institutional factors at play. Abusers are empowered by the ways the church defines masculinity and femininity, constructs theologies of sexuality, and teaches biblical stories about women.

Of course, theologies and social constructions of women, sex, and sin shift through time. Tertullian's critique of remarriage following the death of a spouse did not persist, for instance. The redefinition of White, wealthy women as the moral authorities of the household and society in the nineteenth century briefly challenged the association of all women with Eve's sin (though this shift also vilified women of color and any women who could not afford virtuous domesticity). John Chrysostom, Marie Dentière, and Clara Lucas Balfour challenged the inferiority of women's mental capabilities, creating the potential for women's leadership even if it was not taken up in the church.

Through these developments, the interpretation of the Samaritan woman as (sexual) sinner has maintained its primacy. The ways the church has read and used John 4:4-42 both reflect and contribute to the reductive sexualization of women.

THE SAMARITAN WOMAN AND THE CHURCH

We have been historically taught to characterize [the Samaritan woman]
as a harlot. Could it be because this is the first person to whom Jesus
claimed his messiahship, leading her to become the first city-wide
evangelist? Hence, she too was discredited, lest other women in the
church use her as a model in claiming their spiritual calling to lead.

MIGUEL DE LA TORRE, "SHAMING WOMEN INTO SILENCE"

The majority interpretation of John 4:4-42 from the third century on reveals
a tendency to sexualize the Samaritan woman in negative ways. She is
accused of adultery and prostitution. She is made responsible for the endings
of her multiple marriages in divorce, for her own desire to remarry, and for
her situation of sinful, nonmarital cohabitation.

As a consequence of these choices, in the majority interpretation the
woman's responses to Jesus are condemned as mouthy, rude, and ignorant.
Her questions become attempts to hide her own personal sin. Her testimony
to her neighbors is sometimes minimized as gossip, or (in the case of John
Calvin) dehumanized by comparison with inanimate objects.

Because the woman is defined as a sexual sinner, her words can have no
power. Because interpreters disempower her words, they make her pre-
sumed sexual history an essential concern of her interaction with Jesus. The
Samaritan woman becomes an example of God's amazing grace that can
encompass even a terrible sinner like this.

This message is powerful, to be sure. But, Miguel De La Torre notes, these
interpretive moves prevent men and women in the church from identifying
the Samaritan woman as an example of women's leadership. "After all," he
adds, "if the woman at the well or Mary of Magdala are sluts and whores
(interesting that men are never given these titles), how could they serve as
paragons to emulate or have anything virtuous to contribute to the
conversation?"[1] The reductive sexualization of the Samaritan woman (and

---

[1]Miguel De La Torre, "Shaming Women into Silence," *Baptist News Global,* 3 June 3, 2013, https://
baptistnews.com/article/shaming-women-into-silence/. See also Lucy Peppiatt, *Rediscovering
Scripture's Vision for Women: Fresh Perspectives on Disputed Texts* (Downers Grove, IL: IVP
Academic, 2019), 114.

other biblical women) contributes to the minimization of women in Christian communities.

In part two, I argued that the focus on the Samaritan woman's sin in the majority interpretation fundamentally misrepresents John 4:4-42. This focus ignores important aspects of the social and cultural setting of her story: the limitations of women's marital rights; the involvement of (primarily male) family members in arranging marriages and divorces; the basic definition of marriage around economics rather than relationship.

A focus on the woman's perceived sin also ignores the evidence of John 4:4-42 itself. In contrast to other narratives in the Gospel, there is no mention of "sin" in this story. There is no reason to import it. Jesus' reference to the woman's marital history does not need to be interpreted as an accusation of sin, and her responses to Jesus should not be read through the lens of sin. The Samaritan woman's story is instead about the work of witnessing to Jesus and the new way of being the people of God that Jesus introduces.

RECONSIDERING THE SAMARITAN WOMAN'S STORY

> *Paula entered the church built on the side of Mount Gerizim*
> *around Jacob's well. This is where the Lord sat, thirsty and hungry,*
> *and was satiated by the faith of the woman of Samaria.*
>
> JEROME, *LETTER 108* (AUTHOR'S TRANSLATION)

Without the lens of sin blinding us, we can see John 4:4-42 more clearly. First, the Samaritan woman expresses wisdom, thoughtfulness, and awareness throughout her conversation with Jesus. She is an intelligent partner for Jesus in a way that Nicodemus is not. In this sense, the story challenges the values we place on status and identity.

Second, the emphasis on the division between the Jews and Samaritans throughout John 4:4-42 frames a remarkable message of inclusivity. Worship is open to all, because it is no longer bound to one place. A Samaritan receives Jesus' life-giving water, and it flows out of her into her entire community. The Samaritans' recognition of Jesus as "Savior of the world" reinforces Jesus' statement of purpose in John 3:17.

Third, as Jerome said, the Samaritan woman's faith satisfied Jesus' hunger and thirst (Jn 4:31-34). Within John's Gospel, the Samaritan woman models discipleship through her gradual recognition of Jesus' identity and her response of witnessing to others in her community. Jesus' own metaphor of planting and harvesting in John 4:35-38 further marks the woman as his colleague in the work of witness, of sowing the word of God.

Jerome connected the Samaritan woman with his own colleague Paula. In his letter commemorating Paula after her death, Jerome praised her knowledge of Scripture, her capability as an interpreter, and her leadership over a monastic community for women that she founded in Bethlehem. While Jerome would not necessarily have shared this conclusion, his comparison of Paula with the Samaritan woman implicitly challenges limitations placed on women's responsibility and leadership in the church.

The Samaritan woman's story offers one of many biblical examples of women's work as preachers and teachers in Christian communities. This reading of John 4:4-42 disrupts the perspectives that allow for the victimization of women in Christian communities. Instead of a sexualized sinner, the woman becomes an insightful theologian. Instead of a danger to the men around her, she becomes a teacher who helps others understand the truth. This reconsideration of the Samaritan woman's story encourages and empowers women in the church today.

READING THE BIBLE AFTER #CHURCHTOO

> *Blessed Lord, who caused all holy Scriptures to be written for our*
> *learning: help us so to hear them, to read, mark, learn and inwardly*
> *digest them that, through patience, and the comfort of your holy*
> *word, we may embrace and for ever hold fast the hope of everlasting*
> *life, which you have given us in our Savior Jesus Christ. Amen.*
>
> COLLECT FOR THE SECOND SUNDAY IN ADVENT,
> BOOK OF COMMON PRAYER

The history of the interpretation of John 4:4-42 from the early church until today consistently vilifies, belittles, and silences the Samaritan woman. This pattern endlessly repeats for other biblical women: Dinah,

Vashti, Huldah, Phoebe, the woman in Luke 7:36-50, Mary Magdalene.[2] I have argued in this book that the reductive sexualization and consequent minimization of women in the Bible has contributed to the crisis of sexual abuse revealed by the courageous women and men who have shared their experiences of harassment, assault, and rape in the #ChurchToo movement.

Solving the crisis of abuse requires multiple approaches. We have to listen to victims and survivors. We should lament and grieve as a community. We must also repent and change. We should educate ourselves and our churches on the best practices for protecting the vulnerable and preventing abuse. We need to know what assault is and how to recognize signs of abuse. We need to learn how to support victims and survivors.[3]

We need to listen to ourselves, as well. How do our churches talk about sex, sexuality, and rape? What messages might people in our churches hear in our sermons, prayers, Bible studies, youth programs? We need to recognize and correct the kinds of messages that contribute to the crisis of abuse: the definition of masculinity around uncontrollable sexuality; the objectification of women; the sexualization of young girls.

Finally, as the Book of Common Prayer reminds us, we need to pay attention to our practices of biblical interpretation. We need to look again at the stories that have "always" been taught in one way, to the denigration of female characters and, by extension, the women in Christian communities. We need to commit to interpretive practices that do not victimize women. The reexamination of the Samaritan woman's story in this book offers guidance for this work.

---

[2]Sandra Glahn, ed., *Vindicating the Vixens: Revisiting Sexualized, Vilified, and Marginalized Women of the Bible* (Grand Rapids, MI: Kregel Academic, 2017); Amanda W. Benckhuysen, *The Gospel According to Eve: A History of Women's Interpretation* (Downers Grove, IL: IVP Academic, 2019); and Peppiatt, *Scripture's Vision*, among others, explore the (re)interpretations of some of these biblical women. See also Beth Allison Barr, *The Making of Biblical Womanhood: How the Subjugation of Women Became Gospel Truth* (Grand Rapids, MI: Brazos, 2021), on the long history of women's leadership in the church.

[3]As a reminder, Marie Fortune, *Sexual Violence: The Sin Revisited* (Cleveland: Pilgrim Press, 2005); Mary DeMuth, *We Too: How the Church Can Respond Redemptively to the Sexual Abuse Crisis* (Eugene, OR: Harvest House, 2019); Anne Marie Miller, *Healing Together: A Guide to Supporting Sexual Abuse Survivors* (Grand Rapids, MI: Zondervan Reflective, 2019); and Ruth Everhart, *The #MeToo Reckoning: Facing the Church's Complicity in Sexual Abuse and Misconduct* (Downers Grove, IL: InterVarsity Press, 2020) are all great resources for this work.

As a first step, it is important to resist the reductive, problematic sexualization of women in biblical narratives. The presence of a woman in a story does not make sex an issue of interpretation. Women's lives in the biblical worlds were complex. Their contributions to the stories of the people of God were equally complex. Recognizing women's participation in the household, society, politics, and religious life challenges the minimization of women I have noted in this book.

Of course, sometimes sex is explicitly an issue in a biblical narrative. When sex, sexuality, or marriage are concerns of a story (as in Jn 4:4-42), it is important to consider the historical and cultural contexts. Our modern understandings of sex and marriage, sexual morality, or romance can make us misunderstand or wrongly explain the experiences of women in the biblical worlds. Specifically, interpretations of sex, sexuality, or marriage in the Bible should incorporate power dynamics, family and community involvement, legal possibilities, economic realities, and questions of women's survival in patriarchal contexts.

Considering the contexts of women's lives in the biblical worlds redirects the guilt, shame, and blame that have so often been placed on women with reference to sex, sexuality, and marriage. It allows space for questioning the motivation of the different actors in a story and questioning the social and economic systems that can limit women's options.

Second, we should resist stereotypical slurs. For instance, the Samaritan woman's words should not be dismissed as gossip. Women's actions should not be ascribed to selfishness or an overabundance of emotion. And, of course, women should not be described as seductive or manipulative without very strong, clear evidence. Resisting these kinds of stereotypes allows us to better recognize and appreciate the contributions of women within biblical stories.

Third, the history of biblical interpretation is primarily a history of men's interpretation (all too often, White men's interpretation). Of course, we have much to learn from men. But women's perspectives often help us see the biblical text differently. Marie Dentière, Margaret Fell, Clara Lucas Balfour, Harriet Livermore, Virginia Broughton, and Barbara Essex (among others) challenge the majority interpretation of John 4:4-42 with their recognition of the Samaritan woman's intelligence, engagement, and ministry.

We each bring different perspectives to the Bible, and our perspectives draw our attention to different elements of a text. As readers, we should seek to learn from all interpreters, listening to people of different genders, races, ethnicities, socioeconomic classes, physical abilities, and more. This practice can help us develop fuller understandings of biblical texts, women's place in the Bible, and women's responsibility in the church.

A fourth step for developing more constructive habits of biblical interpretation is to teach biblical stories about women to women and men. John's Gospel presents the Samaritan woman as a model of discipleship. As Origen and Chrysostom emphasized, her search for understanding and her invitation to her neighbors provide an example for all Christians to follow. Challenging men as well as women to learn from biblical women restores the significance of their stories for the church.

The history of the interpretation of the Samaritan woman's story is also the history of the minimization, sexualization, and silencing of women in the church. Counteracting this history requires hard work of questioning ourselves, our theologies, and the explicit and implicit messages we teach. This work is a necessary part of responding to the crisis of #ChurchToo, to recognizing women's equality as image-bearers of God, and to promoting women's full participation in Christian communities.

DISCUSSION QUESTIONS

CHAPTER ONE

1. As you begin this book, take time to read John 4:4-42. What interpretation(s) of the story are you most familiar with? What (or who) has influenced your own understanding of the Samaritan woman?

2. Think about the sermons or Bible studies you've heard that address biblical stories of women. How are the women interpreted? Why do you think pastors (or other teachers) present biblical women as they do? What are the consequences of these interpretations for the church?

3. Do any of the #ChurchToo stories resonate with you? Have you experienced or witnessed similar occurrences? What has the community's response been?

PART ONE (CHAPTERS TWO, THREE, AND FOUR)

1. Which ideas concerning gender and sexuality in these chapters are familiar to you? Which seem the strangest or the most surprising? Why?

2. How would you explain the ways that interpreters' assumptions concerning gender and sex influence their understanding of the Samaritan woman's story? What assumptions have influenced your own understanding of women in the Bible?

3. Which of the interpretations covered in part one were the most difficult for you to engage with? Which interpretations did you like or appreciate? Why do you think you reacted as you did?

4. Racism increases the danger of sexualization for women of color. Why is it important for the church to address this danger? What practical steps could churches take in response?

5 In part one, the author argued that the way the church interprets biblical women intersects with the crisis of sexual assault. What implications of this connection do you see for women and men in the church?

PART TWO (CHAPTERS FIVE, SIX, AND SEVEN)

1. Do you see any common points between the lives of girls and women of the first century and the lives of girls and women today? What do the similarities and differences in women's experience across time suggest about their responsibilities, limitations, and significance in society?

2. Did women's ability to own property, run businesses, and participate in political and community life in the ancient world surprise you? How do the realities of women's experience in the first century complicate our understanding of women in the New Testament?

3. How did you react to the reinterpretation of the Samaritan woman's story in chapter seven? What is the importance of this interpretation for your own understanding?

4. What is the significance of ethnic identity in John 4:4-42? Why do you think the issues of Jewish and Samaritan history and identity are so important in this story? What could this element of the story teach readers today?

5. Removing sin from the Samaritan woman's story does not remove salvation. How do you see the message of salvation in the story apart from the issue of sin?

CONCLUSION

1. As you finished this book, what questions, concerns, or challenges will you continue to consider?

2. Do you know the policies on sexual assault in your church or other communities? What additional policies and procedures might be needed? What do you want to do in response to #ChurchToo?

3. How might the material in this book, specific to the Samaritan woman's story, carry over to other biblical narratives? Whose stories deserve another look? What would the consequences of reinterpreting women's stories be for your own life and for your community?

BIBLIOGRAPHY

PRIMARY SOURCES

Aquinas, Thomas. *Commentary on the Gospel of John Chapters 1–5*. Translated by Fabian Larcher and James A. Weisheipl. With introduction and notes by Daniel Keating and Matthew Levering. Thomas Aquinas in Translation. Washington, DC: Catholic University of America Press, 2010. https://isidore.co/aquinas/english/SSJohn.htm.

Balfour, Clara Lucas. *The Women of Scripture*. London: Houlston and Stoneman, 1847. www.google.com/books/edition/The_Women_of_Scripture/tTJfAAAAcAAJ?hl=en.

Baxter, Elizabeth. *The Women in the Word. A Few Simple Hints from Portraits of Bible Women*. Second edition published 1897 by Christian Herald (London). Excerpt in *Women in the Story of Jesus: The Gospels Through the Eyes of Nineteenth-Century Female Bible Interpreters*, edited by Marion Ann Taylor and Heather E. Weir, 144-47. Grand Rapids, MI: Eerdmans, 2016.

Brock, Sebastian P., and Susan Ashbrook Harvey. *Holy Women of the Syrian Orient*. Berkeley: University of California Press, 1987.

Broughton, Virginia W. *Women's Work: As Gleaned from the Women of the Bible*. In *Virginia Broughton: The Life and Writings of a National Baptist Missionary*. Edited by Tomeiko Ashford Carter. Knoxville: University of Tennessee Press, 2010.

Calvin, John. *Commentaries on the Four Last Books of Moses, Arranged in the Form of a Harmony*. Translated by Charles William Bingham. 4 vols. Edinburgh: Calvin Translation Society, 1853.

———. *The Epistle of Paul the Apostle to the Hebrews and the First and Second Epistles of St. Peter*. Translated by William B. Johnston. Calvin's Commentaries. 1963. Reprint, Grand Rapids, MI: Eerdmans, 1979.

———. *The Epistles of Paul the Apostle to the Romans and to the Thessalonians*. Translated by Ross MacKenzie. Calvin's Commentaries. Grand Rapids, MI: Eerdmans, 1960.

———. *The First Epistle of Paul the Apostle to the Corinthians*. Translated by John W. Fraser. Calvin's Commentaries. 1960. Reprint, Grand Rapids, MI: Eerdmans, 1979.

———. *Genesis*. Translated by John King. 2 vols. 1847. Reprint, Edinburgh: Banner of Truth Trust, 1975.

———. *The Gospel According to St. John 1–10*. Translated by T. H. L. Parker. Calvin's Commentaries. 1961. Reprint, Grand Rapids, MI: Eerdmans, 1978.

———. *The Gospel According to St. John 11–21 and the First Epistle of John*. Translated by T. H. L. Parker. Calvin's Commentaries. 1959. Reprint, Grand Rapids, MI: Eerdmans, 1978.

———. *Institutes of the Christian Religion*. 8th ed. Translated by John Allen. 2 vols. Grand Rapids, MI: Eerdmans, 1949.

———. *John Calvin: Selections from His Writings*. Edited by John Dillenberger. American Academy of Religion Aids for the Study of Religion 2. Atlanta: Scholars Press, 1975.

———. *John Calvin's Works in English*. Meeter Center at Calvin University. https://calvin .edu/centers-institutes/meeter-center/resources/john-calvins-works-in-english/.

———. *Letters of John Calvin*. Edited by Jules Bonnet. Translated by David Constable. 4 vols. Philadelphia: Presbyterian Board of Publication, 1858.

———. *The Second Epistle of Paul the Apostle to the Corinthians and the Epistles to Timothy, Titus, and Philemon*. Translated by T. A. Smail. Calvin's Commentaries. 1964. Reprint, Grand Rapids, MI: Eerdmans, 1979.

———. *Sermons on 1 Timothy*. Translated by Robert White. Carlisle, PA: Banner of Truth, 2018.

Caring Well: A Report from the SBC Sexual Abuse Advisory Group. https://caringwell.com /wp-content/uploads/2019/06/SBC-Caring-Well-Report-June-2019.pdf.

Charles, H. B. "The Woman at the Well." Video. Sermon preached at The Gospel Coalition National Conference, Indianapolis, Indiana, April 3, 2019. https://youtu.be /Xkw8RfgQ3qM.

Chrysostom, John. *Against the Games and Theaters*. In Mayer and Allen, *John Chrysostom*, 118-25.

———. *Baptismal Instructions*. Translated by Paul W. Harkins. Ancient Christian Writers: The Works of the Fathers in Translation 31. Mahwah, NJ: Paulist, 1963.

———. *Commentary on St. John the Apostle and Evangelist, Homilies 1-47*. Translated by Thomas Aquinas Goggin. The Fathers of the Church 33. 1957. Reprint, Washington: Catholic University of America Press, 2000.

———. *Commentary on St. John the Apostle and Evangelist, Homilies 48-88*. Translated by Thomas Aquinas Goggin. The Fathers of the Church 41. 1959. Reprint, Washington: Catholic University of America Press, 2000.

———. *Homilies on Galatians, Ephesians, Philippians, Colossians, Thessalonians, Timothy, Titus, and Philemon*. Vol. 13 of *The Nicene and Post-Nicene Fathers*, Series 1. Edited by Philip Schaff. 14 vols. Edinburgh: T&T Clark, 1886–1889. https://ccel.org/ccel/schaff /npnf113.html.

———. *Homilies on Genesis 1-17*. Translated by Robert C. Hill. Fathers of the Church 74. Washington: Catholic University of America Press, 1986.

———. *Homilies on the Acts of the Apostles and the Epistle to the Romans*. Vol. 11 of *The Nicene and Post-Nicene Fathers*, Series 1. Edited by Philip Schaff. 14 vols. Edinburgh: T&T Clark, 1886–1889. https://ccel.org/ccel/schaff/npnf111.html.

———. *Homilies on the Epistles of Paul to the Corinthians*. Vol. 12 of *The Nicene and Post-Nicene Fathers*, Series 1. Edited by Philip Schaff. 14 vols. Edinburgh: T&T Clark, 1886–1889. https://ccel.org/ccel/schaff/npnf112.html.

———. *Homilies on the Gospel of John and the Epistle to the Hebrews*. Vol. 14 of *The Nicene and Post-Nicene Fathers*, Series 1. Edited by Philip Schaff. 14 vols. Edinburgh: T&T Clark, 1886–1889. https://ccel.org/ccel/schaff/npnf114.html.

———. *Homilies on the Gospel of St. Matthew*. Vol. 10 of *The Nicene and Post-Nicene Fathers*, Series 1. Edited by Philip Schaff. 14 vols. Edinburgh: T&T Clark, 1886–1889. https://ccel.org/ccel/schaff/npnf110.html.

———. *Letter to Theodore*. In vol. 9 of *The Nicene and Post-Nicene Fathers*, Series 1. Edited by Philip Schaff. 14 vols. Edinburgh: T&T Clark, 1886–1889. https://ccel.org/ccel/schaff/npnf109.html.

———. *On Marriage and Family Life*. Translated by Catherine P. Roth and David Anderson. Popular Patristics. Crestwood, NY: St. Vladimir's Seminary Press, 2003.

———. *On Virginity* and *Against Cohabitation*. In *Women in Early Christianity: Translations from Greek Texts*, edited by Patricia Cox Miller, 105-17 and 123-38. Washington: Catholic University of America Press, 2005.

Coughlin, Tyson. "The Story of the Samaritan Woman at the Well Explained." Video. Sermon preached at Vizion Church, Charlotte, North Carolina, December 19, 2017. https://youtu.be/W3jE42chG2w.

Cyril. *Catechetical Lectures*. In vol. 7 of *The Nicene and Post-Nicene Fathers*, Series 2. Edited by Philip Schaff. 14 vols. Edinburgh: T&T Clark, 1886–1889. https://ccel.org/ccel/schaff/npnf207.

Danby, Herbert. *The Mishnah: Translated from the Hebrew with Introduction and Brief Explanatory Notes*. Oxford: Oxford University Press, 1933. https://archive.org/details/DanbyMishnah.

De La Torre, Miguel. "Shaming Women into Silence." *Baptist News Global*. June 3, 2013. https://baptistnews.com/article/shaming-women-into-silence/.

De Pizan, Christine. *The Book of the City of Ladies*. Translated by Jeffrey Richards. New York: Persea, 1982.

Dentière, Marie. *Marie Dentière: Epistle to Marguerite de Navarre and Preface to a Sermon by John Calvin*. Translated and edited by Mary B. McKinley. The Other Voice in Early Modern Europe. Chicago: University of Chicago Press, 2004.

Driscoll, Mark. "John's Gospel – The Woman at the Well – Mark Driscoll 8/34." Video. May 18, 2017. https://youtu.be/0JkFWs5RxZw. Originally "The Woman at the Well," sermon preached at Mars Hill Church, Seattle, WA, December 4, 2000.

———. *The Radical Reformission: Reaching Out Without Selling Out*. Grand Rapids, MI: Zondervan, 2004.

Driscoll, Mark, and Grace Driscoll. *Real Marriage: The Truth About Sex, Friendship, and Life Together*. Nashville: Thomas Nelson, 2012.

Essex, Barbara J. *More Bad Girls of the Bible*. Cleveland: Pilgrim Press, 2009.

Eusebius. *Church History*. In vol. 1 of *The Nicene and Post-Nicene Fathers*, Series 2. Edited by Philip Schaff. 14 vols. Edinburgh: T&T Clark, 1886–1889. Edinburgh: T&T Clark. https://ccel.org/ccel/schaff/npnf201.

Fell, Margaret. *Women's Speaking Justified, Proved, and Allowed of by the Scriptures*. London: 1666. https://digital.library.upenn.edu/women/fell/speaking/speaking.html.

Fructuosus of Braga. *Rule for the Monastery of Compludo*. In *Iberian Fathers, Volume 2*, 155-75. Translated by Claude W. Barlow. The Fathers of the Church 63. Washington, DC: Catholic University of America Press, 1969.

Gardner, Jane F., and Thomas Wiedemann. *The Roman Household: A Sourcebook*. London: Routledge, 1991.

Got Questions Ministries. "What Can We Learn from the Woman at the Well?" *Got Questions*. n.d. www. gotquestions.org/woman-at-the-well.html.

Grumbach, Argula von. *To the University of Ingelstadt*. In *Argula von Grumbach: A Woman's Voice in the Reformation*, edited by Peter Matheson, 56-95. Edinburgh: T&T Clark, 1995. Excerpts available at www.gjlts.com/Church%20History/Reformation%20History/Primary%20Source%20-%20Argula%20%20letter.pdf.

Hemelrijk, Emily A. *Women and Society in the Roman World: A Sourcebook of Inscriptions from the Roman West*. Cambridge: Cambridge University Press, 2021.

Higgs, Liz Curtis. *Bad Girls of the Bible and What We Can Learn from Them*. Colorado Springs: Waterbrook, 1999.

Hoezee, Scott. "John 4:1-38: 'Welling Up.'" Sermon preached at Calvin Christian Reformed Church. http://yardley.cs.calvin.edu/hoezee/2002/john4.html.

Jerome. *Letters*. In vol. 6 of *The Nicene and Post-Nicene Fathers*, Series 2. Edited by Philip Schaff. 14 vols. Edinburgh: T&T Clark, 1886–1889. https://ccel.org/ccel/schaff/npnf206/npnf206.

Josephus. *Against Apion, Jewish Antiquities, The Jewish War*, and *The Life of Josephus*. Translated by H. St. J. Thackeray et al. 10 vols. Loeb Classical Library. Cambridge: Harvard University Press, 1926–1965.

Jussie, Jeanne de. *The Short Chronicle: A Poor Clare's Account of the Reformation of Geneva*. Translated and edited by Carrie S. Klaus. The Other Voice in Early Modern Europe. Chicago: University of Chicago Press, 2006.

Larson, Brad. "How to Have That Hard Conversation." *The Gospel Coalition*. January 27, 2020. www.thegospelcoalition.org/article/hard-conversation/.

Lefkowitz, Mary R., and Maureen B. Fant. *Women's Life in Greece and Rome: A Source Book in Translation*. 3rd edition. Baltimore: Johns Hopkins University Press, 2005. Selections at https://diotima-doctafemina.org/translations/anthologies/womens-life-in-greece-and-rome-selections/.

Lewis, Naphtali. *The Documents from the Bar Kokhba Period in the Cave of Letters: Greek Papyri*. Judean Desert Studies 2. Jerusalem: Israel Exploration Society, 1989.

Livermore, Harriet. *Scriptural Evidence in Favour of Female Testimony in Meetings for Christian Worship*. Portsmouth: R. Foster, 1824. www.google.com/books/edition /Scriptural_Evidence_in_favour_of_female/7llPf0W7zC8C?hl=en.

Locker, Mrs. Frederick (Hannah). *Bible Readings from the Gospels for Mothers' Meetings, Etc.* London: Religious Tract Society, 1877. www.google.com/books/edition/Bible _readings_from_the_Gospels/KKECAAAAQAAJ?hl=en&gbpv=0.

McCracken, Brett. "Exit the Echo Chamber." *The Gospel Coalition*. June 11, 2020. www .thegospelcoalition.org/article/exit-echo-chamber-persuade/.

Moody, Dwight Lyman. *Dwight Lyman Moody's Life Work and Gospel Sermons*. Edited by Richard S. Rhodes. Chicago: Rhodes and McClure, 1907. https://babel.hathitrust .org/cgi/pt?id=loc.ark:/13960/t6b290s4w&view=1up&seq=5.

———. *Glad Tidings Comprising Sermons and Prayer-Meeting Talks Delivered at the N. Y. Hippodrome*. Edited by H. H. Birkins. New York: The Tribune Association, 1876. www .google.com/books/edition/Glad_Tidings/-TwPAAAAIAAJ?hl=en&gbpv=0.

———. *"The Gospel Awakening." Comprising the Sermons and Addresses, Prayer-Meeting Talks and Bible Readings of the Great Revival Meetings Conducted by Moody and Sankey*. 20th ed. Edited by L. T. Remlap. Chicago: Fairbanks and Palmer, 1885. https:// books.google.com/books?id=arIPAAAAIAAJ.

———. *Moody: His Words, Work, and Workers*. Edited by W. H. Daniels. New York: Nelson & Phillips, 1877. www.google.com/books/edition/Moody_His_Words_Work_and _Workers/2eVMAQAAMAAJ?hl=en&gbpv=0.

Origen. *Commentary on the Epistle to the Romans, Books 6–10*. Translated by Thomas P. Scheck. Fathers of the Church 104. Washington: Catholic University of America Press, 2002.

———. *Commentary on the Gospel of John, Books 1–10*. Translated by Ronald E. Heine. Fathers of the Church 80. Washington: Catholic University of America Press, 1989.

———. *Commentary on the Gospel of Matthew*. In vol. 9 of *The Ante-Nicene Fathers*, edited by Alexander Roberts and James Donaldson. 10 vols. Edinburgh: T&T Clark, 1885– 1887. https://ccel.org/ccel/origen/commentary_matt/anf09.

———. *First Principles*. In vol. 4 of *The Ante-Nicene Fathers*, edited by Alexander Roberts and James Donaldson. 10 vols. Edinburgh: T&T Clark, 1885–1887. https://ccel.org /ccel/schaff /anf04.html.

———. *Fragments on 1 Corinthians*. In "Origen on 1 Corinthians," edited by Claude Jenkins. Pts. 1 through 4. *Journal of Theological Studies* 9, no. 34 (January 1908): 231-47; 9, no. 35 (April 1908): 353-73; 9. no. 36 (July 1908): 500-515; 10, no. 37 (October 1908): 29-51.

———. *Homilies on Genesis and Exodus*. Translated by Ronald E. Heine. Fathers of the Church 71. Washington: Catholic University of America Press, 1982.

———. *Homilies on Judges*. Translated by Elizabeth Ann Dively Lauro. Fathers of the Church 119. Washington: Catholic University of America Press, 2010.

———. *Homilies on Luke.* Translated by Joseph T. Lienhard. Fathers of the Church 94. Washington: Catholic University of America Press, 2009.

———. *Homilies on Numbers.* Translated by Thomas P. Sheck. Ancient Christian Texts. Downers Grove, IL: InterVarsity Academic, 2009.

———. *The Song of Songs: Commentary and Homilies.* Translated by R. P. Lawson. New York: Newman, 1956.

Palmer, Phoebe. *The Promise of the Father.* 1859. Reprint, Eugene: Wipf & Stock, 2015.

Papyrus Cattaoui. In *The Marriage of Roman Soldiers (13 BC–AD 235): Law and Family in the Imperial Army.* Translated by Sara Elise Phang. Columbia Studies in the Classical Tradition 24. Brill: Leiden, 2001.

Patrologia Graeca. Edited by J.-P. Migne. 162 vols. Paris, 1857–1886.

Patrologia Latina. Edited by J.-P. Migne. 217 vols. Paris, 1844–1864.

"The Pilgrim from Bordeaux." In *The Pilgrimage of Egeria: A New Translation of the Itinerarium Egeriae with Introduction and Commentary,* by Anne McGowan and Paul F. Bradshaw, 187-204. Collegeville, MN: Liturgical Press, 2018.

Piper, John. "A Vision of Biblical Complementarity: Manhood and Womanhood Defined According to the Bible." In *Recovering Biblical Manhood and Womanhood: A Response to Evangelical Feminism,* edited by John Piper and Wayne Grudem, 31-59. 1991. Reprint, Wheaton, IL: Crossway, 2006.

———. "Can a Woman Preach if Elders Affirm It?" *Ask Pastor John* (podcast). *Desiring God,* February 16, 2015. www.desiringgod.org/interviews/can-a-woman-preach-if -elders-affirm-it.

———. "Did Jesus Teach That Women Are to Be Leaders?" *Desiring God.* January 10, 1984. www.desiringgod.org/articles/did-jesus-teach-that-women-were-to-be -leaders.

———. "Do Men Owe Women a Special Kind of Care?" *Desiring God.* November 6, 2017. www.desiringgod.org/articles/do-men-owe-women-a-special-kind-of-care.

———. "The Food of Christ Is to Give Eternal Life," Message given August 9, 2009. *Desiring God.* www.desiringgod.org/messages/the-food-of-christ-is-to-give-eternal -life.

———. "'The Frank and Manly Mr. Ryle'—The Value of a Masculine Ministry." Message at the Desiring God 2012 Conference for Pastors, January 31, 2012. *Desiring God.* January 31, 2012. www.desiringgod.org/messages/the-frank-and-manly-mr-ryle-the -value-of-a-masculine-ministry.

———. "God Seeks People to Worship Him in Spirit and Truth." *Desiring God.* Message given April 8, 1984. www.desiringgod.org/messages/god-seeks-people-to-worship -him-in-spirit-and-truth.

———. "How Far Is Too Far Before Marriage?" *Ask Pastor John* (podcast). *Desiring God,* April 19, 2013. www.desiringgod.org/interviews/how-far-is-too-far-before -marriage.

———. "I Sought a Prostitute—Am I Doomed?" *Ask Pastor John* (podcast). *Desiring God*, November 2, 2020. www.desiringgod.org/interviews/i-sought-a-prostitute-am-i-doomed.

———. "Is There a Place for Female Professors at Seminary?" *Ask Pastor John* (podcast). *Desiring God*, January 22, 2018. www.desiringgod.org/interviews/is-there-a-place-for-female-professors-at-seminary.

———. "John Piper: Does a Woman Submit to Abuse?" Video. September 1, 2009. https://youtu.be/3OkUPc2NLrM. Originally aired as "What Should a Wife's Submission to Her Husband Look Like if He's an Abuser?" August 19, 2009.

———. "Manhood and Womanhood: Conflict and Confusion After the Fall." Message given May 21, 1989. *Desiring God.* www.desiringgod.org/messages/manhood-and-womanhood-conflict-and-confusion-after-the-fall.

———. "My Wife Is More Spiritual—How Do I Lead Her?" *Ask Pastor John* (podcast). *Desiring God*, November 9, 2020. www.desiringgod.org/interviews/my-wife-is-more-spiritual-how-do-i-lead-her.

———. "Not in This or That Mount, but in Spirit and Truth." Message given June 28, 2009. *Desiring God.* www.desiringgod.org/messages/not-in-this-or-that-mount-but-in-spirit-and-truth.

———. "Sex-Abuse Allegations and the Egalitarian Myth." *Ask Pastor John* (podcast). *Desiring God*, March 16, 2018. www.desiringgod.org/interviews/sex-abuse-allegations-and-the-egalitarian-myth.

———. "The Tragic Cost of Her Cavernous Thirst." *Desiring God.* June 21, 2009. www.desiringgod.org/messages/the-tragic-cost-of-her-cavernous-thirst.

———. "Why Save Sex for Marriage?" *Ask Pastor John* (podcast). *Desiring God*, October 7, 2014. www.desiringgod.org/interviews/why-save-sex-for-marriage.

———. "You Will Never Be Thirsty Again." *Desiring God.* Message given June 14, 2009. www.desiringgod.org/messages/you-will-never-be-thirsty-again.

Pliny the Younger. *Letters* and *Panegyricus.* Translated by Betty Radice. 2 vols. Loeb Classical Library. Cambridge: Harvard University Press, 1969.

Plutarch. *Moralia, Volume 2* and *Life of Tiberius Graccus.* Translated by Bernadotte Perrin et al. 28 vols. Loeb Classical Library. Cambridge: Harvard University Press, 1914–2003.

Quintilian. *The Lesser Declamations.* Translated by D. R. Shackleton Bailey. 2 vols. Loeb Classical Library. Cambridge: Harvard University Press, 2006.

Rowlandson, Jane. *Women and Society in Greek and Roman Egypt: A Sourcebook.* Cambridge: Cambridge University Press, 1998.

Scott, Bobby. "Do You Wish to Be Pure?" *Desiring God.* October 12, 2019. www.desiringgod.org/articles/do-you-wish-to-be-pure.

Seneca. *Moral Essays, Volume 2.* Translated by Richard M. Gummere et al. 10 vols. Loeb Classical Library. Cambridge: Harvard University Press, 1917-2004.

Shelton, Jo-Ann. *As the Romans Did: A Sourcebook in Roman Social History.* 2nd ed. Oxford: Oxford University Press, 1998.

Sodini, George. "George Sodini's Blog: Full Text by Alleged Gym Shooter." *ABC News.* August 5, 2009. https://abcnews.go.com/US/story?id= 8258001&page=1.

Spurgeon, Charles. "Sychar's Sinner Saved." *Spurgeon's Sermons.* Vol. 38. *Christians Classics Ethereal Library.* https://ccel.org/ccel/spurgeon/sermons38/sermons38.xli.html.

Stanton, Elizabeth Cady. *The Women's Bible: A Classic Feminist Perspective.* 1895–1898. Reprint, Mineola, NY: Dover, 2002.

Suetonius. *Lives of the Caesars.* Translated by J. C. Rolfe. 2 vols. Loeb Classical Library. Cambridge: Harvard University Press, 1914.

Tertullian. *On the Apparel of Women, To His Wife, Exhortation to Chastity, On Monogamy, and On Modesty.* In vol. 4 of *The Ante-Nicene Fathers,* edited by Alexander Roberts and James Donaldson. 10 vols. Edinburgh: T&T Clark, 1885–1887. https://ccel.org /ccel/schaff /anf04.html.

———. *On the Veiling of Virgins.* In Dunn, *Tertullian,* 135-61.

———. *The Soul, Against Marcion, Against Praxeas, On Baptism, On Prayer.* In vol. 3 of *The Ante-Nicene Fathers,* edited by Alexander Roberts and James Donaldson. 10 vols. Edinburgh: T&T Clark, 1885–1887. https://ccel.org/ccel/schaff/anf03.html.

———. *The Tertullian Project.* http://tertullian.org/.

Viola, Frank, and Mary DeMuth. *The Day I Met Jesus: The Revealing Diaries of Five Women from the Gospels.* Grand Rapids, MI: Baker, 2015.

Ward, Benedicta. *Harlots of the Desert: A Study of Repentance in Early Monastic Sources.* Cistercian Studies 106. Kalamazoo: Cistercian Publications, 1987.

Wiedemann, Thomas. *Greek and Roman Slavery.* 1981. Reprint, London: Routledge, 2005.

Yadin, Yigael. *The Documents from the Bar Kokhba Period in the Cave of Letters: Hebrew, Aramaic, and Nabatean-Aramaic Papyri.* 2 vols. Jerusalem: Israel Exploration Society, 2002.

ADDITIONAL SOURCES CONSULTED

Barron, Robert. "The Woman at the Well." Video. *Word on Fire.* July 7, 2016. www .wordonfire.org/resources/video/bishop-barron-on-the-woman-at-the-well/5221/.

Breuer, Sarah Dylan. "Third Sunday in Lent, Year A." *Dylan's Lectionary Blog.* February 22, 2005. www.sarahlaughed.net/lectionary/2005/02/third_sunday_in.html.

Buchanan, John. "Conversation at a Well: Salvation Sandwiches." Sermon preached at Fourth Presbyterian Church, Chicago, Illinois. February 21, 2010. fourthchurch.org /sermons/2010/022110.html.

Bullock, Debbie. "Breakthrough at the Well." Video. Sermon preached at Canaan Baptist Church, New Castle, Delaware. May 24, 2013. https://youtu.be/kFJFBe7-bo8.

Crippen, Jeff. "Shame, Abuse Victims, and the Woman at the Well." *A Cry for Justice* (blog). February 18, 2012. https://cryingoutforjustice.blog/2012/02/18/shame -abuse-victims-and-the-woman-at-the-well-by-jeff-crippen/.

Jackson, Wayne. "Jesus and the Samaritan Woman." *Christian Courier.* n.d. www .christiancourier.com/articles/282-jesus-and-the-samaritan-woman.

Jacoby, Douglas. "The Samaritan Woman." New Testament Character Study. Spotify Playlist. *Relate4Ever Publishing*. 2013. https://open.spotify.com/album/3F8bAV0vha UbvmT2dULPOH.

Jones, Natasha Walker. "Insatiable Woman . . . at the Well." Sermon preached at Maranatha Seventh Day Adventist Church, Atlanta, Georgia. May 9, 2020. https:// gethsemanesdachurch.org/insatiable-woman-at-the-well/.

Joslin, Roger. "John 4:5-42." Sermon preached at Holy Trinity Episcopal Church, Greenport, New York. March 15, 2020. www.holytrinitygreenport.com/sermonmarch -15-2020.

Lewis, Karoline. "Commentary on John 4:5-42." *Working Preacher*. February 24, 2008. www.workingpreacher.org/commentaries/revised-common-lectionary/third -sunday-in-lent/commentary-on-john-45-42-2.

Mahler, Naomi. "Jesus and the Samaritan Woman." Video. Sermon preached at Calvary Lutheran Church, Willmar, Minnesota. September 12, 2020. https://youtu.be /ECOlxtzR30Y.

McGonigle, Robin. "Bad Girls, Good Stories: The Woman at the Well." Sermon preached at University Congregational Church, Wichita, Kansas. January 26, 2014. https:// ucchurch.org/sermons/bad-girls-good-stories-the-woman-at-the-well/.

McKenzie, Alyce. "The Secrets We Keep: Reflections on John 4:1-30." *Patheos*. March 22, 2011. www.patheos.com/resources/additional-resources/2011/03/the-secrets-we -keep-alyce-mckenzie-3-21-2011.

McNeil, Brenda Salter. "The Woman at the Well." Video. Sermon preached at Anchor Church, Kaneohe, Hawaii. 26 August 2018. https://youtu.be/Ncrdme9CGgY.

Moore, Russell. "Man, Woman, and the Mystery of Christ: An Evangelical Protestant Perspective." *The Gospel Coalition*. November 18, 2014. www.thegospelcoalition.org /article/man-woman-and-the-mystery-of-christ-an-evangelical-protestant -perspective/.

Morris, Robert. "The Samaritan Woman's Story." Video. Sermon preached at Gateway Church, Dallas/Fort Worth, Texas. March 9, 2013. https://youtu.be/_8WIp9dEvxQ.

Newbell, Trillia. "The Samaritan Woman and Our Barrier-Smashing Savior." *The Gospel Coalition*. October 25, 2019. www.thegospelcoalition.org/article/samaritan -woman-savior/.

Odhner, Calvin. "The Samaritan Woman at the Well." Sermon preached at Pittsburgh New Church, Pittsburgh, Pennsylvania. February 2, 2020. www.pittsburghnewchurch .org/sermons/2020/2/10/sermon-the-samaritan-woman-at-the-well.

Parshall, Janet. "The Woman at the Well." Video. Lecture presented at Revive Our Hearts True Woman '12, Indianapolis, Indiana. September 21, 2012. www.reviveourhearts .com/events/true-woman-12/woman-well/.

Pitre, Brant. "Jesus and the Samaritan Woman." Video. *Catholic Productions*. March 4, 2020. https://youtu.be/UV_mZtnTPBQ.

Powell, Barnabas. "The Samaritan Woman at the Well." Video. St. Raphael, Nicholas, and Irene Greek Orthodox Church, Cumming, Georgia. May 17, 2012. https://youtu.be /7kjYn3F2Mlg.

Runyan, Tania. "Before the Well" and "After the Well." In *A Thousand Vessels: Poems*. Seattle: WordFarm, 2011.

Smith, Dan. "The Woman at the Well." Video. Sermon preached at United Methodist Church, Louisa, Kentucky. May 6, 2018. https://youtu.be/HZgrzkTPd0E.

Smith, Scottie. "A Prayer About Grace Allergies." *The Gospel Coalition*. July 27, 2010. www .thegospelcoalition.org/blogs/scotty-smith/a-prayer-about-grace-allergies-2/.

Taylor, Diana Wallis. *Journey to the Well: A Novel*. Grand Rapids, MI: Revell, 2009.

Thomas, Debie. "The Woman at the Well." *Journey with Jesus*. March 8, 2020. www .journeywithjesus.net/essays/2561-the-woman-at-the-well-2.

Thompson, Sudie Niesen. "At the Well." Sermon preached at Westminster Presbyterian Church, Wilmington, Delaware. March 19, 2017. www.wpc.org/sermons/detail /At-the-Well/64.

Trigilio, John, and Kenneth Brighenti. *Women in the Bible for Dummies*. Hoboken, NJ: Wiley, 2005.

Vallotton, Kris. "Jesus and the Samaritan Woman." Video. Sermon preached at Bethel Church, Redding, California. January 5, 2017. https://youtu.be/FoapaeDxNCg.

Weidner, Robin. "Out of the Bushes and into the Light." *Focus on the Family*. January 1, 2008. www.focusonthefamily.com/marriage/out-of-the-bushes-and-into-the-light/.

Woods, Peter. "High Noon at Jacob's Well." *The Listening Hermit* (blog). March 24, 2011. https://thelisteninghermit.com/2011/03/24/high-noon-at-jacobs-well/.

Workman, Stephanie. "John 4:5-42." Sermon preached at Second Presbyterian Church, Richmond, Virginia. March 15, 2020. www.2presrichmond.org/sermons/2020/3/15 /wxctexh9xxkhdsb11ma03j5il9gz2b.

SECONDARY SOURCES

Akelaitis, Algirdas. "The Practice and Experience of the Menstrual Rituals in the Ancient Israel." *Soter* 73 (2020): 5-19.

Allison, Emily Joy. *#ChurchToo: How Purity Culture Upholds Abuse and How to Find Healing*. Minneapolis: Broadleaf, 2021.

Anderson, Robert T., and Terry Giles. *The Keepers: An Introduction to the History and Culture of the Samaritans*. Peabody, MA: Hendrickson, 2002.

———. *The Samaritan Pentateuch: An Introduction to Its Origin, History, and Significance for Biblical Studies*. SBL Resources for Biblical Study 72. Atlanta: Society of Biblical Literature, 2012.

Asian American Christian Collaborative. "AACC Statement on the Atlanta Massacre and Ongoing Anti-Asian Hate." March 22, 2021. www.asianamericanchristiancollaborative .com/atlantastatement.

Bacon, Brenda Socachevsky. "Reader Response: How Shall We Tell the Story of Beruriah's End?" *Nashim* 5 (2002): 231-39.

Balch, David L. and Carolyn Osiek, eds. *Early Christian Families in Context: An Interdisciplinary Dialogue*. Religion, Marriage, and Family. Grand Rapids, MI: Eerdmans, 2003.

Barr, Beth Allison. *The Making of Biblical Womanhood: How the Subjugation of Women Became Gospel Truth*. Grand Rapids, MI: Brazos, 2021.

Beasley-Murray, George R. *John*. Word Biblical Commentary 36. Waco: Word, 1987.

Bebbington, D. W. "Moody as Transatlantic Evangelical." In George, *Mr. Moody*, 75-92.

Beirne, Margaret M. *Women and Men in the Fourth Gospel: A Genuine Discipleship of Equals*. Journal for the Study of the New Testament Supplement Series 242. London: Sheffield Academic, 2003.

Benckhuysen, Amanda W. *The Gospel According to Eve: A History of Women's Interpretation*. Downers Grove, IL: IVP Academic, 2019.

Bendroth, Margaret Lamberts. *Fundamentalism and Gender: 1875 to the Present*. New Haven: Yale University Press, 1993.

Boer, Wietse de. *The Conquest of the Soul: Confession, Discipline, and Public Order in Counter-Reformation Milan*. Studies in Medieval and Reformation Thought 84. Leiden: Brill, 2001.

————. "The Catholic Church and Sexual Abuse, Then and Now." *Origins* 12, no. 6 (2019). http://origins.osu.edu/article/catholic-church-sexual-abuse-pope-confession -priests-nuns.

Bowler, Sarah. "Bathsheba: Vixen or Victim?" In Glahn, *Vixens*, 81-100.

Brown, Callum G. *The Death of Christian Britain: Understanding Secularisation 1800– 2000*. Christianity and Society in the Modern World. Abingdon: Routledge, 2001.

Brown, Peter. *The Body and Society: Men, Women, and Sexual Renunciation in Early Christianity*. Lectures on the History of Religions. New York: Columbia University Press, 1988.

Brown, Raymond E. *The Gospel According to John (I–XII)*. Anchor Bible 29. New York: Doubleday, 1966.

Burns, J. Patout, and Robin M. Jensen. *Christianity in Roman Africa: The Development of Its Practices and Beliefs*. Grand Rapids, MI: Eerdmans, 2014.

Caldwell, Lauren. *Roman Girlhood and the Fashioning of Femininity*. Cambridge: Cambridge University Press, 2015.

Carroll, Maureen. *Infancy and Earliest Childhood in the Roman World: 'A Fragment of Time.'* Oxford: Oxford University Press, 2018.

Carson, D. A. *The Gospel According to John*. Pillar New Testament Commentary. Grand Rapids, MI: Eerdmans, 1991.

Chaves, Mark, and Diana Garland. "The Prevalence of Clergy Sexual Advances Toward Adults in Their Congregations." *Journal for the Scientific Study of Religion* 48 (2009): 817-24.

Cohick, Lynn. "The 'Woman at the Well': Was the Samaritan Woman Really an Adulteress?" In Glahn, *Vixens*, 249-53.

——. *Women in the World of the Earliest Christians.* Grand Rapids, MI: Baker Academic, 2009.

Conybeare, Catherine. "Tertullian on Flesh, Spirit, and Wives." In *Severan Culture*, edited by Simon Swain, Stephen Harrison, and Jaś Elsner, 430-39. Cambridge: Cambridge University Press, 2007.

Coontz, Stephanie. *Marriage, a History: From Obedience to Intimacy or How Love Conquered Marriage.* New York: Viking, 2005.

Cooper-White, Pamela. *Cry of Tamar: Violence Against Women and the Church's Response.* 2nd ed. Minneapolis: Fortress, 2012.

Corts, Thomas E. "D. L. Moody: Payment on Account." In George, *Mr. Moody*, 51-73.

Daniel-Hughes, Carly. "'We Are Called to Monogamy': Marriage, Virginity, and the Resurrection of the Fleshly Body in Tertullian of Carthage." In *Coming Back to Life: The Permeability of Past and Present, Mortality and Immortality, Death and Life in the Ancient Mediterranean*, edited by Frederick S. Tappenden and Carly Daniel-Hughes, 239-64. Montreal: McGill University Library, 2017.

Davis, Tamie. "Why Equality Is Not Enough When You've Been Abused." *Lausanne Global Analysis* 7, no. 4 (2018). https://lausanne.org/content/lga/2018-07/why-equality-is-not-enough-when-youve-been-abused.

Day, Janeth Norfleete. *The Woman at the Well: Interpretation of John 4:1-42 in Retrospect and Prospect.* Biblical Interpretation Series 61. Leiden: Brill, 2002.

De Wet, Chris L. *Preaching Bondage: John Chrysostom and the Discourse of Slavery in Early Christianity.* Oakland: University of California Press, 2015.

DeMuth, Mary. *We Too: How the Church Can Respond Redemptively to the Sexual Abuse Crisis.* Eugene, OR: Harvest House, 2019.

Denhollander, Rachael. *What Is a Girl Worth?* Carol Stream, IL: Tyndale Momentum, 2019.

DeRogatis, Amy. *Saving Sex: Sexuality and Salvation in American Evangelicalism.* Oxford: Oxford University Press, 2015.

Dixon, Suzanne. *The Roman Family.* Baltimore: Johns Hopkins University Press, 1992.

Doern, Kristin G. "Balfour, Clara Lucas." In *Oxford Dictionary of National Biography*, edited by David Cannadine, vol. 3. Oxford: Oxford University Press, 2004.

Douglass, Jane Dempsey. *Women, Freedom, and Calvin.* Philadelphia: Westminster, 1985.

Du Mez, Kristen Kobes. *Jesus and John Wayne: How White Evangelicals Corrupted a Faith and Fractured a Nation.* New York: Liveright, 2020.

Dube, Muse W. "Reading for Decolonization (John 4:1-42)." *Semeia* 75 (1996): 37-59.

Dunn, Geoffrey D. *Tertullian.* The Early Church Fathers. London: Routledge, 2004.

Dunning, Benjamin H. *Specters of Paul: Sexual Difference in Early Christian Thought.* Philadelphia: University of Pennsylvania Press, 2011.

Elliott, Dyan. *The Bride of Christ Goes to Hell: Metaphor and Embodiment in the Lives of Pious Women, 200–1500*. The Middle Ages. Philadelphia: University of Pennsylvania Press, 2012.

Evensen, Bruce J. *God's Man for the Gilded Age: D. L. Moody and the Rise of Modern Mass Evangelism*. Oxford: Oxford University Press, 2003.

Everhart, Ruth. *The #MeToo Reckoning: Facing the Church's Complicity in Sexual Abuse and Misconduct*. Downers Grove, IL: InterVarsity Press, 2020.

Farmer, Craig S. "Changing Images of the Samaritan Woman in Early Reformed Commentaries on John." *Church History* 65 (1996): 365-75.

Fehribach, Adeline. *The Women in the Life of the Bridegroom: A Feminist Historical-Literary Analysis of the Female Characters in the Fourth Gospel*. Collegeville, MN: Liturgical, 1998.

Finlay, Barbara. "Was Tertullian a Misogynist? A Reconsideration." *Journal of the Historical Society* 3 (2003): 503-25.

Fortune, Marie. *Sexual Violence: The Sin Revisited*. Cleveland: Pilgrim Press, 2005.

Freedman, Estelle B. *Redefining Rape: Sexual Violence in the Era of Suffrage and Segregation*. Cambridge: Harvard University Press, 2013.

Garland, Diana. "The Prevalence of Clery Sexual Misconduct with Adults: A Research Study Executive Summary." *Clergy Sexual Misconduct*. www.baylor.edu/clergysexual misconduct/index.php?id=67406.

Garnsey, Peter, and Richard Saller, with Jaś Elsner, Martin Goodman, Richard Gordon, and Greg Woolf. *The Roman Empire: Economy, Society, and Culture*. 2nd ed. Oakland: University of California Press, 2015.

Gench, Frances. *Back to the Well: Women's Encounters with Jesus in the Gospels*. Louisville: Westminster John Knox, 2004.

George, Timothy, ed. *Mr. Moody and the Evangelical Tradition*. London: T&T Clark, 2004.

Glahn, Sandra, ed. *Vindicating the Vixens: Revisiting Sexualized, Vilified, and Marginalized Women of the Bible*. Grand Rapids, MI: Kregel Academic, 2017.

Glancy, Jennifer. *Slavery in Early Christianity*. Minneapolis: Fortress, 2006. First published 2002 by Oxford University Press (Oxford). Citations refer to the 2006 edition.

Groot, Christiana de. "Deborah: A Lightning Rod for Nineteenth-Century Women's Issues." In *Faith and Feminism in Nineteenth-Century Religious Communities*, edited by Michaela Sohn-Kronthaler and Ruth Albrecht, 63-98. The Bible and Women: An Encyclopedia of Exegesis and Cultural History 8.2. Atlanta: SBL Press, 2019.

Grubbs, Judith Evans. "The Dynamics of Infant Abandonment: Motives, Attitudes, and (Unintended) Consequences." In *The Dark Side of Childhood in Late Antiquity and the Middle Ages: Unwanted, Disabled, and Lost*, edited by Katariina Mustakallio and Christian Laes, 21-36. Childhood in the Past 2. Oxford: Oxbow, 2011.

Grubbs, Judith Evans and Tim Parkin, eds. *The Oxford Handbook of Childhood and Education in the Classical World.* Oxford: Oxford University Press, 2013.

Haenchen, Ernst. *John 1: A Commentary on the Gospel of John Chapters 1–6.* Hermeneia. Philadelphia: Fortress, 1984.

Hallett, Judith P. "Women in Augustan Rome." In James and Dillon, *Companion to Women,* 372-84.

Helm, Paul. *Calvin: A Guide for the Perplexed.* New York: Bloomsbury, 2008.

Hernández-Truyol, Berta Esperanza. "Latinas—Everywhere Alien: Culture, Gender, and Sex." In *Critical Race Feminism: A Reader,* edited by Adrien Katherine Wing, 57-69. New York: New York University Press, 2003.

Hezser, Catherine. *Jewish Slavery in Antiquity.* Oxford: Oxford University Press, 2005.

Hobbs, R. Gerald. "The Biblical Canon of Early Evangelical Feminists." *Reformation & Renaissance Review* 18 (2016): 216-32.

Hoffman, Daniel L. *The Status of Women and Gnosticism in Irenaeus and Tertullian.* Studies in Women and Religion 36. Lewiston, NY: Edwin Mellen, 1995.

Hung, Eugene. "Defending My Daughters Against Rape Culture." *Mutuality* 24 (2017): 14-15.

Hunter, David G. "The Reception and Interpretation of Paul in Late Antiquity: 1 Corinthians 7 and the Ascetic Debates." In *The Reception and Interpretation of the Bible in Late Antiquity,* edited by Lorenzo DiTommaso and Lucian Turcescu, 163-91. The Bible in Ancient Christianity 6. Leiden: Brill, 2008.

Hylen, Susan E. *A Modest Apostle: Thecla and the History of Women in the Early Church.* Oxford: Oxford University Press, 2015.

James, Sharon L. and Sheila Dillon, eds. *A Companion to Women in the Ancient World.* Blackwell Companions to the Ancient World. Oxford: Wiley-Blackwell, 2012.

Johnson, Elizabeth A. *She Who Is: The Mystery of God in Feminist Theological Discourse.* 1992. Reprint, New York: Crossroad, 2018.

Kalleres, Dayna S. *City of Demons: Violence, Ritual, and Christian Practice in Late Antiquity.* Oakland: University of California Press, 2015.

Kantor, Jodi, and Megan Twohey. "Harvey Weinstein Paid Off Sexual Harassment Accusers for Decades." *New York Times.* October 5, 2017. www.nytimes.com/2017/10/05 /us/ harvey-weinstein-harassment-allegations.html.

———. *She Said: Breaking the Sexual Harassment Story That Helped Ignite a Movement.* New York: Penguin, 2019.

Keener, Craig. *The Gospel of John: A Commentary.* 2 vols. Grand Rapids, MI: Baker Academic, 2003.

Kingdon, Robert M. *Adultery and Divorce in Calvin's Geneva.* Cambridge: Harvard University Press, 1995.

Klein, Linda Kay. *Pure: Inside the Evangelical Movement That Shamed a Generation of Young Women and How I Broke Free.* New York: Touchstone, 2018.

Knust, Jennifer. "Marriage as a Social Good: Origen of Alexandria and John Chrysostom, Revisited." *Marriage, Families & Spirituality* 26 (2020): 7-25.

Kraemer, Ross S. "Typical and Atypical Jewish Family Dynamics: The Cases of Babatha and Berenice." In Balch and Osiek, *Early Christian Families*, 130-56.

Kreider, Glen. "Eve: The Mother of All Seducers?" In Glahn, *Vixens*, 129-46.

Kuefler, Mathew. *The Manly Eunuch: Masculinity, Gender Ambiguity, and Christian Ideology in Late Antiquity.* Chicago: University of Chicago Press, 2001.

Lehtipuu, Outi. "To Remarry or not to Remarry? 1 Timothy 5:14 in Early Christian Ascetic Discourse." *Studia Theologica* 71 (2017): 29-50.

Levine, Amy-Jill. *A Feminist Companion to John.* Feminist Companion to the New Testament and Early Christian Writings 4. 2 vols. London: Sheffield Academic, 2003.

Lieber, Laura S. "Jewish Women: Texts and Contexts." In James and Dillon, *Companion to Women*, 329-42.

Lipscomb, Suzannah. "Subjection and Companionship: The French Reformed Marriage." *Reformation & Renaissance Review* 6 (2004): 349-60.

Lomax, Tamura. *Jezebel Unhinged: Loosing the Black Female Body in Religion & Culture.* Durham: Duke University Press, 2018.

Lose, David. "Misogyny, Moralism and the Woman at the Well." *HuffPost.* March 21, 2011. www.huffpost.com/entry/misogyny-moralism-and-the_b_836753.

MacHaffie, Barbara J. *Her Story: Women in Christian Tradition.* 2nd ed. Minneapolis: Fortress, 2006.

Malina, Bruce J., and Richard L. Rohrbaugh. *Social-Science Commentary on the Gospel of John.* Minneapolis: Fortress, 1998.

Mayer, Wendy, and Pauline Allen. *John Chrysostom.* The Early Church Fathers. London: Routledge, 2000.

Mayfield, D. L. "Focus on the Family." *Christ and Pop Culture* (blog). August 7, 2015. https://christandpopculture.com/focus-on-the-family/.

McHugh, John F. *A Critical and Exegetical Commentary on John 1–4.* International Critical Commentary. London: T&T Clark, 2009.

McWilliam, Janette. "The Socialization of Roman Children." In Grubbs and Parkin, *Oxford Handbook of Childhood and Education*, 264-85.

Michaels, J. Ramsey. *The Gospel of John.* New International Commentary on the New Testament. Grand Rapids, MI: Eerdmans, 2010.

Miller, Anne Marie. *Healing Together: A Guide to Supporting Sexual Abuse Survivors.* Grand Rapids, MI: Zondervan Reflective, 2019.

Morris, Leon. *The Gospel According to John.* New International Commentary on the New Testament. Rev. ed. Grand Rapids, MI: Eerdmans, 1995.

Moslener, Sara. *Virgin Nation: Sexual Purity and American Adolescence.* Oxford: Oxford University Press, 2015.

Myers, Alicia D. *Blessed Among Women? Mothers and Motherhood in the New Testament.* Oxford: Oxford University Press, 2017.

National Resource Center on Domestic Violence. "Gender Based Violence and Intersecting Challenges Impacting Native American and Alaskan Village Communities: Sexual Assault." *VAWNet.* Accessed July 6, 2021. https://vawnet.org/sc /gender-based-violence-and-intersecting-challenges-impacting-native-american -alaskan-village-1.

Newsom, Carol A. "Women as Biblical Interpreters Before the Twentieth Century." In *Women's Bible Commentary,* 3rd ed., edited by Carol A. Newsom, Sharon H. Ringe, and Jacqueline E. Lapsley, 11-24. Louisville: Westminster John Knox, 2012.

Neyrey, Jerome H. "What's Wrong with This Picture? John 4, Cultural Stereotypes of Women, and Public and Private Space." In Levine, *Feminist Companion,* 98-125.

Novakovic, Lidija. "Jews and Samaritans." In *The World of the New Testament: Cultural, Social, and Historical Contexts,* edited by Joel B. Green and Lee Martin McDonald, 207-16. Grand Rapids, MI: Baker Academic, 2013.

O'Day, Gail R., and Susan E. Hylen. *John.* Westminster Bible Companion. Louisville: Westminster John Knox, 2006.

Okure, Teresa. "Jesus and the Samaritan Woman (Jn 4:1-42) in Africa." *Theological Studies* 70 (2009): 401-18.

O'Malley, Roberta Liggett, Karen Holt, and Thomas J. Holt. "An Exploration of the Involuntary Celibate (Incel) Subculture Online." *Journal of Interpersonal Violence.* September 24, 2020. https://doi.org/10.1177/0886260520959625.

Osiek, Carolyn. "Female Slaves, *Porneia,* and the Limits of Obedience." In Balch and Osiek, *Early Christian Families,* 255-74.

Oudshoorn, Jacobine G. *The Relationship Between Roman and Local Law in the Babatha and Salome Komaise Archives: General Analysis and Three Case Studies on Laws of Succession, Guardianship, and Marriage.* Studies on the Texts of the Desert of Judah 69. Leiden: Brill, 2007.

Paasch, Hannah. "Sexual Abuse Happens in #ChurchToo." *HuffPost.* December 4, 2017. www .huffpost.com/entry/sexual-abuse-churchtoo_n_5a205b30e4b03350e0b53131.

Parker, T. H. L. *Calvin: An Introduction to His Thought.* Outstanding Christian Thinkers. 1995. Reprint, London: Continuum, 2002.

Parkin, Tim. "The Roman Life Course and the Family." In Rawson, *Companion to Families,* 276-90.

Peppiatt, Lucy. *Rediscovering Scripture's Vision for Women: Fresh Perspectives on Disputed Texts.* Downers Grove, IL: IVP Academic, 2019.

Ramelli, Ilaria L. E. "Colleagues of Apostles, Presbyters, and Bishops: Women *Syzygoi* in Ancient Christian Communities." In *Patterns of Women's Leadership in Early Christianity,* edited by Joan E. Taylor and Ilaria L. E. Ramelli, 26-58. Oxford: Oxford University Press, 2021.

Rape, Abuse, and Incest National Network. "More Statistics." *RAINN*. Accessed July 6, 2021. www.rainn.org/statistics.

Rawson, Beryl. *Children and Childhood in Roman Italy*. Oxford: Oxford University Press, 2003.

———, ed. *A Companion to Families in the Greek and Roman Worlds*. Blackwell Companions to the Ancient World. Chichester: Wiley-Blackwell, 2011.

Reeder, Caryn A. "1 Peter 3:1-6: Biblical Authority and Battered Wives." *Bulletin for Biblical Research* 25 (2015): 519-39.

———. "Child, Children." In *Dictionary of Jesus and the Gospels*, 2nd ed., edited by Joel B. Green, Jeannine K. Brown, and Nicholas Perrin, 109-13. Downers Grove, IL: InterVarsity Press, 2013.

———. *Gendering War and Peace in the Gospel of Luke*. Cambridge: Cambridge University Press, 2019.

———. *Slavery in the New Testament*. Grove Biblical. Cambridge: Grove Books, 2019.

———. *The Enemy in the Household: Family Violence in Deuteronomy and Beyond*. Grand Rapids, MI: Baker Academic, 2012.

Ross, Susan A. "Feminist Theology and the Clergy Sexual Abuse Crisis." *Theological Studies* 80 (2019): 632-52.

Saller, Richard. "The Roman Family as Productive Unit." In Rawson, *Companion to Families*, 116-28.

Sandwell, Isabella. *Religious Identity in Late Antiquity*. Cambridge: Cambridge University Press, 2007.

Schneiders, Sandra M. *Written That You May Believe: Encountering Jesus in the Fourth Gospel*. New York: Crossroad, 1999.

Schwartz, Seth. "The Political Geography of Rabbinic Texts." In *The Cambridge Companion to the Talmud and Rabbinic Literature*, edited by Charlotte Elisheva Fonrobert and Martin S. Jaffee, 75-96. Cambridge: Cambridge University Press, 2007.

Sigismund-Nielson, Hanne. "Slave and Lower-Class Roman Children." In Grubbs and Parkin, *Oxford Handbook of Childhood and Education*, 286-301.

Smith, D. Moody. *John*. Abingdon New Testament Commentaries. Nashville: Abingdon, 1999.

Smith, Jeremy. "Godly Men and Smokin' Hot Wives." *Hacking Christianity* (blog). August 5, 2013. https://hackingchristianity.net/2013/08/godly-men-and-smokin-hot-wives.html.

Spencer, F. Scott. "'You Just Don't Understand' (or Do You?): Jesus, Women, and Conversation in the Fourth Gospel." In Levine, *Feminist Companion to John*, 15-47.

Stjerna, Kirsi. *Women and the Reformation*. Oxford: Blackwell, 2009.

Styler, Rebecca. "A Scripture of Their Own: Nineteenth-Century Bible Biography and Feminist Bible Criticism." *Christianity and Literature* 57 (2007): 65-85.

Taylor, Marion Ann, and Heather E. Weir. *Let Her Speak for Herself: Nineteenth-Century Women Writing on Women in Genesis*. Waco: Baylor University Press, 2006.

Thompson, John Lee. "Calvin as a Biblical Interpreter." In *The Cambridge Companion to John Calvin*, edited by Donald K. McKim, 58–73. Cambridge: Cambridge University Press, 2004.

———. *"Creata ad Imaginem Dei, Licet Secundo Gradu*: Woman as the Image of God According to John Calvin." *Harvard Theological Review* 81 (1988): 125-43.

———. *John Calvin and the Daughters of Sarah: Women in Regular and Exceptional Roles in the Exegesis of Calvin, his Predecessors, and his Contemporaries*. Travaux d'Humanisme et Renaissance 259. Geneva: Librairie Droz, 1992.

———. *Reading the Bible with the Dead: What You Can Learn from the History of Exegesis That You Can't Learn from Exegesis Alone*. Grand Rapids, MI: Eerdmans, 2007.

Thompson, Marianne Meye. *John: A Commentary*. New Testament Library. Louisville: Westminster John Knox, 2015.

Topping, Eva Catafyglotu. *Saints and Sisterhood: The Lives of Forty-Eight Holy Women*. Minneapolis: Light and Life, 1990.

Trigg, Joseph W. *Origen*. The Early Church Fathers. London: Routledge, 1998.

Valenti, Jessica. *The Purity Myth: How America's Obsession with Virginity Is Hurting Young Women*. Berkeley: Seal, 2010.

Vorster, Nico. "John Calvin on the Status and Role of Women in Church and Society." *Journal of Theological Studies* 68 (2017): 178-211.

Watt, Jeffrey R. *The Consistory and Social Discipline in Calvin's Geneva*. Perspectives on Early Modern Europe. Rochester: University of Rochester Press, 2020.

Witte, John, and Robert M. Kingdon. *Courtship, Engagement, and Marriage*. Vol. 1 of *Sex, Marriage, and Family in John Calvin's Geneva*. Grand Rapids, MI: Eerdmans, 2005.

Yuen, Nancy Wang. "Atlanta Spa Shooting Suspect's 'Bad Day' Defense, and America's Sexualized Racism Problem." *Think* (blog). *NBC News*. March 18, 2021. www.nbcnews .com/think/opinion/atlanta-spa-shooting-suspect-s-bad-day-defense-america -s-ncna1261362.

Zamfir, Korinna. "Women Teaching—Spiritually Washing the Feet of the Saints? The Early Christian Reception of 1 Timothy 2:11-12." *Annali di Storia dell'Esegesi* 32 (2015): 353-79.

Zazueta, Karla. "Mary Magdalene: Repainting Her Portrait of Misconceptions." In Glahn, *Vixens*, 255-72.

INTERPRETER INDEX

SCRIPTURE INDEX